Phil Ballard

Sams **Teach Yourself**

JavaScript

Barnes & Noble Exclusive Edition

Seventh Edition

in **24** **Hours**

Pearson

Sams Teach Yourself JavaScript in 24 Hours, Barnes & Noble Exclusive Edition

Seventh Edition

ISBN-13: 978-0-672-33810-6

ISBN-10: 0-672-33810-6

Library of Congress Control Number: 2018951300

1   18

Trademarks

All terms mentioned in this book that are known to be trademarks or service marks have been appropriately capitalized. Pearson cannot attest to the accuracy of this information. Use of a term in this book should not be regarded as affecting the validity of any trademark or service mark.

Warning and Disclaimer

Every effort has been made to make this book as complete and as accurate as possible, but no warranty or fitness is implied. The information provided is on an "as is" basis. The author and the publisher shall have neither liability nor responsibility to any person or entity with respect to any loss or damages arising from the information contained in this book.

Special Sales

For information about buying this title in bulk quantities, or for special sales opportunities (which may include electronic versions; custom cover designs; and content particular to your business, training goals, marketing focus, or branding interests), please contact our corporate sales department at corpsales@pearsoned.com or (800) 382-3419.

For government sales inquiries, please contact governmentsales@pearsoned.com.

For questions about sales outside the U.S., please contact intlcs@pearson.com.

Editor
Mark Taber

Managing Editor
Sandra Schroeder

Senior Project Editor
Tonya Simpson

Copy Editor
Chuck Hutchinson

Indexer
Erika Millen

Proofreader
Abigail Manheim

Technical Editor
Jesse Smith

Editorial Assistant
Cindy Teeters

Cover Designer
Chuti Prasertsith

Compositor
codemantra

Contents at a Glance

Table of Contents

Part IV: Manipulating Web Pages with JavaScript

About the Author

Phil Ballard, the author of several books, graduated in 1980 with an honors degree in electronics from the University of Leeds, England. Following an early career as a research scientist with a major multinational, he spent a few years in commercial and managerial roles within the high technology sector, later working full time as a software engineering consultant.

Accessing the Free Web Edition

Your purchase of this book in any format, print or electronic, includes access to the corresponding Web Edition, which provides several special features to help you learn:

▶ The complete text of the book online

▶ Interactive quizzes and exercises to test your understanding of the material

▶ Updates and corrections as they become available

The Web Edition can be viewed on all types of computers and mobile devices with any modern web browser that supports HTML5.

To get access to the Web Edition of *Sams Teach Yourself JavaScript in 24 Hours*, Barnes & Noble Exclusive Edition, all you need to do is register this book:

1. Go to www.informit.com/register.

2. Sign in or create a new account.

3. Enter the ISBN: **9780672338090**.

4. Answer the questions as proof of purchase.

The Web Edition will appear under the Digital Purchases tab on your Account page.

Click the Launch link to access the product.

Figure Credits

Chapter 1, "Introducing JavaScript," Figures 1.2 through 1.4 courtesy of Google, LLC.

Chapter 2, "Writing Simple Scripts," Figures 2.3 through 2.6 courtesy of Google, LLC.

Chapter 3, "Introducing Functions," Figures 3.1 and 3.2 courtesy of Google, LLC.

Chapter 4, "More Fun with Functions," Figures 4.1, and 4.3 through 4.7 courtesy of Google, LLC.

Chapter 5, "DOM Objects and Built-in Objects," Figures 5.3 and 5.4 courtesy of Google, LLC.

Chapter 6, "Dealing with Numbers," Figures 6.1 through 6.3 courtesy of Google, LLC.

Chapter 7, "Working with Character Strings," Figures 7.2 and 7.3 courtesy of Google, LLC.

Chapter 8, "Storing Data in Arrays," Figure 8.1 courtesy of Mozilla Corporation. Figure 8.2 courtesy of Google, LLC.

Chapter 9, "Handling Events in JavaScript," Figures 9.1 through 9.4 courtesy of Google, LLC.

Chapter 10, "Controlling Program Flow," Figures 10.1 and 10.2 courtesy of Google, LLC.

Chapter 11, "Introducing Object-Oriented Programming," Figures 11.3 and 11.4 courtesy of Google, LLC.

Chapter 12, "Learning More About Objects," Figures 12.1 and 12.2 courtesy of Google, LLC. Figure 12.3 courtesy of Microsoft Corporation.

Chapter 13, "Scripting with the DOM," Figures 13.1, 13.3, 13.5, and 13.6 courtesy of Mozilla Corporation. Figures 13.7 and 13.8 courtesy of Google, LLC.

Chapter 15, "Programming HTML with JavaScript," Figures 15.2 through 15.4 courtesy of Google, LLC.

Chapter 16, "Manipulating CSS in JavaScript," Figures 16.1 through 16.3 courtesy of Google, LLC. Figure 16.4 courtesy of Mozilla Corporation.

Chapter 17, "More Advanced Control of CSS," Figures 17.1 through 17.9 courtesy of Google, LLC.

Chapter 18, "Reading and Writing Cookies," Figures 18.1 through 18.3 courtesy of Google, LLC.

Chapter 19, "Matching Patterns Using Regular Expressions," Figures 19.1 through 19.4 courtesy of Google, LLC.

Chapter 20, "Understanding and Using Closures," Figures 20.1 through 20.6 courtesy of Google, LLC.

Chapter 21, "Organizing Code with Modules," Figure 21.1 courtesy of Google, LLC.

Chapter 22, "Good Coding Practice," Figure 22.1 courtesy of Mozilla Corporation.

Chapter 23, "Debugging Your Code," Figures 23.2 through 23.4, 23.6 through 23.9, 23.11 through 23.13 courtesy of Google, LLC. Figure 23.5 courtesy of Mozilla Corporation. Figure 23.10 courtesy of Google, LLC.

Chapter 24, "Where to Go Next," Figure 24.1 courtesy of Google, LLC.

Chapter 25, "Data Visualization Using JavaScript," Figures 25.2 through 25.6 courtesy of Google, LLC.

Chapter 26, "Game Programming Using EaselJS," Figures 26.1 through 26.6 courtesy of Google, LLC.

Introduction

Before you begin reading, let's look at who this book was written for, why it was written, the conventions employed, how the content is organized, and the tools you need to create JavaScript.

Who This Book Is For

If you're interested in learning JavaScript, chances are that you've already gained at least a basic understanding of HTML and web page design in general, and want to move on to adding some extra interactivity to your pages. Or maybe you currently code in another programming language and want to see what additional capabilities JavaScript can add to your armory.

If you've never tinkered with HTML at all, nor done any computer programming, it would be helpful to browse through an HTML primer before getting into the book. Don't worry—HTML is very accessible, and you don't need to be an expert in it to start experimenting with the JavaScript examples in this book.

JavaScript is an ideal language to use for your first steps in programming, and in case you get bitten by the bug, pretty much all the fundamental concepts that you learn in JavaScript will later be applicable in a wide variety of other languages such as C, Java, and PHP.

Our Aims

When JavaScript was first introduced, it was somewhat limited in what it could do. With basic features and rather haphazard browser support, it gained a reputation in some quarters as being something of a toy or gimmick. Now, due to much better browser support for W3C standards and improvement in the JavaScript implementations used in recent browsers, JavaScript is finally being treated as a serious programming language.

Many advanced programming disciplines used in other programming languages can readily be applied to JavaScript; for example, object-oriented programming promotes the writing of solid, readable, maintainable, and reusable code.

So-called unobtrusive scripting techniques and the use of Document Object Model (DOM) scripting focus on adding interaction to web pages while keeping the HTML simple to read and well separated from the program code.

This series of lessons aims to teach the fundamental skills relevant to all the important aspects of JavaScript as it's used today. You'll start from basic concepts and gradually learn the best practices for writing JavaScript programs in accordance with current web standards.

Many programming tutorials are daunting for anybody but experienced programmers due to the complexity of the code examples and exercises. For maximum clarity and accessibility, the examples offered here are intended to illustrate the key points of each lesson while using as little code complexity as possible.

Conventions Used

All the code examples in the book are written as HTML5 and the sixth edition of the ECMAScript JavaScript standard.

In addition to the main text of each lesson, you will find a number of boxes labeled Notes, Tips, and Cautions.

NOTE
These sections provide additional comments that might help you understand the text and examples.

TIP
These blocks give additional hints, shortcuts, or workarounds to make coding easier.

CAUTION
These blocks help you avoid common pitfalls by using the relevant information.

▼ TRY IT YOURSELF

Each lesson contains at least one section that walks you through the process of implementing your own script. This will help you gain confidence in writing your own JavaScript code based on the techniques you've learned.

Q&A, Workshop, and Exercises

After each lesson, you'll find three final sections:

▶ The "Q&A" section answers a few of the more common questions about the lesson's topic.

▶ The "Workshop" section includes a quiz that tests your knowledge of what you learned in that lesson.

▶ The "Exercises" section offers suggestions for further experimentation, based on the lesson, that you might like to try on your own.

How Things Are Organized

The book is divided into six parts, gradually increasing in the complexity of the techniques taught.

▶ **Part I: Your First Steps with JavaScript**

This part of the book provides an introduction to the JavaScript language and how to write simple scripts using the language's common functions. It is aimed mainly at readers with little or no prior programming knowledge and no knowledge of the JavaScript language.

▶ **Part II: Cooking with Code**

Here JavaScript's data types are introduced, such as numbers, strings, and arrays. More sophisticated programming paradigms such as event handling, program control loops, and timers are also covered.

▶ **Part III: Understanding JavaScript Objects**

This part of the book concentrates on creating and handling objects, including navigating and editing the objects belonging to the DOM.

▶ **Part IV: Manipulating Web Pages with JavaScript**

Here you learn in greater depth how JavaScript can interact with HTML (including HTML5) and Cascading Style Sheets (CSS), including the latest CSS3 specification.

▶ **Part V: Some Advanced Techniques for Your JavaScript Toolkit**

In this part of the book, you learn some specialized programming techniques including the use of cookies, regular expressions, closures, and modules.

▶ **Part VI: Learning the Trade**

In the final part, you explore aspects of professional JavaScript development such as good coding practices and the debugging of your programs.

Tools You'll Need

Writing JavaScript does not require any expensive and complicated tools such as Integrated Development Environments (IDEs), compilers, or debuggers.

The examples in this book can all be created in a text-editing program, such as the Windows Notepad program. At least one such application ships with just about every operating system, and countless more are available for no or low cost via download from the Internet.

NOTE

Appendix A, "Tools for JavaScript Development," lists some additional, easily obtainable tools and resources for use in JavaScript development.

To see your program code working, you'll need a modern, standards-compliant web browser such as Microsoft Edge, Mozilla Firefox, Opera, Apple Safari, or Google Chrome. It is recommended that you upgrade your browser to the latest current stable version. In particular, Microsoft's obsolescent Internet Explorer is best avoided in favor of the company's later and much more standards-compliant Edge browser, or an alternative such as Chrome or Firefox.

The vast majority of the book's examples do not need an Internet connection to function. Simply storing the source code file in a convenient location on your computer and opening it with your chosen browser is generally sufficient. The few exceptions to this include the lesson on cookies and the examples in the book that demonstrate Ajax; to explore all the sample code will require a web connection (or a connection to a web server on your local area network) and a little web space in which to post the sample code. If you've done some HTML coding, you may already have that covered; if not, a hobby-grade web hosting account costs very little and will be more than adequate for trying out the examples in this book.

LESSON 1
Introducing JavaScript

What You'll Learn in This Lesson:

▶ What server-side and client-side programming are

▶ How JavaScript can improve your web pages

▶ The history of JavaScript

▶ The basics of the Document Object Model (DOM)

▶ What the window and document objects are

▶ How to add content to your web pages using JavaScript

▶ How to alert the user with a dialog box

The modern Web has little to do with its original, text-only ancestor. Modern web pages can involve audio, video, animated graphics, interactive navigation, and much more—and more often than not, JavaScript plays a big part in making it all possible. This first lesson describes what JavaScript is, briefly reviews the language's origins, and explains the kinds of things it can do to improve your web pages. You also dive right in and write some working JavaScript code.

Web Scripting Fundamentals

Since you've decided to learn JavaScript, there's a pretty good chance that you're already familiar with using the World Wide Web and have at least a basic understanding of writing web pages in some variant of HTML.

Hypertext Markup Language (HTML) is not a programming language but (as the name indicates) a markup language; you can use it to mark parts of your page to indicate to the browser that these parts should be shown in a particular way—using bold or italic text, for instance, or as a heading, a list of bullet points, a table of data, or using many other markup options.

Once written, these pages by their nature are static. They can't respond to user actions, make decisions, or modify the display of their page elements. The markup they contain will always be interpreted and displayed in the same way whenever a user visits the page.

As you know from using the World Wide Web, modern websites can do much more; the pages you routinely visit are often far from static. They can contain "live" data, such as share prices or flight arrival times, animated displays with changing colors and fonts, or interactive capabilities such as the ability to click through a gallery of photographs or sort a column of data.

These clever capabilities are provided to the user by programs—often known as scripts—operating behind the scenes to manipulate what's displayed in the browser.

NOTE

Scripts and Programs

The term *script* has no doubt been borrowed from the world of theater and TV, where the script defines the actions of the presenters or performers. In the case of a web page, the protagonists are the elements on the page, with a script provided by a scripting language such as, in this case, JavaScript. *Program* and *script* are, for our purposes, pretty much interchangeable terms, as are *programming* and *scripting*. You'll find all these terms used in the course of these lessons.

Server- Versus Client-Side Programming

There are two fundamental ways of adding scripts to otherwise static web content:

▶ You can have the web server execute a script before delivering your page to the user. Such scripts can define what information is sent to the browser for display to the user—for example, by retrieving product prices from the database of an online store, checking a user's identity credentials before logging her in to a private area of the website, or retrieving the contents of an email mailbox. These scripts are generally run at the web server before generating the requested web page and serving it to the user. You won't be surprised to learn that we refer to this as *server-side* scripting.

▶ Alternatively, the scripts themselves, rather than being run on the server, can be delivered to the user's browser along with the markup code that defines the page. Such scripts are then executed by the browser and operate on the page's already-delivered content. The many functions such scripts can perform include animating page sections, reformatting page layouts, allowing the user to drag and drop items within a page, validating user input on forms, redirecting users to other pages, and much more. You have probably already guessed that this is referred to as *client-side* scripting, and you're correct.

This book is all about JavaScript, the most-used language for client-side scripting on the Internet.

NOTE

JavaScript and Java

Although the names are similar, JavaScript doesn't have much, if anything, to do with the Java language developed by Sun Microsystems. The two languages share some aspects of syntax, but no more so than either of them do with a whole host of other programming languages.

JavaScript in a Nutshell

A program written in JavaScript can access the elements of a web page and the browser window in which it is running; it also can perform actions on those elements and create new page elements. A few examples of JavaScript's capabilities include

- ▶ Opening new windows with a specified size, position, and style (for example, whether the window has borders, menus, toolbars, and so on)

- ▶ Providing user-friendly navigation aids such as drop-down menus

- ▶ Validating data entered into a web form to make sure that it is of an acceptable format before the form is submitted to the web server

- ▶ Changing how page elements look and behave when particular events occur, such as the mouse cursor moving over them

- ▶ Detecting and exploiting advanced features supported by the particular browser being used, such as third-party plug-ins or native support for new technologies

Because JavaScript code runs locally inside the user's browser, the page tends to respond quickly to JavaScript instructions, enhancing the user's experience and making the application seem more like one of the computer's native applications rather than simply a web page. Also, JavaScript can detect and utilize certain user actions that HTML can't, such as individual mouse clicks and keyboard actions.

Virtually every web browser in common use has support for JavaScript.

Where JavaScript Came From

The ancestry of JavaScript dates back to the mid-1990s, when version 1.0 was introduced for Netscape Navigator 2.

The European Computer Manufacturers Association (ECMA) became involved, defining ECMAScript, the great-granddaddy of the current language. At the same time, Microsoft introduced JScript, its own version of the language, for use in its Internet Explorer range of browsers.

NOTE

JavaScript and VBScript

JavaScript is not the only client-side scripting language. Microsoft browsers have supported (in addition to jScript, Microsoft's version of JavaScript) a scripting-oriented version of the company's own
Visual Basic language, called VBScript.

JavaScript, however, has much better browser support; a version of JavaScript is supported by nearly
every modern browser.

The Browser Wars

In the late 1990s, Netscape Navigator 4 and Internet Explorer 4 both claimed to offer major
improvements over earlier browser versions in terms of what could be achieved with JavaScript.

Unfortunately, the two sets of developers had gone in separate directions, each defining its own
additions to the JavaScript language and how it interacted with a web page.

This ludicrous situation forced developers to essentially write two versions of each of their scripts,
and use some clumsy and often error-prone routines to try to determine which browser was
being used to view the page, and subsequently switch to the most appropriate version of their
JavaScript code.

Thankfully, the World Wide Web Consortium (the W3C) worked hard with the individual browser
manufacturers to standardize the way web pages were constructed and manipulated, by means of
the Document Object Model (DOM). Level 1 of the new standardized DOM was completed in late
1998, and Level 2 in late 2000.

Don't worry if you're not sure what the DOM is or what it does; you learn a lot about it later this
lesson.

NOTE

About the W3C

The World Wide Web Consortium (W3C) is an international community that exists to develop open
standards to support the long-term growth of the World Wide Web.

Its website at www.w3.org/ is a vast resource of information and tools relating to web standards.

The `<script>` Tag

Whenever a user requests a page, any JavaScript programs that page contains are passed to the
browser along with page content.

You can include JavaScript statements directly into your HTML code by placing them between `<script>` and `</script>` tags within the HTML:

```
<script>
    ... JavaScript statements ...
</script>
```

NOTE

Interpreted and Compiled Languages

JavaScript is an interpreted language, rather than a compiled language such as C++ or Java. This means that the JavaScript instructions are passed to the browser as plain text and are interpreted sequentially; they do not need to first be "compiled" into condensed machine code only readable by the computer's processor. This capability offers big advantages in that JavaScript programs are easy to read, they can be edited swiftly, and their operation can be retested simply by reloading the web page in the browser.

The examples in this book are all written to validate correctly as HTML5, in which no obligatory attributes are specified for the `<script>` element (the `type` attribute is optional in HTML5 and has been excluded from the examples in this book to aid clarity). However, if you write JavaScript for inclusion in HTML 4.x or XHTML pages, you should add the `type` attribute to your `<script>` elements:

```
<script type="text/javascript">
    ... JavaScript statements ...
</script>
```

You'll also occasionally see `<script>` elements having the attribute `language="JavaScript"`. This attribute has long been deprecated, so unless you think you need to support ancient browsers such as Navigator and Mosaic, you don't need to continue writing code like this.

NOTE

About Deprecated Code

The term *deprecated* is applied to software features or practices to indicate that they are best avoided, usually because they have been superseded.

Although still supported to provide backward compatibility, their deprecated status often implies that such features will be removed in the near future.

The examples in this lesson place their JavaScript code within the `<body>` section of the HTML document, but JavaScript code can appear elsewhere in the document too; you can also use the `<script>` element to load JavaScript code saved in an external file. We'll discuss how to include JavaScript in your pages in much more detail in Lesson 2, "Writing Simple Scripts."

Introducing the DOM

A Document Object Model (DOM) is a conceptual way of visualizing a document and its contents.

Each time your browser is asked to load and display a page, it needs to interpret (we usually use the word *parse*) the source code contained in the HTML file comprising the page. As part of this parsing process, the browser creates a type of internal model known as a DOM representation based on the content of the loaded document. It is this model that the browser then refers to when rendering the visible page. You can use JavaScript to access and edit the various parts of the DOM representation, at the same time changing the way the user sees and interacts with the page in view.

In the early days, JavaScript provided rather primitive access to certain parts of a web page. JavaScript programs could gain access, for example, to the images and forms contained in a web page; a JavaScript program could contain statements to select "the second form on the page" or "the form called 'registration.'"

Web developers sometimes refer to this as DOM Level 0, in backward-compatible homage to the W3C's subsequent Level 1 DOM definition. As well as DOM Level 0, you might also see reference to the BOM, or Browser Object Model. Since then, the W3C has gradually extended and improved the DOM specification. The W3C's much more ambitious definition has produced a DOM that is valid not just for web pages and JavaScript, but for any programming language and for XML, in addition to HTML, documents.

NOTE

About DOM Levels

In this book, we concentrate on the W3C's Level 1 and 2 DOM definitions. If you're interested in the details of the various DOM levels, you can find a good overview at https://developer.mozilla.org/en/DOM_Levels.

The W3C and Standards Compliance

The browser vendors have incorporated much-improved support for DOM in their most recent versions. At the time of writing, Internet Explorer has been replaced by the much more standards-compliant Edge browser; Netscape Navigator has evolved into Mozilla Firefox (currently in version 58.0); and other competitors in the market include Opera, Apple's Safari, and Google's Chrome and Chromium. All of these offer excellent support for the DOM.

The situation has improved markedly for web developers. Apart from a few irritating quirks, you can now largely forget about writing special code for individual browsers provided that you follow the DOM standards.

NOTE

Beware of Old Browsers

The use of early browsers such as Netscape Navigator (any version) or Internet Explorer (up to version 8) has now virtually disappeared. This book concentrates on more modern browsers that are compatible with DOM Level 1 or better, such as Microsoft Edge, Mozilla Firefox, Google Chrome, Apple Safari, and Opera. You are recommended to upgrade your browser to one of these at the latest stable version.

The `window` and `document` Objects

Each time your browser loads and displays a page, it creates in memory an internal representation of the page and all its elements, the DOM. In the DOM, elements of your web page have a logical, hierarchical structure, like a tree of interconnected parent and child objects. These objects, and their interconnections, form a conceptual model of the web page and the browser that contains and displays it. Each object also has a list of properties that describe it, and a number of methods you can use to manipulate those properties using JavaScript.

Right at the top of the hierarchical tree is the browser `window` object. This object is a parent or ancestor to everything else in the DOM representation of your page.

The `window` object has various child objects, some of which are visualized in Figure 1.1. The first child object shown in Figure 1.1, and the one we'll use most in this book, is the `document` object. Any HTML page loaded into the browser creates a `document` object containing all the HTML and other resources that go into making up the displayed page. All this information is accessible via JavaScript as a parent-child hierarchy of objects, each with its own properties and methods.

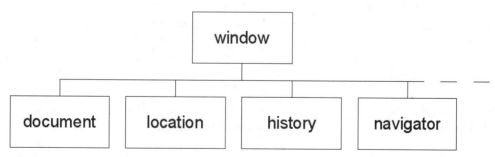

FIGURE 1.1
The `window` object and some of its children

The other children of the `window` object visible in Figure 1.1 are the `location` object (containing details of the URL of the currently loaded page), the `history` object (containing details of the browser's previously visited pages), and the `navigator` object (which stores details of the browser type, version, and capabilities). We'll look in detail at these objects in Lesson 5, "DOM Objects and Built-in Objects," and use them again at intervals throughout the book, but for now let's concentrate on the `document` object.

Object Notation

The notation to represent objects within the tree uses the dot or period:

```
parent.child
```

As an example, referring to Figure 1.1, the `location` object is a child of the `window` object, so in the DOM it is referred to like this:

```
window.location
```

TIP

Extending Dot Notation

This notation can be extended as many times as necessary to represent any object in the tree. For example,

```
object1.object2.object3
```

represents `object3`, whose parent is `object2`, which is itself a child of `object1`.

Since the `<body>` section of your HTML page is represented in the DOM as a child element of the `document` object, you would access it like this:

```
window.document.body
```

The last item in the sequence can also be, instead of another object, a property or method of the parent object:

```
object1.object2.property
object1.object2.method
```

For example, suppose that you want to access the `title` property of the current document, as specified by the HTML `<title>...</title>` tags. You can simply use

```
window.document.title
```

NOTE

The Best Is Yet to Come

Don't worry if object hierarchy and dot notation don't seem too clear right now. You'll be seeing many examples in the lessons that follow!

TIP

A Handy Shortcut

The `window` object always contains the current browser window, so you can refer to `window.document` to access the current document. As a shortcut, you can also simply use `document` instead of `window.document`; this also refers to the current document.

If you have several windows open, or if you are using a frameset, separate `window` and `document` objects exist for each window or frame. To refer to one of these documents, you need to use the relevant window name and document name belonging to the window or frame in question.

Talking to the User

Let's look at some of the methods associated with the `window` and `document` objects. We begin with two methods, each of which provides a means to talk to the user:

```
window.alert()
```

Even if you don't realize it, you've seen the results of the `window` object's `alert` method on many occasions. The `window` object, you'll recall, is at the top of the DOM hierarchy and represents the browser window that's displaying your page. When you call the `alert()` method, the browser pops open a dialog displaying your message, along with an OK button. Here's an example:

```
<script>window.alert("Here is my message");</script>
```

This is our first working example of the dot notation. Here we are calling the `alert()` method of the `window` object, so our object.method notation becomes `window.alert`.

TIP

Another Handy Shortcut

In practice, you can leave out the `window.` part of the statement. Because the `window` object is the top of the DOM hierarchy (it's sometimes referred to as the *global object*), any methods called without direct reference to their parent object are assumed to belong to `window`. So

```
<script>alert("Here is my message");</script>
```

works just as well.

Notice that the line of text inside the parentheses is contained within quotation marks. These can be single or double quotes, but they must be there; otherwise, an error will be produced.

This line of code, when executed in the browser, pops up a dialog like the one in Figure 1.2.

FIGURE 1.2
A `window.alert()` dialog

TIP
Different Browsers Display Differently

Figure 1.2 shows the alert generated by the Chrome browser running on Ubuntu Linux. The appearance of the dialog changes in detail depending on the particular browser, operating system, and display options you are using, but it always contains the message along with a single OK button.

TIP
Understanding Modal Dialogs

Until the user clicks OK, he is prevented from doing anything else with the page. A dialog that behaves this way is known as a modal dialog.

document.write()

You can probably guess what the `write` method of the `document` object does, simply from its name. This method, instead of popping up a dialog, writes characters directly into the DOM of the document, as shown in Figure 1.3.

```
<script>document.write("Here is another message");</script>
```

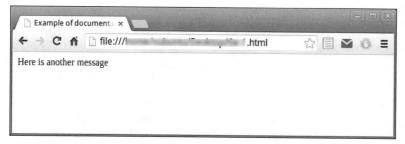

FIGURE 1.3
Using `document.write()`

NOTE

In fact, `document.write` is a pretty dumb way to write content to the page; it has a lot of limitations, both in terms of its function and in terms of coding style and maintainability. It has largely fallen into disuse for "serious" JavaScript programming. By the time you're ready to write more advanced JavaScript programs, you'll have learned much better ways to put content into your pages using JavaScript and the DOM. However, we use `document.write` quite a lot during Part I of the book, while you come to grips with some of the basic principles of the language.

TRY IT YOURSELF ▼

"Hello World!" in JavaScript

It seems almost rude to introduce a programming language without presenting the traditional "Hello World" example. Have a look at the simple HTML document of Listing 1.1.

LISTING 1.1 "Hello World!" in an `alert()` Dialog

```
<!DOCTYPE html>
<html>
<head>
    <title>Hello from JavaScript!</title>
</head>
<body>
    <script>
        alert("Hello World!");
    </script>
</body>
</html>
```

Create a document called `hello.html` in your text editor, and enter the code from Listing 1.1. Save it to a convenient place on your computer, and then open it with your web browser.

CAUTION

Take Care with File Extensions

Some text editor programs might try to add a .txt extension to the filename you specify. Be sure your saved file has the extension .html; otherwise, the browser will probably not open it correctly.

Many popular operating systems allow you to right-click on the icon of the HTML file and choose Open With or a similarly worded option. Alternatively, fire up your chosen browser, and use the File > Open options from the menu bar to navigate to your file and load it into the browser.

You should see a display similar to Figure 1.2, but with the message "Hello World!" in the dialog. If you have more than one browser installed on your computer, try them all and compare the display. The dialogs will probably look a little different, but the message, and the operation of the OK button, should be just the same.

CAUTION

Watch Out for Warnings

The default security settings in some browsers cause them to show a security warning when they are asked to open local content, such as a file on your own computer. If your browser does this, just choose the option that allows the content to be shown.

Reading a Property of the `document` Object

You may recall from earlier in the lesson that objects in the DOM tree have properties and methods. You saw how to use the `write` method of the `document` object to output text to the page; now let's try reading one of the properties of the `document` object. Now you're going to use the `document.title` property, which contains the title as defined in the HTML `<title>` element of the page.

Edit `hello.html` in your text editor, and change the call to the `window.alert()` method:

```
alert(document.title);
```

Notice that `document.title` is NOT now enclosed in quotation marks. If it were, JavaScript would infer that you wanted to output the string "document.title" as literal text. Without the quote marks, JavaScript sends to the `alert()` method the value contained in the `document.title` property. The result is shown in Figure 1.4.

FIGURE 1.4
Displaying a property of the `document` object

Summary

In this first lesson, you were introduced to the concepts of server-side and client-side scripting and read a brief history of JavaScript and the Document Object Model. You had an overview of the sorts of things JavaScript can do to enhance your web pages and improve the experience for your users.

Additionally, you learned about the basic structure of the Document Object Model and how JavaScript can access particular objects and their properties and use the methods belonging to those objects.

In the lessons that follow, we'll build on these fundamental concepts to get into more advanced scripting projects.

Q&A

Q. If I use server-side scripting (in a language such as Java, PHP, or ASP), can I still use JavaScript on the client side?

A. Most definitely. In fact, the combination of server-side and client-side scripting provides a potent platform, capable of producing powerful applications. Google's Gmail is a good example.

Q. How many different browsers should I test in?

A. As many as you practically can. Writing standards-compliant code that avoids browser-specific features will go a long way toward making your code run smoothly in different browsers. However, one or two minor differences between browser implementations of certain features are likely to always exist.

Q. Won't the inclusion of JavaScript code slow down the load time of my pages?

A. Yes, though usually the difference is small enough not to be noticeable. If you have a particularly large piece of JavaScript code, you may feel it's worthwhile testing your page on the slowest connection a user is likely to have. Other than in extreme circumstances, it's unlikely to be a serious issue.

Workshop

Quiz questions and exercises to test your understanding and to stretch your skills.

Quiz

1. Is JavaScript a compiled or an interpreted language?

    a. A compiled language

    b. An interpreted language

    c. Neither

    d. Both

2. What extra tags must be added to an HTML page to include JavaScript statements?

    a. `<script>` and `</script>`

    b. `<type="text/javascript">`

    c. `<!--` and `-->`

3. The top level of the DOM hierarchy is occupied by

    a. The `document` property

    b. The `document` method

    c. The `document` object

    d. The `window` object

4. The `window.alert()` method is used to

    a. Send a message to the user in a modal dialog box.

    b. Send a message to the user in the taskbar of the browser.

    c. Write characters into the text of a web page.

5. Which of these statements is true?

    a. The window object is a child of the document object.

    b. The document object is a child of the window object.

    c. Neither of the above.

Answers

1. b. JavaScript is an interpreted language. The program code is written in plain text, and the statements are read and executed one at a time.

2. a. JavaScript statements are added between `<script>` and `</script>` tags.

3. d. The `window` object is at the top of the DOM tree, and the `document` object is one of its child objects.

4. a. Send a message to the user in a modal dialog box.

5. b. The document object is a child of the window object.

Exercises

In the "Try It Yourself" section of this lesson, you used the line

```
alert(document.title);
```

to output the title property of the `document` object. Try rewriting that script to instead output the `document.lastModified` property, which contains the date and time that the web page was last changed. (Be careful—property names are case sensitive. Note the capital *M*.) See whether you can then modify the code to use `document.write()` in place of `alert()` to write the property directly into the page, as in Figure 1.3.

Try the sample code from this lesson in as many different browsers as you have access to. What differences do you note in how the sample pages are displayed?

LESSON 2
Writing Simple Scripts

What You'll Learn in This Lesson:

▶ Various ways to include JavaScript in your web pages

▶ The basic syntax of JavaScript statements

▶ How to declare and use variables

▶ Ways to use mathematical operators

▶ How to comment your code

▶ How to capture mouse events

You learned in Lesson 1, "Introducing JavaScript," that JavaScript is a scripting language capable of making web pages more interactive.

In this lesson you learn more about how to add JavaScript to your web pages and then about some of the fundamental syntax of JavaScript programs such as statements, variables, operators, and comments. You'll also get your hands dirty with more code examples.

Including JavaScript in Your Web Page

In the previous lesson, you learned that JavaScript programs are passed to the browser along with page content. But how do you achieve that? Actually, two basic methods associate JavaScript code with your HTML page, both of which use the `<script></script>` element introduced in Lesson 1.

One method is to include the JavaScript statements directly into the HTML file, just like you did in the previous lesson:

```
<script>
    ... Javascript statements are written here ...
</script>
```

A second, and usually preferable, way to include your code is to save your JavaScript into a separate file and use the `<script>` element to include that file by name using the `src` (source) attribute:

```
<script src='mycode.js'></script>
```

The preceding example includes the file mycode.js, which contains the JavaScript statements. If your JavaScript file is not in the same folder as the calling script, you can also add a (relative or absolute) path to it:

```
<script src='/path/to/mycode.js'></script>
```

or

```
<script src='http://www.example.com/path/to/mycode.js'></script>
```

Placing your JavaScript code in a separate file offers some important advantages:

▶ When the JavaScript code is updated, the updates are immediately available to any page using that same JavaScript file. This capability is particularly important in the context of JavaScript libraries, which we look at in a later lesson.

▶ The code for the HTML page is kept cleaner and therefore is easier to read and maintain.

▶ Performance is slightly improved because your browser caches the included file, therefore storing a local copy in memory until the next time it is needed by this or another page.

NOTE

File Extensions

It is customary to give files of JavaScript code the file extension .js, as in this example. However, your included code files can have any extension, and the browser will try to interpret the contents as JavaScript.

CAUTION

Take Care with Markup

The JavaScript statements in the external file must NOT be surrounded by `<script>` ... `</script>` tags. In addition, you cannot place any HTML markup within the external file. Just include the raw JavaScript code.

Listing 2.1 shows the simple web page used in Lesson 1, but now with a file of JavaScript code included in the `<body>` section. JavaScript can be placed in either the head or body of the HTML page. In fact, it is more common—and generally recommended—for JavaScript code to be placed in the head of the page, where it provides a number of functions that can be called from elsewhere in the document. You'll learn about functions in Lesson 3, "Introducing Functions"; until then, you can limit yourself to adding sample code into the body of the document.

LISTING 2.1   An HTML Document with a JavaScript File Included

```
<!DOCTYPE html>
<html>
<head>
    <title>A Simple Page</title>
</head>
<body>
    <p>Some content ...</p>
    <script src='mycode.js'></script>
</body>
</html>
```

When JavaScript code is added into the body of the document, the code statements are interpreted and executed as they are encountered while the page is being rendered. For this reason, it's important that JavaScript instructions do not try to access DOM elements that haven't yet been defined. Instead, JavaScript statements must be included *after* the HTML that defines such items.

After the code has been read and executed, page rendering continues until the page is complete.

TIP

Multiple Scripts

You're not limited to using a single script element. You can have as many of them on your page as you need.

NOTE

HTML Comments

You sometimes see HTML-style comment notation `<!--` and `-->` inside script elements, surrounding the JavaScript statements, like this:

```
<script>

    <!--

    ... Javascript statements are written here ...

    -->

</script>
```

This notation is for the benefit of ancient browsers that didn't recognize the `<script>` tag. This HTML "comment" syntax prevented such browsers from displaying the JavaScript source code on the screen along with the page content. Unless you have a reason to support very old browsers, this technique is no longer required.

Writing JavaScript Statements

JavaScript programs are lists of individual instructions that we refer to as *statements*. To interpret statements correctly, the browser expects to find each statement written on a separate line:

```
this is statement 1
this is statement 2
```

Alternatively, they can be combined in the same line by terminating each with a semicolon:

```
this is statement 1; this is statement 2;
```

To ease the readability of your code and to help prevent hard-to-find syntax errors, it's good practice to combine both methods by giving each statement its own line and terminating the statement with a semicolon too:

```
this is statement 1;
this is statement 2;
```

Commenting Your Code

Some statements are not intended to be executed by the browser's JavaScript interpreter but are there for the benefit of anybody who may be reading the code. We refer to such lines as *comments*, and there are specific rules for adding comments to your code.

A comment that occupies just a single line of code can be written by placing a double forward slash before the content of the line:

```
// This is a comment
```

NOTE

Comment Syntax

JavaScript can also use the HTML comment syntax for single-line comments:

```
<!-- this is a comment -->
```

However, this is not commonly used in JavaScript programs.

To add a multiline comment in this way, you need to prefix every line of the comment:

```
// This is a comment
// spanning multiple lines
```

A more convenient way of entering multiline comments to your code is to prefix your comment with /* and terminate it with */. A comment written using this syntax can span multiple lines:

```
/* This comment can span
multiple lines without
the need to mark up
every individual line */
```

Adding comments to your code is really a good thing to do, especially when you're writing larger or more complex JavaScript applications. Comments can act as reminders to you, and also as instructions and explanations to anybody else reading your code at a later date.

NOTE

File Size

It's true that comments add a little to the size of your JavaScript source file, and this larger file size can have an adverse effect on page-loading times and code performance. Generally, the difference is so small as to be barely noticeable, but if it really matters, you can always strip out all the comments from a "production" version of your JavaScript file—that is, a version to use with live, rather than development, websites. Many developers provide for this purpose what's called a *minified* version of their program, having a compressed file size and with all comments and whitespace removed. You can often spot such minified files because they usually have a filename with a .min.js suffix.

Using Variables

You can think of a variable as a named "pigeon-hole" where you keep a particular piece of data. Such data can take many different forms—an integer or decimal number, a string of characters, or various other data types discussed later in this lesson or in those that follow. You can call variables pretty much anything you want, so long as you use only alphanumeric characters, the dollar sign ($), or underscores in the name.

NOTE

Case Sensitivity

JavaScript is case sensitive; a variable called `mypetcat` is a different variable from `Mypetcat` or `MYPETCAT`.

Many coders of JavaScript and other programming languages like to use the so-called *CamelCase* convention (also called *mixedCase*, *BumpyCaps*, and various other terms) for variable names.

In CamelCase, compound words or phrases have the elements joined without spaces, with each element's initial letter capitalized except the first letter, which can be either upper- or lowercase. In this example, the variable would be named `MyPetCat` or `myPetCat`.

Suppose you have a variable called `netPrice`. You can set the value stored in `netPrice` with a simple statement:

```
netPrice = 8.99;
```

We call this *assigning a value* to the variable.

NOTE

Assigning a Value and Testing Equality

It's important to note that the = character is used only for **assigning** a value. When you need to instead **test** whether two values or expressions are equal, it's incorrect to use just the = character. Instead, you need == to test equality:

```
if(a == b) { … do something … }   // correct, tests whether a and b are equal
if(a = b) { … do something … }    // incorrect, assigns value of b to a
```

You'll see how to use **conditional statements** like this in Lesson 10, "Controlling Program Flow."

Note that you don't have to declare the existence of this variable before assigning a value, as you would have to in some other programming languages. However, doing so is possible in JavaScript. One way is by using the `var` keyword, and in most cases it's good programming practice:

```
var netPrice;
netPrice = 8.99;
```

Alternatively, you can combine these two statements conveniently and readably into one:

```
var netPrice = 8.99;
```

To assign a character string as the value of a variable, you need to include the string in single or double quotation marks:

```
var productName = "Leather wallet";
```

You could then, for example, write a line of code sending the value contained in that variable to the `window.alert` method:

```
alert(productName);
```

The generated dialog would evaluate the variable and display it (this time, in Mozilla Firefox) as in Figure 2.1.

FIGURE 2.1
Displaying the value of variable `productName`

TIP

Variable Names

Choose readable variable names. Having variable names such as `productName` and `netPrice` makes code much easier to read and maintain than if the same variables were called `var123` and `myothervar49`, even though the latter names are entirely valid.

Working with Operators

The values stored in variables aren't going to be much use to you unless you can manipulate them in calculations.

Arithmetic Operations

First, JavaScript allows you to carry out operations using the standard arithmetic operators of addition, subtraction, multiplication, and division:

```
var theSum = 4 + 3;
```

As you've surely guessed, after this statement is executed, the variable `theSum` will contain a value of 7. You can use variable names in operations too:

```
var productCount = 2;
var subtotal = 14.98;
var shipping = 2.75;
var total = subtotal + shipping;
```

You can use JavaScript to subtract (–), multiply (*), and divide (/) in a similar manner:

```
subtotal = total - shipping;
var salesTax = total * 0.15;
var productPrice = subtotal / productCount;
```

To calculate the remainder from a division, you can use JavaScript's modulus division operator. It is denoted by the % character:

```
var itemsPerBox = 12;
var itemsToBeBoxed = 40;
var itemsInLastBox = itemsToBeBoxed % itemsPerBox;
```

In this example, the variable itemsInLastBox would contain the number 4 after the last statement completes.

JavaScript also has convenient operators to increment (++) or decrement (--) the value of a variable:

```
productCount++;
```

is equivalent to the statement

```
productCount = productCount + 1;
```

Similarly,

```
items--;
```

is just the same as

```
items = items - 1;
```

TIP

Combining Operators

If you need to increment or decrement a variable by a value other than one, JavaScript also allows you to combine other arithmetic operators with the = operator—for example, += and -=.

The following two lines of code are equivalent:

```
total = total + 5;
total += 5;
```

So are these two:

```
counter = counter - step;
counter -= step;
```

You can use this notation for other arithmetic operators such as multiplication and division too:

```
price = price * uplift;
price *= uplift;
```

Operator Precedence

When you use several operators in the same calculation, JavaScript uses precedence rules to determine in what order the calculation should be done. For example, consider the statement

```
var average = a + b + c / 3;
```

If, as the variable's name implies, you're trying to calculate an average, this would not give the desired result; the division operation would be carried out on c before adding the values of a and b to the result. To calculate the average correctly, you would have to add parentheses to the statement, like this:

```
var average = (a + b + c) / 3;
```

If you have doubts about the precedence rules, I recommend that you always use parentheses liberally. There is no cost to doing so, it makes your code easier to read (both for you and for anyone else who later has to edit or decipher it), and it ensures that precedence issues don't spoil your calculations.

NOTE

Precedence Rules

If you have programming experience in another language such as PHP or Java, you'll find that the precedence rules in JavaScript are pretty much identical to the ones you're used to. You can find detailed information on JavaScript precedence at http://msdn.microsoft.com/en-us/library/z3ks45k7(v=vs.94).aspx.

Using the + Operator with Strings

Arithmetic operators don't make much sense if the variables they operate on contain strings rather than numeric values. The exception is the + operator, which JavaScript interprets as an instruction to concatenate (join together sequentially) two or more strings:

```
var firstname = "John";
var surname = "Doe";
var fullname = firstname + " " + surname;
// the variable fullname now contains the value "John Doe"
```

If you try to use the + operator on two variables, one of which is a string and the other numeric, JavaScript converts the numeric value to a string and concatenates the two:

```
var name = "David";
var age = 45;
alert(name + age);
```

Figure 2.2 shows the result of using the + operator on a string and a numeric value.

FIGURE 2.2
Concatenating a string and a numeric value

You'll learn about JavaScript data types and string operations in general, much more in Lesson 7, "Working with Character Strings."

▼ TRY IT YOURSELF

Convert Celsius to Fahrenheit

To convert a temperature in degrees Celsius to one measured in degrees Fahrenheit, you need to multiply by 9, divide by 5, and then add 32. Let's do that in JavaScript:

```
var cTemp = 100; // temperature in Celsius
// Let's be generous with parentheses
var hTemp = ((cTemp * 9) /5 ) + 32;
```

In fact, you could omit all the parentheses from this calculation and it will still work fine:

```
var hTemp = cTemp*9/5 + 32;
```

However, the parentheses make the code easier to understand and help prevent errors caused by operator precedence.

Let's test the code in a web page, as shown in Listing 2.2.

LISTING 2.2   Calculating Fahrenheit from Celsius

```
<!DOCTYPE html>
<html>
<head>
    <title>Fahrenheit From Celsius</title>
</head>
<body>
    <script>
        var cTemp = 100; // temperature in Celsius
```

```
      // Let's be generous with parentheses
      var hTemp = ((cTemp * 9) /5 ) + 32;
      document.write("Temperature in Celsius: " + cTemp + " degrees<br/>");
      document.write("Temperature in Fahrenheit: " + hTemp + " degrees");
   </script>
</body>
</html>
```

Save this code as a file named temperature.html and load it into your browser. You should get the result shown in Figure 2.3.

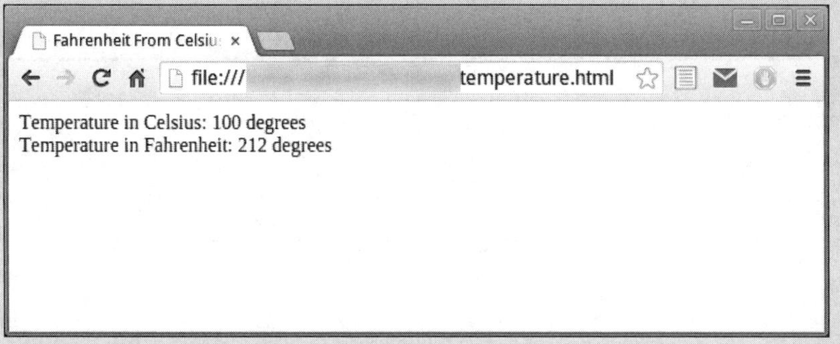

FIGURE 2.3
The output of Listing 2.2

Edit the file a few times to use different values for cTemp, and check that everything works okay.

Capturing Mouse Events

One of the fundamental purposes of JavaScript is to help make your web pages more interactive for the user. To achieve this, you need to have some mechanisms to detect what the user and the program are doing at any given moment—where the mouse is in the browser window, whether the user has clicked a mouse button or pressed a keyboard key, whether a page has fully loaded in the browser, and so on.

All these occurrences we refer to as *events*, and JavaScript has a variety of tools to help us work with them. Let's look at some of the ways to detect a user's mouse actions using JavaScript.

JavaScript deals with events by using so-called event handlers. We are going to investigate three of these: onClick, onMouseOver, and onMouseOut.

The onClick Event Handler

The onClick event handler can be applied to nearly all HTML elements visible on a page. One way you can implement it is to add one more attribute to the HTML element:

```
onclick=" ...some JavaScript code... "
```

NOTE

Adding Event Handlers to HTML Elements

While adding event handlers directly into HTML elements is perfectly valid, doing so is not regarded these days as good programming practice. This approach serves us well for the examples in Part I of this book, but later in the book you'll learn more powerful and elegant ways to use event handlers.

Let's look at the example in Listing 2.3.

LISTING 2.3   Using the onClick Event Handler

```html
<!DOCTYPE html>
<html>
<head>
    <title>onClick Demo</title>
</head>
<body>
    <input type="button" onclick="alert('You clicked the button!')" value="Click Me" />
</body>
</html>
```

The HTML code adds a button to the <body> element of the page and supplies that button with an onclick attribute. The value given to the onclick attribute is the JavaScript code you want to run when the HTML element (in this case a button) is clicked. When the user clicks on the button, the onclick event is activated (we normally say the event has been "fired") and the JavaScript statements listed in the value of the attribute are executed.

In this case, there's just one statement:

```
alert('You clicked the button!')
```

Figure 2.4 shows the result of clicking the button.

FIGURE 2.4
Using the onClick event handler

NOTE

Case Sensitivity

You may have noticed that we call the handler onClick but that we write it in lowercase as onclick when adding it to an HTML element. This convention has arisen because, although HTML *is not* case sensitive, XHTML *is* case sensitive and requires all HTML elements and attribute names to be written in lowercase.

onMouseOver **and** onMouseOut **Event Handlers**

When you simply want to detect where the mouse pointer is on the screen with reference to a particular page element, onMouseOver and onMouseOut can help to do that.

The onMouseOver event is fired when the user's mouse cursor enters the region of the screen occupied by the element in question. The onMouseOut event, as you've already probably guessed, is fired when the cursor leaves that same region.

Listing 2.4 provides a simple example of the onMouseOver event in action.

LISTING 2.4   Using onMouseOver

```
<!DOCTYPE html>
<html>
<head>
    <title>onMouseOver Demo</title>
</head>
<body>
    <img src="image1.png" alt="image 1" onmouseover="alert('You entered the image!')" />
</body>
</html>
```

The result of running the script is shown in Figure 2.5. Replacing onmouseover with onmouseout in the code will, of course, simply fire the event handler—and therefore pop up the alert dialog—as the mouse leaves the image, rather than doing so as it enters.

FIGURE 2.5
Using the onMouseOver event handler

▼ TRY IT YOURSELF

Creating an Image Rollover

You can use the onMouseOver and onMouseOut events to change how an image appears while the mouse pointer is above it. To achieve this, you use onMouseOver to change the src attribute of the HTML <img> element as the mouse cursor enters and onMouseOut to change it back as the mouse cursor leaves. The code is shown in Listing 2.5.

LISTING 2.5 An Image Rollover Using onMouseOver **and** onMouseOut

```
<!DOCTYPE html>
<html>
<head>
    <title>OnMouseOver Demo</title>
</head>
<body>
    <img src="tick.gif" alt="tick" onmouseover="this.src='tick2.gif';"
    onmouseout="this.src='tick.gif';" />
</body>
</html>
```

You may notice something new in the syntax used here. Within the JavaScript statements for `onMouseOver` and `onMouseOut` is the keyword `this`.

When you use `this` within an event handler added via an attribute of an HTML element, `this` refers to the HTML element itself; in this case, you can read it as "this image," and `this.src` refers (using the "dot" notation that we've already met) to the `src` (source) property of this image object.

In this example we used two images—tick.gif and tick2.gif. You can use any images you have on hand, but the demonstration works best if they are the same size and not too large.

Use your editor to create an HTML file containing the code of Listing 2.5. You can change the image names tick.gif and tick2.gif to the names of your two images, if different; just make sure the images are saved in the same folder as your HTML file. Save the HTML file and open it in your browser.

You should see that the image changes as the mouse pointer enters and changes back as it leaves, as depicted in Figure 2.6.

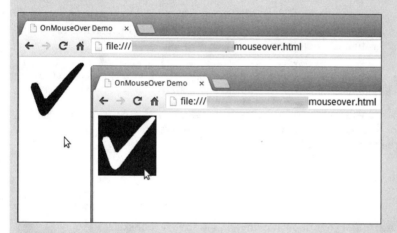

FIGURE 2.6
An image rollover using `onMouseOver` and `onMouseOut`

NOTE

Image Rollovers

At one time image rollovers were regularly done this way, but these days they can be achieved much more efficiently using Cascading Style Sheets (CSS). Still, it's a convenient way to demonstrate the use of the `onMouseOver` and `onMouseOut` event handlers. You'll learn about using CSS with JavaScript in later lessons.

Summary

This lesson covered quite a lot of ground.

First, you learned various ways to include JavaScript code in your HTML pages.

You studied how to declare variables in JavaScript, assign values to those variables, and manipulate them using arithmetic operators.

Finally, you used some of JavaScript's event handlers and learned how to detect certain actions of the user's mouse.

Q&A

Q. Some of the listings and code snippets list opening and closing `<script>` tags on the same line; other times they are on separate lines. Does it matter?

A. JavaScript completely ignores empty spaces such as the space character, tabs, and blank lines. You can use such blank space, which programmers usually call whitespace, to lay out your code in such a way that it's more readable and easy to follow.

Q. Can I use the same `<script>` element both to include an external JavaScript file and to contain JavaScript statements?

A. No. If you use the script element to include an external JavaScript file by using the `src` attribute, you cannot also include JavaScript statements between `<script>` and `</script>`. This region must be left empty.

Workshop

Quiz questions and exercises to test your understanding and to stretch your skills.

Quiz

1. What is an `onClick` event handler?

    a. An object that detects the mouse's location in the browser

    b. A script that executes in response to the user clicking the mouse

    c. An HTML element that the user can click

2. How many `<script>` elements are permitted on a page?

    a. None

    b. Exactly one

    c. Any number

3. Which of these is NOT a true statement about variables?

   a. Their names are case sensitive.

   b. They can contain numeric or non-numeric information.

   c. Their names may contain spaces.

4. Which of these is a valid comment in a JavaScript program?

   a. `// this is a comment`

   b. `/* this is a comment */`

   c. Both of the above

   d. Neither of the above

5. When a + operator is used between a numeric and a non-numeric quantity, JavaScript

   a. Converts the numeric value to a string and concatenates the two

   b. Converts the string to a numeric value and adds the two

   c. Reports an error

TIP

Register Your Book

Just a reminder for those of you reading these words in the print or e-book edition of this book: If you go to www.informit.com/register and register this book (using ISBN 978-0-672-33809-0), you can receive free access to an online Web Edition that not only contains the complete text of this book but also features an interactive version of this quiz.

Answers

   1. b. An `onClick` event handler is a script that executes when the user clicks the mouse.

   2. c. You can use as many `<script>` elements as you need.

   3. c. Variable names in JavaScript must not contain spaces.

   4. c. Both of the above.

   5. a. Converts the numeric value to a string and concatenates the two.

Exercises

Starting with Listing 2.4, remove the `onMouseOver` handler from the `<img>` element. Instead, add an `onClick` handler to set the title property of the image to `My New Title`. (Hint: You can access the image title using `this.title`.)

Can you think of an easy way to test whether your script has correctly set the new image title?

LESSON 3
Introducing Functions

What You'll Learn in This Lesson:

▶ What functions are and what they do

▶ How to define functions

▶ How to call (execute) functions

▶ How functions receive data

▶ How to return values from functions

▶ How to create anonymous functions

Commonly, programs carry out the same or similar tasks repeatedly during the course of their execution. For you to avoid rewriting the same piece of code over and over again, JavaScript has the means to parcel up parts of your code into reusable units, called *functions*. Once you've written a function, it is available for the rest of your program to use, as if it were itself a part of the JavaScript language.

Using functions also makes your code easier to debug and maintain. Suppose you've written an application to calculate shipping costs; when the tax rates or haulage prices change, you'll need to make changes to your script. There may be 50 places in your code where such calculations are carried out. When you attempt to change every calculation, you're likely to miss some instances or introduce errors. However, if all such calculations are wrapped up in a few functions used throughout the application, then you just need to make changes to those functions. Your changes will automatically be applied all through the application.

Functions are one of the basic building blocks of JavaScript and will appear in virtually every script you write. In this lesson you see how to create and use functions.

General Syntax

Creating a function is similar to creating a new JavaScript command that you can use in your script. Here's the basic syntax for creating a function:

```
function sayHello() {
    alert("Hello");
    // ... more statements can go here ...
}
```

You begin with the keyword `function`, followed by your chosen function name with parentheses appended, then a pair of curly braces, `{ }`. Inside the braces go the JavaScript statements that make up the function. The preceding example simply has one line of code to pop up an alert dialog, but you can add as many lines of code as are necessary to make the function...well, function!

CAUTION

Take Care with Case

The keyword `function` must always be used in lowercase; otherwise, an error will be generated.

To keep things tidy, you can collect together as many functions as you like into one `<script>` element:

```
<script>
    function doThis() {
        alert("Doing This");
    }
    function doThat() {
        alert("Doing That");
    }
</script>
```

Calling Functions

Code wrapped up in a function definition will not be executed when the page loads. Instead, it waits quietly until the function is called.

To call a function (you will sometimes hear programmers say "invoke" a function), you simply use the function name, with the parentheses, wherever you want to execute the statements contained in the function:

```
sayHello();
```

For example, you may want to add a call to your new function `sayHello()` to the `onClick` event of a button:

```
<input type="button" value="Say Hello" onclick="sayHello()" />
```

TIP

Function Names

Function names, like variable names, are case sensitive. A function called `MyFunc()` is different from another called `myFunc()`. Also, as with variable names, it's really helpful to the readability of your code to choose meaningful function names.

TIP

About Methods

You've already seen numerous examples of using the *methods* associated with JavaScript objects, such as `document.write()` and `window.alert()`.

Methods are simply functions that "belong" to a specific object. You'll learn much more about objects in the lessons to come.

Putting JavaScript Code in the Page <head>

Up to now, our examples have all placed the JavaScript code into the <body> part of the HTML page. Using functions lets you employ the much more common, and usually preferable, practice of storing your JavaScript code in the <head> of the page. Functions contained within a <script> element in the page head, or in an external file included via the src attribute of a <script> element in the page head, are available to be called from anywhere on the page. Putting functions in the document's head section ensures that they have been defined prior to any attempt being made to execute them.

CAUTION

Multiple Definitions

Be careful that none of your JavaScript functions are defined more than once. This can sometimes happen when you include more than one script element in a page, especially where one or more of these references an external file of JavaScript commands.

If you call a function that has been defined multiple times, JavaScript won't issue an error message. It will simply use the latest definition of the function, so these can be difficult bugs to find!

Listing 3.1 shows an example of a function defined in the head section of the page.

LISTING 3.1   Functions in the Page Head

```
<!DOCTYPE html>
<html>
<head>
    <title>Calling Functions</title>
    <script>
        function sayHello() {
            alert("Hello");
        }
    </script>
</head>
<body>
    <input type="button" value="Say Hello" onclick="sayHello()" />
</body>
</html>
```

In this listing, you can see that the function definition has been placed inside a `<script>` element in the page head, but the call to the function has been made from a different place entirely—on this occasion, from the `onClick` event handler of a button in the body section of the page.

The result of clicking the button is shown in Figure 3.1.

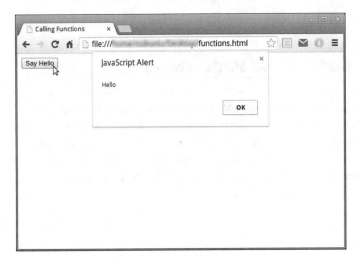

FIGURE 3.1
Calling a JavaScript function

Passing Arguments to Functions

It would be rather limiting if your functions could only behave in an identical fashion each and every time they were called, as would be the case in the preceding example.

Fortunately, you can extend the capabilities of functions a great deal by passing data to them. You do this when the function is called, by passing to it one or more *arguments*:

```
functionName(arguments)
```

Let's write a simple function to calculate the cube of a number and display the result:

```
function cube(x) {
    alert(x * x * x);
}
```

Now you can call the function, replacing the variable x with a number. Calling the function as in the following line results in a dialog being displayed that contains the result of the calculation, in this case 27:

```
cube(3);
```

Of course, you could equally pass a *variable name* as an argument. The following code would also generate a dialog containing the number 27:

```
var length = 3;
cube(length);
```

What's in a Name?

You'll sometimes see or hear the word *parameters* used in place of arguments, but it means essentially the same thing. (In fact, *parameters* are the values the function expects and are baked into function definitions from the beginning, whereas *arguments* are the values provided for those parameters when the function is called. In practice, most programmers use the two terms interchangeably.)

Multiple Arguments

Functions are not limited to a single argument. When you want to send multiple arguments to a function, all you need to do is separate them with commas:

```
function times(a, b) {
    alert(a * b);
}
times(3, 4); // alerts '12'
```

You can use as many arguments as you need.

CAUTION

Count Your Arguments

Make sure that your function calls contain enough argument values to match the parameters specified in the function definition. If any of the parameters in the definition are left without a value, JavaScript may issue an error, or the function may perform incorrectly. If your function call is issued with too many arguments, JavaScript will ignore the extra ones.

It's important to note that the names given to parameters in the definition of your function have nothing to do with the names of any variables whose values are passed to the function. The variable names in the argument list act like placeholders for the actual values that will be passed when the function is called. The names that you give to arguments are only used inside the function definition to specify how it works.

We'll talk about this in more detail in the next lesson when we discuss variable *scope*.

▼ TRY IT YOURSELF

A Function to Output User Messages

Now you can use what you've learned so far in this lesson by creating a function that can send the user a message about a button she has just clicked. You place the function definition in the `<head>` section of the page and call it with multiple arguments.

Here's the function:

```
function buttonReport(buttonId, buttonName, buttonValue) {
    // information about the id of the button
    var userMessage1 = "Button id: " + buttonId + "\n";
    // then about the button name
    var userMessage2 = "Button name: " + buttonName + "\n";
    // and the button value
    var userMessage3 = "Button value: " + buttonValue;
    // alert the user
    alert(userMessage1 + userMessage2 + userMessage3);
}
```

The function `buttonReport` takes three arguments, those being the id, name, and value of the button element that has been clicked. With each of these three pieces of information, a short message is constructed. These three messages are then concatenated into a single string, which is passed to the `alert()` method to pop open a dialog containing the information.

TIP

Special Characters

You may have noticed that the first two message strings have the element `"\n"` appended to the string; this is a *new line* character, forcing the message within the alert dialog to return to the left and begin a new line. Certain special characters like this one must be prefixed with \ if they are to be correctly interpreted when they appear in a string. Such a prefixed character is known as an *escape sequence*. You'll learn more about escape sequences in Lesson 7, "Working with Character Strings."

To call the function, you put a button element on the HTML page, with its id, name, and value defined:

```
<input type="button" id="id1" name="Button 1" value="Something" />
```

You need to add an `onClick` event handler to this button from which to call the function. Here, you can use the `this` keyword, as discussed in Lesson 2, "Writing Simple Scripts":

```
onclick = "buttonReport(this.id, this.name, this.value)"
```

The complete example is shown in Listing 3.2.

LISTING 3.2   **Calling a Function with Multiple Arguments**

```
<!DOCTYPE html>
<html>
<head>
    <title>Calling Functions</title>
    <script>
        function buttonReport(buttonId, buttonName, buttonValue) {
            // information about the id of the button
            var userMessage1 = "Button id: " + buttonId + "\n";
            // then about the button name
            var userMessage2 = "Button name: " + buttonName + "\n";
            // and the button value
            var userMessage3 = "Button value: " + buttonValue;
            // alert the user
            alert(userMessage1 + userMessage2 + userMessage3);
        }
    </script>
</head>
<body>
    <input type="button" id="id1" name="Left Hand Button" value="Left" onclick
    ➡ = "buttonReport(this.id, this.name, this.value)"/>
    <input type="button" id="id2" name="Center Button" value="Center" onclick
    ➡ = "buttonReport(this.id, this.name, this.value)"/>
    <input type="button" id="id3" name="Right Hand Button" value="Right" onclick
    ➡ = "buttonReport(this.id, this.name, this.value)"/>
</body>
</html>
```

Use your editor to create the file buttons.html and enter the preceding code. You should find that it generates output messages like the one shown in Figure 3.2, but with different message content depending on which button has been clicked.

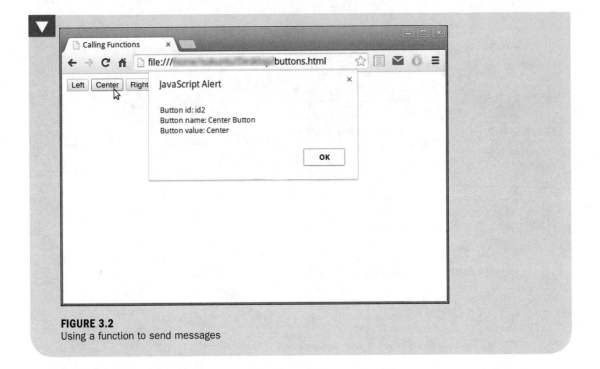

FIGURE 3.2
Using a function to send messages

Returning Values from Functions

Okay, now you know how to pass information to functions so that they can act on that information for you. But how can you get information back from your function? You won't always want your functions to be limited to popping open a dialog!

To achieve this, you can use a mechanism to collect data from a function call—the *return value*. Let's see how it works using a modified version of the cube() function:

```
function cube(x) {
    return x * x * x;
}
```

Instead of using an alert() dialog within the function, as in the previous example, this time the required result is prefixed with the return keyword. To access this value from outside the function, you simply assign to a variable the value returned by the function:

```
var answer = cube(3);
```

After this line is executed, the variable answer will contain the value 27.

Remember that to call a function, you must add the parentheses to the function name as in the preceding example. If you use the function name without the parentheses, JavaScript will assume you're referring to the definition of the function, rather than the value it returns. Suppose that, in the preceding code snippet, you had instead used

```
var answer = cube;    // note no parentheses!
```

When this line is executed, instead of the number 27 the variable answer will contain an identical function definition to that of cube(), so the following line, when executed, would alert a value of 27:

```
alert(answer(3));  // alerts 27
```

NOTE

Data Types of Return Values

The values returned by functions are not restricted to numerical quantities as in this example. In fact, functions can return values having any of the data types supported by JavaScript. If no return statement is included in a function, it will by default return a value of undefined. We'll discuss this and other data types in the lessons of Part II, "Cooking with Code."

TIP

Passing Return Values to Other Statements

Where a function returns a value, you can use the function call to pass the return value directly to another statement in the code. For example, instead of

```
var answer = cube(3);
alert(answer);
```

you could simply use

```
alert(cube(3));
```

The value of 27 returned from the function call cube(3) immediately becomes the argument passed to the alert() method.

Anonymous Functions

There is a more convenient and elegant way to define a function, without having to create a separate named function and then later assign it by name to the required method.

In Listing 3.1 you used this line of code:

```
<input type="button" value="Say Hello" onclick="sayHello()" />
```

You'll recall that this was the function definition:

```
function sayHello() {
    alert("Hello");
}
```

An alternative way to achieve the same effect would be like this:

```
var sayHello = function() { alert("Hello"); };
```

Because you haven't needed to give a name to your function prior to assigning it, this technique is referred to as using an *anonymous function*.

This way of defining functions can be concise and useful, and you'll see it a lot in the lessons to come.

Summary

In this lesson you learned about what functions are and how to create them in JavaScript. You learned how to call functions from within your code and pass information to those functions in the form of arguments. You also found out how to return information from a function to its calling statement.

Finally, you learned about anonymous functions.

Q&A

Q. Can one function contain a call to another function?

A. Most definitely; in fact, such calls can be nested as deeply as you need them to be.

Q. What characters can I use in function names?

A. Function names must start with a letter or an underscore and can contain letters, digits, and underscores in any combination. They cannot contain spaces, punctuation, or other special characters.

Workshop

Quiz questions and exercises to test your understanding and to stretch your skills.

Quiz

1. Functions are called using

   a. The function keyword

   b. The call command

   c. The function name, with parentheses

2. What happens when a function executes a return statement?

    a. An error message is generated.

    b. A value is returned and function execution continues.

    c. A value is returned and function execution stops.

3. A function can return

    a. Only a number

    b. Only a number or a string

    c. Any valid JavaScript data type

4. An argument is

    a. A piece of logical reasoning used within a function

    b. A value passed to a function as a parameter

    c. A value returned by a function

5. A function defined without being named

    a. Is referred to as an anonymous function

    b. Never returns a value

    c. Will cause an error

TIP

Register Your Book

Just a reminder for those of you reading these words in the print or e-book edition of this book: If you go to www.informit.com/register and register this book (using ISBN 978-0-672-33809-0), you can receive free access to an online Web Edition that not only contains the complete text of this book but also features an interactive version of this quiz.

Answers

    1. c. A function is called using the function name, with parentheses.

    2. c. After executing a return statement, a function returns a value and then ceases function execution.

    3. c. A functtion can return any valid JavaScript data type.

    4. b. An argument is a value passed to a function as a parameter.

    5. a. A function defined without being named is referred to as an anonymous function.

Exercises

Write a function to take a temperature value in Celsius as an argument and return the equivalent temperature in Fahrenheit, basing it on the code from Lesson 2.

Test your function in an HTML page having three buttons that, when clicked, pass values of 10, 20, and 30 degrees Celsius, respectively, to the function. Check that everything works to your satisfaction.

LESSON 4
More Fun with Functions

What You'll Learn in This Lesson:

▶ The scope of variables
▶ How to use `let` and `const`
▶ How to make your syntax more concise with arrow functions
▶ Ways to give your functions default parameters

In Lesson 3, "Introducing Functions," you learned a little about identifying parts of your code with distinct, reusable objectives and parceling up—the term programmers usually use is *abstracting*—those processes into functions.

In this lesson you first dig deeper into functions to see how they affect the accessibility of variables in your code. You also see a few new tricks to make your functions more concise and productive.

Scope of Variables

You have already seen how to declare variables with the `var` keyword. There is a golden rule to remember when using functions:

"Variables declared inside a function using the keyword `var` exist only inside that function."

This limitation is known as the *scope* of the variable. Let's look at an example:

```
// Define our function addTax()
function addTax(subtotal, taxRate) {
    var total = subtotal * (1 + (taxRate/100));
    return total;
}
// now let's call the function
var invoiceValue = addTax(50, 10);

alert(invoiceValue); // works correctly
alert(total); // doesn't work
```

If you run this code, you first see an `alert()` dialog with the value of the variable `invoiceValue` (which should be 55, but in fact will probably be something like 55.000000001 because the code doesn't ask JavaScript to round the result).

You do not, however, then see an `alert()` dialog containing the value of the variable total. Instead, JavaScript simply produces an error. Whether you see this error reported depends on your browser settings—you'll learn more about error handling later in the book—but JavaScript is unable to display an `alert()` dialog with the value of your variable total.

The reason is that the declaration of the variable total is placed inside the instruction block that forms the definition of the `addTax()` function. Outside the function the variable total simply doesn't exist (or, as JavaScript puts it, "is not defined"). The `return` keyword passes back just the *value* stored in the variable `total`, and that value is then stored in another variable, `invoiceValue`.

We refer to variables declared inside a function definition as being *local variables*, that is, local to that function. Variables declared outside any function are known as *global variables*. To add a little more confusion, local and global variables can have the same name but still be different variables!

The range of situations in which a variable is defined is known as the *scope* of the variable—for example, you can refer to a variable as having *local scope* or having *global scope*.

▼ TRY IT YOURSELF

Demonstrating the Scope of Variables

To illustrate the issue of a variable's scope, let's look at the following piece of code:

```
var a = 10;
var b = 10;
function showVars() {
        var a = 20; // declare a new local variable 'a'
        b = 20; // change the value of global variable 'b'
        return "Local variable 'a' = " + a + "\nGlobal variable 'b' = " + b;
    }
var message = showVars();
alert(message + "\nGlobal variable 'a' = " + a);
```

Within the `showVars()` function, two variables, a and b, are manipulated. The variable a is defined inside the function; this is a local variable that exists only inside the function, quite separate from the global variable (also called a) that is declared at the beginning of the script.

The variable b is not declared inside the function, but outside; it is a **global** variable.

Listing 4.1 shows the preceding code within an HTML page.

LISTING 4.1   Global and Local Scope

```html
<!DOCTYPE html>
<html>
<head>
    <title>Variable Scope</title>
</head>
<body>
    <script>
        var a = 10;
        var b = 10;
        function showVars() {
            var a = 20; // declare a new local variable 'a'
            b = 20; // change the value of global variable 'b'
            return "Local variable 'a' = " + a + "\nGlobal variable 'b' = " + b;
        }
        var message = showVars();
        alert(message + "\nGlobal variable 'a' = " + a);
    </script>
</body>
</html>
```

When the page is loaded, `showVars()` returns a message string containing information about the updated values of the two variables `a` and `b`, as they exist inside the function—`a` with local scope and `b` with global scope.

A message about the current value of the other global variable, `a`, is then appended to the message, and the message displayed to the user.

Copy the code into the file `scope.html` and load it into your browser. Compare your results with Figure 4.1.

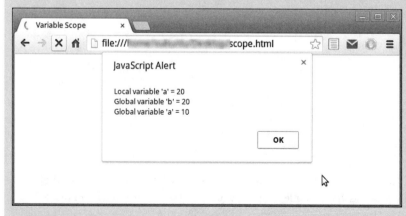

FIGURE 4.1
Local and global scope

Using the `this` Keyword

You may recall that you used such a keyword in Lesson 2, "Writing Simple Scripts," while you were defining an inline event handler:

```
<img src="tick.gif" alt="tick" onmouseover="this.src='tick2.gif';" />
```

When used in that way, `this` refers to the HTML element itself—in the preceding case the `<img>` element.

When you use `this` inside a function, the keyword `this` refers to whatever "owns" the function—something we refer to as the *parent scope* of the function.

In Listing 4.1, the `showVars()` function was created at the "top level." In other words, it belongs to the global object (the object that also owns any variables that are in global scope). In a web browser the global object is normally the browser's `window` object.

So what would happen if you asked the function to return the value of `this.a`, as in the following code snippet?

```
function showVars() {
    var a = 20; // declare a new local variable 'a'
    b = 20; // change the value of global variable 'b'
    return "this.a = " + this.a + "\nLocal variable 'a' = " + a + "\nGlobal
    ➡ variable 'b' = " + b;
}

var message = showVars();
alert(message + "\nGlobal variable 'a' = " + a);
```

Since `this` refers here to the global object, `this.a` refers to the variable a, which is in global scope. The output from the program would be something like that shown in Figure 4.2.

FIGURE 4.2
Showing that `this.a` refers to the global variable a

If this explanation all seems a little confusing, don't worry. We'll be revisiting the keyword `this` at several points throughout the upcoming lessons, especially when we start to deal in more detail with objects in Lesson 11, "Introducing Object-Oriented Programming."

Declaring Variables Using `let`

Until recently, JavaScript had only two types of scope—namely, the *function scope* and *global scope* that you've already heard about.

Having only these two types was a nuisance to many programmers, especially those more familiar with other languages. Many other programming languages allow variables to have so-called block scope (a block in JavaScript constitutes the entire contents of a pair of curly braces { }). A variable with block scope would be accessible only to program statements occurring within the same block as the variable definition.

Recent updates to the JavaScript language have seen this omission corrected with a new keyword `let`, which allows you to define a variable with exactly this block scope.

Now look at the following code snippet. It introduces something you haven't seen before: the `if()` statement. Don't worry too much about the syntax at this point, because you'll be reading about such conditional statements in much more detail in Lesson 10, "Controlling Program Flow." Suffice to say that such a statement allows your program to execute a block of statements only if a particular condition is met—in this case that variable x has a value greater than 50.

```
function myFunction(x) {
    var y = x;
    if(x > 50) {
        var y = 10;
        alert("Inner y = " + y);  // alerts 10
    }
    alert("Outer y = " + y);  // alerts 10
    ... more statements ...
}
```

What will the program display in the alert dialogs if we call the function with an argument of 100? The value of y will initially be set to 100, with *function scope*; that is, its value will be accessible anywhere within the function.

Since the value of x is greater than 50, the inner block of code will then be executed. The first command within that inner block will redeclare y, and since the `var` keyword gives the declared variable function scope, the new value will be accessible throughout the entire function `myFunction`. The result is that, when you leave the inner code block and the second alert is executed, the new value of y (that is, a value of 10) will be displayed. Any further lines of code in the outer block will "see" this new value of y.

Now consider what happens if instead you use `let` in the inner block:

```
function myFunction(x) {
    var y = x;
    if(x > 50) {
        let y = 10;
```

```
        alert("Inner y = " + y);  // alerts 10
    }
    alert("Outer y = " + y);  // alerts 100
    ... more statements ...
}
```

Here, the variable y declared within the inner code block has only *block scope*; when execution leaves the inner block and performs the second alert, a value of 100 will be reported for y and seen by any subsequent lines of code in the outer block.

Declaring Constants with the const Keyword

Sometimes you need to store a value that simply can't be changed by later code. Examples might include, for instance, the initial setup parameters of your program, such as the width and height of a page element for displaying output.

You can achieve this result by using the keyword const. A const declaration creates a *constant*—a value that can't be changed by reassignment or redeclaration later in the code. Any attempt to change the value of a variable declared using const will result in an error:

```
function myFunction() {
    const x = 300;
    x = 400;   // an error is generated at this line

    ... more statements ...
}
```

▼ TRY IT YOURSELF

Checking Out const

Let's look at how const operates. At the time of writing, it works in most browsers, but here we're going to use Google Chrome.

Instead of writing code in a text file, open the JavaScript Console for your browser, as shown in Figure 4.3. In the case of Chrome, you can do that by pressing Ctrl+Shift+J.

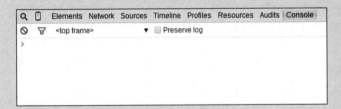

FIGURE 4.3
Chrome's JavaScript Console

First, define a constant using the `const` keyword. You can call it anything you like and choose any value. The one here is called `MYCONST` and it has a value of 10 (see Figure 4.4).

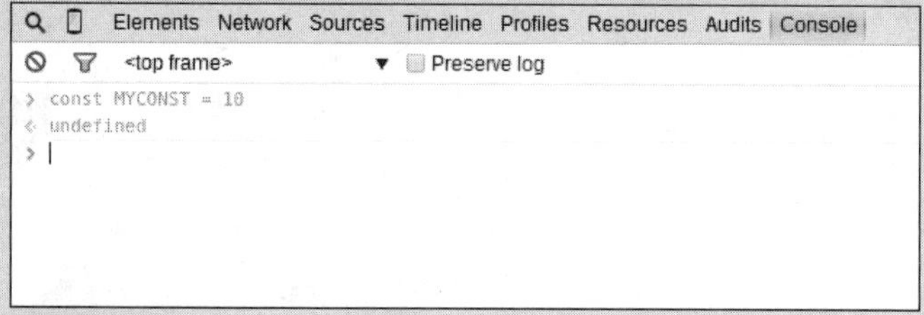

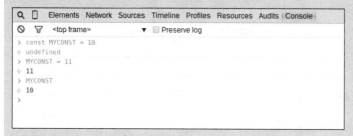

FIGURE 4.4
Setting a constant

The console issues `undefined` because the declaration of a `const` does not return a value.

Now try to redefine the value of `MYCONST`, as shown in Figure 4.5.

FIGURE 4.5
The constant can't be reassigned.

As you can see, the constant `MYCONST` couldn't be reassigned a new value. Now try to redeclare it instead (see Figure 4.6).

FIGURE 4.6
Redeclaration of a constant doesn't work.

Nope, you can't do that either. Finally, try to reinitialize it (see Figure 4.7).

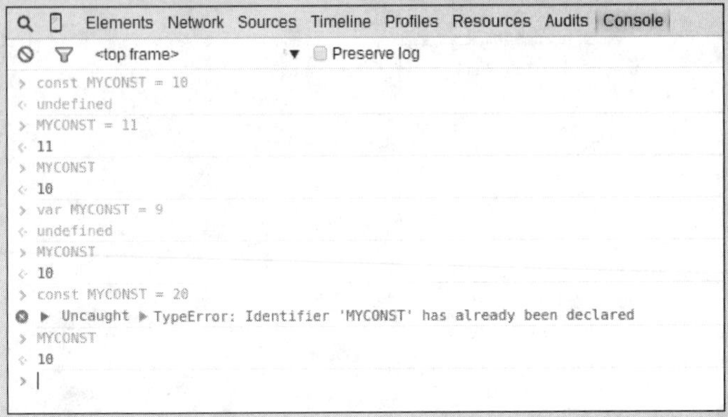

```
Q  ☐   Elements  Network  Sources  Timeline  Profiles  Resources  Audits │ Console │
⊘  ▽   <top frame>              ▼ ☐ Preserve log
>  const MYCONST = 10
⊲  undefined
>  MYCONST = 11
⊲  11
>  MYCONST
⊲  10
>  var MYCONST = 9
⊲  undefined
>  MYCONST
⊲  10
>  const MYCONST = 20
❶ ▶ Uncaught ▶ TypeError: Identifier 'MYCONST' has already been declared
>  MYCONST
⊲  10
>  |
```

FIGURE 4.7
Trying to reinitialize throws an error.

JavaScript throws an error.

Values declared using the `const` keyword, as you can see, cannot be reinitialized, redeclared, or reassigned.

Arrow Functions

In the preceding lesson you learned about anonymous functions.

Here's the example used in that lesson:

```
var sayHello = function() { alert("Hello"); };
```

A recent inclusion in JavaScript is a more concise syntax for writing this sort of function, in which the arrow symbol (=>) is shorthand for an anonymous function. These are generally known as *arrow functions*.

NOTE
Lambda Functions

If you've come to JavaScript from another programming language such as C#, Java, or Python, you may recognize a similarity between the arrow functions of JavaScript and the Lambda functions available in other languages.

The preceding line of code could be rewritten like this:

```
var sayHello = () => alert('Hello');
```

Notice that you don't have to include the keyword function or (in this case) the curly braces.

NOTE

The Fat Arrow

The `=>` symbol is often referred to as the *fat arrow* symbol.

In more general terms, arrow functions are written like this:

```
param => statements/expression
```

First, let's look at `param`, the name of a parameter (or parameters) to be passed to the function. Where a function requires no arguments, as in the previous example of the alert box, you indicate this with an empty pair of parentheses `()`.

If only one parameter is passed to the function, the parentheses aren't required; you can simply write something like this:

```
myFunc = x => alert(x);
```

On the right side, you need curly braces only where more than one expression is included. Where there's only one statement or expression, like in the `alert()` example, they're not required.

Here's an example with two parameters:

```
myFunc = (x, y) => alert(x + y);
```

More complex functions can use the familiar curly braces and return parameter, if required, as in this example:

```
myFunc = (x, y, z) => {
    let area = x*y + 5;
    let boxes = area / z;
    return boxes;
}
```

Setting Default Parameters

Sometimes it's useful to have your functions assign a default value to a parameter where no argument is given.

As an example, consider a function that outputs user messages:

```
function warn(temp) {
    alert("Warning:\nA Temperature of " + temp + " is too high");
}
```

Programs can call this function easily to create the user message:

```
warn(95);
```

The output of the script would be an alert dialog something like the one in Figure 4.8.

FIGURE 4.8
A simple warning dialog

On rare occasions you might want to change the wording to something more eye-catching. To do so, you can rewrite the function to add an option to change part of the message. To specify a default parameter, you just assign the default value to the parameter in the function definition:

```
function warn(temp, headline='Warning') {
    alert(headline + ":\nA Temperature of " + temp + " is too high");
}
```

The function can be called in exactly the same way as previously:

```
warn(95);
```

Once again, the result is as in Figure 4.8, since the default value for `headline` has been used in the absence of any submitted argument. However, you can now, when required, change the message by overwriting the default argument for the second parameter, `headline`:

```
warn(105, '***DANGER***');
```

The result is shown in Figure 4.9.

FIGURE 4.9
Overwriting a default value

Remember that parameters having defaults specified should always come after nondefault parameters in the function definition.

Summary

In this lesson you learned about the local or global scope of a variable and how the scope of variables affects how functions work with them.

You also found out how the `this` keyword works in the context of a function.

Finally, you learned how to make function syntax more concise by using arrow functions.

Q&A

Q. Is it possible to design functions that will work for an arbitrary number of arguments?

A. Yes, it is, but it's a little beyond the scope of this lesson. We'll return to the subject in Lesson 8, "Storing Data in Arrays."

Q. Why must parameters having defaults specified always come after nondefault parameters in the function definition?

A. Consider a function definition like this one:

```
function myFunc(a=10, b) {
    … statements
}
```

You now try to call `myFunc` with b equal to 20:

```
myFunc(20);
```

The value of `a` will be overwritten with 20, but no value will then be provided for `b`, and the function will fail. To make it work, you'd have to include arguments for both parameters:

```
myFunc(10, 20);
```

This approach will work, but it negates the advantage of having default parameters in the first place!

Workshop

Quiz questions and exercises to test your understanding and to stretch your skills.

Quiz

1. A variable declared inside a function definition is called

  a. A local variable

  b. A global variable

  c. An argument

2. A variable declared using the `const` keyword

  a. Is always numeric

  b. Is read-only

  c. Can be redeclared

3. Declaring a variable by using the `let` keyword creates a variable with

   a. Local scope

   b. Block scope

   c. Global scope

4. When you use `this` within a function definition, `this` refers to

   a. The variables declared inside the function

   b. The function itself

   c. The object that "owns" the function

5. An arrow function

   a. Is an anonymous function

   b. Cannot accept arguments

   c. Both of the above

TIP
_____

Register Your Book

Just a reminder for those of you reading these words in the print or e-book edition of this book: If you go to www.informit.com/register and register this book (using ISBN 978-0-672-33809-0), you can receive free access to an online Web Edition that not only contains the complete text of this book but also features an interactive version of this quiz.
_____

Answers

1. a. A variable defined within a function has local scope.

2. b. Is read-only.

3. b. Block scope.

4. c. The object that "owns" the function.

5. a. Is an anonymous function.

Exercise

Revisit the script you wrote in the exercise for Lesson 3. Modify the script so that your temperature conversion function now has a default value of zero for its argument. Add an extra button to the page that, when clicked, calls the function without passing any argument. Check that the script correctly outputs 32 (the Fahrenheit equivalent of zero degrees Celsius) and that all the other buttons operate as they did previously.

DOM Objects and Built-in Objects

In Lesson 1, "Introducing JavaScript," we talked a little about the DOM and introduced the top-level object in the DOM tree, the `window` object. We also looked at one of its child objects, `document`.

In this lesson, you learn about some more of the utility objects and methods that you can use in your scripts.

Interacting with the User

Among the methods belonging to the `window` object, some are designed specifically to help your page communicate with the user by assisting with the input and output of information.

alert()

You've already used the `alert()` method to pop up an information dialog for the user. You'll recall that this modal dialog simply shows your message with a single OK button. The term *modal* means that script execution pauses, and all user interaction with the page is suspended until the user clears the dialog. The `alert()` method takes a message string as its argument:

```
alert("This is my message");
```

`alert()` does not return a value.

`confirm()`

The `confirm()` method is similar to `alert()`, in that it pops up a modal dialog with a message for the user. The `confirm()` dialog, though, provides the user with a choice; instead of a single OK button, the user may select between OK and Cancel, as shown in Figure 5.1. Clicking on either button clears the dialog and allows the calling script to continue, but the `confirm()` method returns a different value depending on which button was clicked—Boolean `true` in the case of OK, or `false` in the case of Cancel. We'll look at JavaScript's data types in the next lesson, but for the moment you just need to know that a Boolean variable can take only one of two values, `true` or `false`.

FIGURE 5.1
The `confirm()` dialog

The `confirm()` method is called in a similar way to `alert()`, passing the required message as an argument:

```
var answer = confirm("Are you happy to continue?");
```

Note that here, though, you pass the returned value of `true` or `false` to a variable so you can later test its value and have the script take appropriate action depending on the result.

`prompt()`

The `prompt()` method is yet another way to open a modal dialog. In this case, though, the dialog invites the user to enter information.

A `prompt()` dialog is called in just the same manner as `confirm()`:

```
var answer = prompt("What is your full name?");
```

The `prompt()` method also allows for an optional second argument, giving a default response in case the user clicks OK without typing anything:

```
var answer = prompt("What is your full name?", "John Doe");
```

The return value from a `prompt()` dialog depends on what option the user takes:

▶ If the user types in input and clicks OK or presses Enter, the user input string is returned.

▶ If the user clicks OK or presses Enter without typing anything into the prompt dialog, the method returns the default response (if any), as optionally specified in the second argument passed to `prompt()`.

▶ If the user dismisses the dialog (that is, by clicking Cancel or pressing Escape), then the `prompt()` method returns `null`.

NOTE

The `null` Value

JavaScript uses the `null` value on certain occasions to denote an empty value. When treated as a number, it takes the value 0; when used as a string, it evaluates to the empty string (`""`); and when used as a Boolean value, it becomes `false`.

The `prompt()` dialog generated by the previous code snippet is shown in Figure 5.2.

FIGURE 5.2
The `prompt()` dialog

Selecting Elements by Their ID

In later lessons you'll learn a lot about navigating around the DOM using the various methods of the `document` object. For now, we limit ourselves to looking at one in particular—the `getElementById()` method.

To select an element of your HTML page having a specific ID, all you need to do is call the document object's `getElementById()` method, specifying as an argument the ID of the required element. The method returns the DOM object corresponding to the page element with the specified ID.

Let's look at an example. Suppose your web page contains a `<div>` element:

```
<div id="div1">
    ... Content of DIV element ...
</div>
```

In your JavaScript code, you can access this `<div>` element using `getElementById()`, passing the required ID to the method as an argument:

```
var myDiv = document.getElementById("div1");
```

You now have access to the chosen page element and all its properties and methods.

CAUTION

Make Sure There Is an ID Value

Of course, for this approach to work, the page element must have its ID attribute set. Because ID values of HTML page elements are required to be unique, the method should always return a single page element, provided a matching ID is found.

The `innerHTML` Property

A handy property that exists for many DOM objects, `innerHTML` allows you to get or set the value of the HTML content inside a particular page element. Imagine your HTML contains the following element:

```
<div id="div1">
    <p>Here is some original text.</p>
</div>
```

You can access the HTML content of the `<div>` element using a combination of `getElementById()` and `innerHTML`:

```
var myDivContents = document.getElementById("div1").innerHTML;
```

The variable `myDivContents` will now contain the string value:

```
"<p>Here is some original text.</p>"
```

You can also use `innerHTML` to set the contents of a chosen element:

```
document.getElementById("div1").innerHTML = "<p>Here is some new text instead!</p>";
```

Executing this code snippet erases the previous HTML content of the `<div>` element and replaces it with the new string.

Accessing Browser History

The browser's history is represented in JavaScript by the `window.history` object, which is essentially a list of the URLs previously visited. Its methods enable you to use the list, but not to manipulate the URLs explicitly.

The only property owned by the `history` object is its length. You can use this property to find how many pages the user has visited:

```
alert("You've visited " + history.length + " web pages in this browser session");
```

The `history` object has three methods.

`forward()` and `back()` are equivalent to pressing the Forward and Back buttons on the browser; they take the user to the next or previous page in the history list.

```
history.forward();
```

The third method, `go`, takes a single parameter. This can be an integer, positive or negative, and it takes the user to a relative place in the history list:

```
history.go(-3); // go back 3 pages
history.go(2); // go forward 2 pages
```

The method can alternatively accept a string, which it uses to find the first matching URL in the history list:

```
history.go("example.com"); // go to the nearest URL in the history
                           // list that contains 'example.com'
```

Using the `location` Object

The `location` object contains information about the URL of the currently loaded page.

You can think of the page URL as a series of parts:

```
[protocol]//[hostname]:[port]/[pathname][search][hash]
```

Here's a sample URL:

```
http://www.example.com:8080/tools/display.php?section=435#list
```

The list of properties of the location object includes data concerning the various parts of the URL. The properties are listed in Table 5.1.

TABLE 5.1 Properties of the `location` Object

Property	Description
`location.href`	'http://www.example.com:8080/tools/display.php?section=435#list'
`location.protocol`	'http:'
`location.host`	'www.example.com:8080'
`location.hostname`	'www.example.com'
`location.port`	'8080'
`location.pathname`	'/tools/display.php'
`location.search`	'?section=435'
`location.hash`	'#list'

Navigating Using the `location` Object

There are two ways to take the user to a new page using the `location` object.

First, you can directly set the `href` property of the object:

```
location.href = 'www.newpage.com';
```

Using this technique to transport the user to a new page maintains the original page in the browser's history list, so the user can return simply by using the browser's Back button.

If you prefer that the sending page is removed from the history list and replaced with the new URL, you can instead use the location object's `replace()` method:

```
location.replace('www.newpage.com');
```

This method replaces the old URL with the new one both in the browser and in the history list.

Reloading the Page

To reload the current page into the browser—the equivalent of having the user click the "reload page" button—you can use the `reload()` method:

```
location.reload();
```

TIP

Avoiding Cache Problems

Using `reload()` without any arguments retrieves the current page from the browser's cache, if it's available there. To avoid this and get the page directly from the server, you can call `reload()` with the argument `true`:

```
document.reload(true);
```

Obtaining Browser Information—The navigator Object

Whereas the location object stores information about the current URL loaded in the browser, the navigator object's properties contain data about the browser application itself.

Displaying Information Using the navigator Object

We're going to write a script that allows you to find out what the navigator object knows about your own browsing setup. Use your editor to create the file navigator.html containing the code from Listing 5.1. Save the file and open it in your browser.

LISTING 5.1   Using the navigator Object

```
<!DOCTYPE html>
<html>
<head>
    <title>window.navigator</title>
    <style>
        td {border: 1px solid gray; padding: 3px 5px;}
    </style>
</head>
<body>
    <script>
        document.write("<table>");
        document.write("<tr><td>appName</td><td>"+navigator.appName + "</td></tr>");
        document.write("<tr><td>appCodeName</td><td>"+navigator.appCodeName
        ➥ + "</td></tr>");
        document.write("<tr><td>appVersion</td><td>"+navigator.appVersion
        ➥ + "</td></tr>");
        document.write("<tr><td>language</td><td>"+navigator.language
        ➥ + "</td></tr>");
        document.write("<tr><td>cookieEnabled</td><td>"+navigator.cookieEnabled
        ➥ + "</td></tr>");
        document.write("<tr><td>cpuClass</td><td>"+navigator.cpuClass
        ➥ + "</td></tr>");
        document.write("<tr><td>onLine</td><td>"+navigator.onLine + "</td></tr>");
        document.write("<tr><td>platform</td><td>"+navigator.platform
        ➥ + "</td></tr>");
        document.write("<tr><td>No of Plugins</td><td>"+navigator.plugins.length
        ➥ + "</td></tr>");
        document.write("</table>");
    </script>
</body>
</html>
```

Compare your results to mine, shown in Figure 5.3.

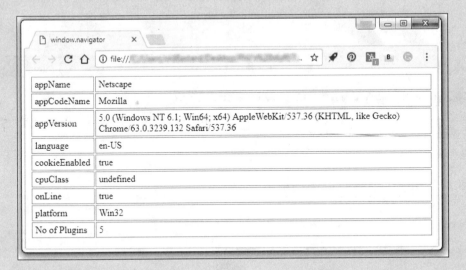

FIGURE 5.3
Browser information from the `navigator` object

Whoa, what's going on here? I loaded the page into the Chromium browser on my Windows PC. Why is it reporting the `appName` property as Netscape and the `appCodeName` property as Mozilla? Also, the `cpuClass` property has come back as `undefined`. What's that all about?

There's a lot of history and politics behind the `navigator` object. The result is that the object provides, at best, an unreliable source of information about the user's platform. Not all properties are supported in all browsers (hence the failure to report the `cpuClass` property in the preceding example), and the names reported for browser type and version rarely match what you would intuitively expect.

Although cross-browser standards compliance is closer than it was a few years ago, there still remain occasions when you need to know the capabilities of your user's browser. Querying the `navigator` object is nearly always the wrong way to do it.

NOTE

Feature Detection

In a later lesson, we'll talk about feature detection, a much more elegant and cross-browser way to have your code make decisions based on the capabilities of the user's browser.

Using Dates and Times

The `Date` object is used to work with dates and times. There is no `Date` object already created for you as part of the DOM, as was the case with the examples so far. Instead, you create your own `Date` objects as and when you need them. Each `Date` object you create can represent a different date and time.

Creating a `Date` Object with the Current Date and Time

The simplest way to create a new `Date` object containing information about the date and time looks like this:

```
var mydate = new Date();
```

The variable `mydate` is an object containing information about the date and time at the moment the object was created. JavaScript has a long list of methods for retrieving, setting, and editing data within `Date` objects. Let's look at a few simple examples:

```
var year = mydate.getFullYear(); // four-digit year e.g. 2018
var month = mydate.getMonth(); // month number 0 - 11; 0 is Jan, etc.
var date = mydate.getDate(); // day of the month 1 - 31
var day = mydate.getDay(); // day of the week 0 - 6; Sunday = 0, etc.
var hours = mydate.getHours(); // hours part of the time, 0 - 23
var minutes = mydate.getMinutes(); // minutes part of time, 0 - 59
var seconds = mydate.getSeconds(); // seconds part of time, 0 - 59
```

Creating a `Date` Object with a Given Date and Time

You can easily create `Date` objects representing arbitrary dates and times by passing arguments to the `Date()` statement. There are several ways to do this:

```
new Date(milliseconds) //milliseconds since January 1st 1970
new Date(dateString)
new Date(year, month, day, hours, minutes, seconds, milliseconds)
```

Here are a few examples.

You can use a date string like this:

```
var d1 = new Date("October 22, 1995 10:57:22")
```

When you use separate arguments for the parts, trailing arguments are optional; any missing arguments are replaced with zero:

```
var d2 = new Date(95,9,22) // 22nd October 1995 00:00:00
var d3 = new Date(95,9,22,10,57,0) // 22nd October 1995 10:57:00
```

Setting and Editing Dates and Times

The `Date` object also has an extensive list of methods for setting or editing the various parts of the date and time:

```
var mydate = new Date(); // current date and time
document.write("Object created on day number " + mydate.getDay() + "<br />");
mydate.setDate(15); // change day of month to the 15th
document.write("After amending date to 15th, the day number is " + mydate.getDay());
```

The preceding code snippet initially creates the object `mydate` representing the date and time of its creation, but with the day of the month subsequently changed to the 15th; if you retrieve the day of the week before and after this operation, you'll see that it has been correctly recalculated to take account of the changed date:

```
Object created on day number 5
After amending date to 15th, the day number is 0
```

So in this example, the object was created on a Friday; whereas the 15th of the month corresponded to a Sunday.

You can also carry out date and time arithmetic, letting the `Date` object do all the heavy lifting:

```
var mydate=new Date();
document.write("Created: " + mydate.toDateString() + " " + mydate.toTimeString()
➡ + "<br />");
mydate.setDate(mydate.getDate()+33); // add 33 days to the 'date' part
document.write("After adding 33 days: " + mydate.toDateString() + " "
➡ + mydate.toTimeString());
```

The preceding example calculates a date 33 days in the future, automatically amending the day, date, month, and/or year as necessary. Note the use of `toDateString()` and `toTimeString()`; they are useful methods for converting dates into a readable format. The preceding example produces output like the following:

```
Created: Mon Jun 18 2018 14:59:24 GMT+0100 (CET)
After adding 33 days: Sat Jul 21 2018 14:59:24 GMT+0100 (CET)
```

Simplifying Calculation with the `Math` Object

JavaScript's `Math` object can save you a lot of work when performing many sorts of calculations that frequently occur.

Unlike the `Date` object, the `Math` object does not need to be created before use; it already exists, and you can call its methods directly.

Table 5.2 shows some of the methods available.

TABLE 5.2   Some Methods of the `Math` Object

Method	Description
`ceil(n)`	Returns n rounded up to the nearest whole number
`floor(n)`	Returns n rounded down to the nearest whole number
`max(a, b, c, ...)`	Returns the largest number
`min(a, b, c, ...)`	Returns the smallest number
`round(n)`	Returns n rounded up or down to the nearest whole number
`random()`	Returns a random number between 0 and 1

Let's work through some examples.

Rounding

The methods `ceil()`, `floor()`, and `round()` are useful for truncating the decimal parts of numbers:

```
var myNum1 = 12.55;
var myNum2 = 12.45;
alert(Math.floor(myNum1)); // shows 12
alert(Math.ceil(myNum1)); // shows 13
alert(Math.round(myNum1)); // shows 13
alert(Math.round(myNum2)); // shows 12
```

Note that when you use `round()`, if the fractional part of the number is 0.5 or greater, the number is rounded to the next highest integer. If the fractional part is less than 0.5, the number is rounded to the next lowest integer.

Finding Minimum and Maximum

You can use `min()` and `max()` to pick the largest and smallest number from a list:

```
var ageDavid = 23;
var ageMary = 27;
var ageChris = 31;
var ageSandy = 19;
document.write("The youngest person is " + Math.min(ageDavid, ageMary, ageChris,
➥ ageSandy) + " years old<br />");
document.write("The oldest person is " + Math.max(ageDavid, ageMary, ageChris,
➥ ageSandy) + " years old<br />");
```

The output as written to the page looks like this:

```
The youngest person is 19 years old
The oldest person is 31 years old
```

Generating Random Numbers

To generate a random number, you can use `Math.random()`, which generates a random number between 0 and 1.

Normally, you would specify the possible range of random numbers; for example, you might want to generate a random integer between 0 and 100.

As `Math.random()` generates a random number between 0 and 1, it's helpful to wrap it in a small function that suits your needs. The following function takes the `Math` object's randomly generated number, scales it up by multiplying by the variable range (passed to the function as an argument), and finally uses `round()` to remove any fractional part:

```
function myRand(range) {
    return Math.round(Math.random() * range);
}
```

To generate a random integer between 0 and 100, you can then simply call

```
myRand(100);
```

CAUTION

Use `Math` Methods Directly

You always use `Math` methods directly, for example, `Math.floor()`, rather than as a method of an object you created. In other words, the following example is wrong:

```
var myNum = 24.77;
myNum.floor();
```

The code would provoke a JavaScript error.

Instead,

```
<p>Math.floor(myNum);</p>
```

will work correctly.

Mathematical Constants

Various often-used mathematical constants are available as properties of `Math`. They are listed in Table 5.3.

TABLE 5.3   Mathematical Constants

Constant	Description
E	Base of natural logs, approximately 2.718
LN2	Natural log of 2, approximately 0.693
LN10	Natural log of 10, approximately 2.302
LOG2E	Base 2 log of E, approximately 1.442
LOG10E	Base 10 log of E, approximately 0.434
PI	Approximately 3.14159
SQRT1_2	1 over the square root of 2, approximately 0.707
SQRT2	Square root of 2, approximately 1.414

These constants can be used directly in your calculations:

```
var area = Math.PI * radius * radius; // area of circle
var circumference = 2 * Math.PI * radius; // circumference
```

The `with` Keyword

Although you can use the `with` keyword with any object, the `Math` object is an ideal object to use as an example. By using `with`, you can save yourself some tedious typing.

The keyword `with` takes an object as an argument and is followed by a code block wrapped in braces. The statements within that code block can call methods without specifying an object, and JavaScript assumes that those methods belong to the object passed as an argument.

Here's an example:

```
with (Math) {
    var myRand = random();
    var biggest = max(3,4,5);
    var height = round(76.35);
}
```

This example calls `Math.random()`, `Math.max()`, and `Math.round()` simply by using the method names, because all method calls in the code block have been associated with the `Math` object.

▼ TRY IT YOURSELF

Reading the Date and Time

Now you can put into practice some of what we have covered in this lesson by creating a script to get the current day and date when the page is loaded. You can also implement a button to reload the page, refreshing the time and date information.

Take a look at Listing 5.2.

LISTING 5.2   Getting Date and Time Information

```
<!DOCTYPE html>
<html>
<head>
    <title>Current Date and Time</title>
        <style>
            p {font: 14px normal arial, verdana, helvetica;}
        </style>
        <script>
            function telltime() {
                var out = "";
                var now = new Date();
                out += "<br />Date: " + now.getDate();
                out += "<br />Month: " + now.getMonth();
                out += "<br />Year: " + now.getFullYear();
                out += "<br />Hours: " + now.getHours();
                out += "<br />Minutes: " + now.getMinutes();
                out += "<br />Seconds: " + now.getSeconds();
                document.getElementById("div1").innerHTML = out;
            }
        </script>
</head>
<body>
    The current date and time are:<br/>
    <div id="div1"></div>
    <script>
        telltime();
    </script>
    <input type="button" onclick="location.reload()" value="Refresh" />
</body>
</html>
```

The first statement in the function `telltime()` creates a new `Date` object called `now`. As you will recall, since the object is created without passing any parameters to `Date()`, it will have properties pertaining to the current date and time at the moment of its creation.

```
var now = new Date();
```

You can access the individual parts of the time and date using `getDate()`, `getMonth()`, and similar methods. As you do so, you assemble the output message as a string stored in the variable `out`:

```
out += "<br />Date: " + now.getDate();
out += "<br />Month: " + now.getMonth();
out += "<br />Year: " + now.getFullYear();
out += "<br />Hours: " + now.getHours();
out += "<br />Minutes: " + now.getMinutes();
out += "<br />Seconds: " + now.getSeconds();
```

Finally, you use `getElementById()` to select the (initially empty) `<div>` element having `id="div1"`, and write the contents of variable `out` into it using the `innerHTML` method:

```
document.getElementById("div1").innerHTML = out;
```

The function `telltime()` is called by a small script embedded in the `<body>` part of the page:

```
<script>
    telltime();
</script>
```

To refresh the date and time information, you simply need to reload the page into the browser. At that point the script runs again, creating a new instance of the `Date` object with the current date and time. You could just click Refresh on the browser's menu, but since you know how to reload the page using the `location` object, you can do that by calling

```
location.reload()
```

from a button's `onClick` method.

Figure 5.4 shows the script in action. Note that the month is displayed as 1. Remember that JavaScript counts months starting at 0 (January) and ending in 11 (December).

FIGURE 5.4
Getting date and time information

Summary

In this lesson you looked at some useful objects either built into JavaScript or available via the DOM, and how their properties and methods can help you write code more easily.

You saw how to use the `window` object's modal dialogs to exchange information with the user.

You also learned how to select page elements by their ID using the `document.getElementById` method, and how to get and set the HTML inside a page element using the `innerHTML` property.

In addition, you worked with browser information from the `navigator` object and page URL information from the `location` object.

Finally, you saw how to use the `Date` and `Math` objects.

Q&A

Q. Does `Date()` have methods to deal with time zones?

A. Yes, it does. In addition to the `get...()` and `set...()` methods discussed in this lesson (such as `getDate()`, `setMonth()`), there are UTC (Coordinated Universal Time, previously called GMT) versions of the same methods (`getUTCDate()`, `setUTCMonth()`, and so on). You can retrieve the difference between your local time and UTC time by using the `getTimezoneOffset()` method.

Q. Why does `Date()` have the methods called `getFullYear()` and `setFullYear()` instead of just `getYear()` and `setYear()`?

A. The methods `getYear()` and `setYear()` do exist; they deal with two-digit years instead of the four-digit years used by `getFullYear()` and `setFullYear()`. Because of the potential problems with dates spanning the millennium, these functions have been deprecated. You should use `getFullYear()` and `setFullYear()` instead.

Workshop

Quiz questions and exercises to test your understanding and to stretch your skills.

Quiz

1. What happens when a user clicks OK in a confirm dialog?

   a. A value of `true` is returned to the calling program.

   b. The displayed message is returned to the calling program.

   c. Nothing.

2. Which method of the `Math()` object always rounds a number up to the next integer?

   a. `Math.round()`

   b. `Math.floor()`

   c. `Math.ceil()`

3. If my loaded page is http://www.example.com/documents/letter.htm?page=2, what will the `location.pathname` property of the `location` object contain?

   a. `http`

   b. `www.example.com`

   c. `/documents/letter.htm`

   d. `page=2`

4. How would you create a `Date` object with the current date and time?

   a. `var mydate = new Date();`

   b. `var mydate = new Date(now);`

   c. `var mydate = new Date(0);`

5. The `innerHTML` property of a `<div>` element can be used

   a. To set the HTML content of the `div`

   b. To get the HTML content of the `div`

   c. Either of the above

TIP

Register Your Book

Just a reminder for those of you reading these words in the print or e-book edition of this book: If you go to www.informit.com/register and register this book (using ISBN 978-0-672-33809-0), you can receive free access to an online Web Edition that not only contains the complete text of this book but also features an interactive version of this quiz.

Answers

1. a. A value of `true` is returned when OK is clicked. The dialog is cleared and control is returned to the calling program.

2. c. `Math.ceil()` always rounds a number up to the next higher integer.

3. c. The `location.pathname` property contains /documents/letter.htm.

4. a. `var mydate = new Date();`

5. c. Either of the above.

Exercises

Modify Listing 5.2 to output the date and time as a single string, with the following format:

`mm/dd/yyyy hh:mm:ss`

Use the `Math` object to write a function to return the volume of a round chimney, given its radius and height in meters as arguments. The volume returned should be rounded up to the nearest cubic meter.

Use the `history` object to create a few pages with their own Forward and Back buttons. After you've navigated to these pages (to put them in your browser's history list), do your Forward and Back buttons operate exactly like the browser's?

LESSON 6
Dealing with Numbers

What You'll Learn in This Lesson:

▶ The numeric types supported by JavaScript

▶ Conversion between number types

▶ Boolean data types

▶ The meaning of `null` and `undefined`

▶ How to use the negation operator

We use the term *data type* to talk about the nature of the data that a variable contains. A string variable contains a character string, a number variable contains a numerical value, and so forth. However, the JavaScript language is what's called a *loosely typed* language, meaning that JavaScript variables can be interpreted as different data types in differing circumstances.

In JavaScript, you don't have to declare the data type of a variable before using it because the JavaScript interpreter will make its best guess. If you put a string into your variable and later want to interpret that value as a number, that's okay with JavaScript, provided that the variable actually contains a string that's "like" a numerical value (for example, `"200px"` or `"50 cents"`, but not something such as your name). Later you can use it as a string again, if you want.

In this lesson you learn about dealing with numbers in JavaScript; in the following lesson you'll get to know about strings; and in Lesson 8 you'll look at the array data type. In each lesson you find out about some built-in methods for handling values of these types.

Numbers

Mathematicians have all sorts of names for different types of numbers. From the so-called *natural numbers* 1, 2, 3, 4 ..., you can add 0 to get the *whole numbers* 0, 1, 2, 3, 4 ..., and then include the negative values –1, –2, –3, –4 ... to form the set of *integers*.

To express numbers falling between the integers, you commonly use a decimal point with one or more digits following it:

3.141592654

Calling such numbers *floating point* indicates that they can have an arbitrary number of digits before and after the decimal point; that is, the decimal point can "float" to any location in the number.

JavaScript supports both integers and floating-point numbers.

Integers

An integer is a whole number—positive, negative, or zero. To put it another way, an integer is any numerical value without a fractional part.

All the following are valid integers:

- ▶ 33
- ▶ –1,000,000
- ▶ 0
- ▶ –1

Floating-Point Numbers

Unlike integers, floating-point numbers have a fractional part, even if that fractional part is zero. They can be represented in the traditional way, like 3.14159, or in exponential notation, like 35.4e5.

NOTE

Exponential Notation

In exponential notation, e represents "times 10 to the power," so 35.4e5 can be read as 35.4×10^5. Exponential notation provides a compact way to express numbers from the very large to the very small.

All the following are valid floating-point numbers:

- ▶ 3.0
- ▶ 0.00001
- ▶ –99.99

► 2.5e12

► 1e-12

Hexadecimal, Binary, and Octal Numbers

JavaScript also has the capability to handle hexadecimal (base 16), binary (base 2), and octal (base 8) numbers in addition to the more familiar decimal (base 10) numbers.

Hexadecimal numbers begin with the prefix `0x`—for instance, `0xFF` represents the number 255. Hexadecimals have been part of JavaScript for some time, but more recently the language has also gained the ability to deal with binary and octal numbers.

Binary values are prefixed with `0b`, such as `0b111`, which represents 7.

Octal (base 8) numbers are perhaps less common, but they too can be used in your programs. You prefix an octal number with `0o` (zero followed by lowercase letter o), so for instance `0o77` is the octal representation for 63.

NOTE

Unix-style File Permissions

If you've ever dealt with the Unix operating system or one of its siblings such as Linux or Mac OS, you're probably already familiar with octal numbers. The read, write, and execute (rwx) permissions allocated to files in such systems are each associated with the three bits of a binary number. The resulting binaries are more often shown as octal values as follows:

Octal Digit	Binary(rwx)	Permission
0	000	none
1	001	execute only
2	010	write only
3	011	write and execute
4	100	read only
5	101	read and execute
6	110	read and write
7	111	read, write, and execute

Global Methods

JavaScript has a range of methods available for you to use in manipulating numerical values. These are *global* methods; that is, they are available to you at any point in your code.

NOTE

Primitive Values Can Use Methods

So-called primitive values such as numbers are not objects and so cannot, strictly speaking, have their own properties and methods. But JavaScript treats primitive values as objects, thus enabling the execution of the methods described in this section.

Let's take a brief look at some of these methods.

`toString()`

The `toString()` method returns a number as a character string. You'll read all about string types in the next lesson; it's enough for now to see how the conversion works.

The method works just fine on either a variable or when directly applied to a numerical value:

```
var num = 666;
num.toString();          // returns string "666"

(666).toString();        // returns string "666"
```

You can use `toString()` directly with an expression too:

```
(333 * 2).toString();    // returns string "666"
```

TIP

Using a Radix with `toString()`

The `toString()` method can optionally be passed an argument, an integer between 2 and 36, as a *radix value*. The string conversion will then also convert the numerical base of the number.

Here are a few examples:

```
var x = 13;
alert(x.toString());     // alerts 13
alert(x.toString(2));    // alerts 1101
alert(x.toString(16));   // alerts d
```

Note that the conversion does not add the prefix described earlier for binary (prefix `0b`), octal (`0o`), or hexadecimal (`0x`) numbers.

toFixed()

The toFixed() method also returns a string, but with the number written with a specified number of decimal places. You specify that number in the argument passed to the method:

```
x.toFixed(0); // returns "666"
x.toFixed(3); // returns "666.000"
```

toExponential()

Exponential notation was mentioned earlier in the lesson. The toExponential() method works as you would imagine, the number being rounded and written out using exponential notation. The argument passed to the method defines the number of characters behind the decimal point after the conversion:

```
var num = 666;
num.toExponential(4);     // returns "6.6600e+2"
num.toExponential(6);     // returns "6.660000e+2"
```

The Number **Object**

JavaScript uses the Number object to represent any kind of numerical data, including integers or floating-point numbers. Usually, you don't need to worry about creating Number objects yourself because JavaScript converts numerical values to instances of the class Number.

NOTE

Global Methods Versus Number Methods

Some of the methods of the Number object are also available as methods of the global object. In other words, you could simply use

```
isFinite(666)
```

and get the same result as if you had used

```
Number.isFinite(666)
```

However, while the global methods remain active, some of the equivalent number methods contain subtle improvements that make them preferable in use. For example, the global version of the isNaN() method often gives a misleading result because it tries to convert the argument to a numerical value before testing, whereas Number.isNaN() does not.

The Number object has a range of useful properties and methods that you can use to analyze and manipulate numbers, some of which are described next.

Number.isNaN()

NaN (standing for *Not a Number*) is the value returned when your script tries to treat something as a number but can't make any sense of it as a numerical value. For example, the result of trying to multiply a string by an integer is not numerical. You can test for non-numerical values with the Number.isNaN() function:

```
Number.isNaN(3);        // returns false
Number.isNaN(3.14159);  // returns false
Number.isNaN(0 / 0);    // returns true
Number.isNaN(3*'blah'); // returns true
```

Number.isInteger()

The Number.isInteger() method determines whether a value or expression passed to it evaluates to an integer, returning true if the value is numerical and is an integer, and false otherwise. Here are some examples:

```
Number.isInteger(666)      // true
Number.isInteger(-666)     // true
Number.isInteger(12*7)     // true
Number.isInteger(0)        // true
Number.isInteger(3/4)      // false
Number.isInteger('666')    // false
Number.isInteger(Infinity) // false
```

CAUTION

Upgrade Your Browser

The Number.isInteger() method is, at the time of writing, a recent addition to the JavaScript standard and is not supported in Internet Explorer 11 and earlier versions.

Number.parseFloat() **and** Number.parseInt()

JavaScript offers two functions with which you can force the conversion of a string into a number format.

The Number.parseFloat() function parses a string and returns a floating-point number.

If the first character in the specified string is a number, it parses the string until it reaches the end of that number, and returns the value as a number instead of a string:

```
Number.parseFloat("21.4") // returns 21.4
Number.parseFloat("76 trombones") // returns 76
Number.parseFloat("The magnificent 7") // returns NaN
```

Using `parseInt()` is similar, but returns either an integer value or `NaN`. This function allows you to optionally include, as a second argument, the base (radix) of the number system you're using, and can therefore be used to return the base 10 values of other number formats:

```
Number.parseInt(18.95, 10); // returns 18
Number.parseInt("12px", 10); // returns 12
Number.parseInt("1110", 2); // returns 14
Number.parseInt("Hello") // returns NaN
```

Infinity

`Infinity` is a value larger than the largest number that JavaScript can represent. In most JavaScript implementations, this is an integer of plus or minus 2^{53}. Okay, that's not quite infinity, but it is pretty big.

There is also the keyword literal `-Infinity` to signify the negative infinity.

You can test for infinite values with the `Number.isFinite()` function. The `Number.isFinite()` function takes the value to test as an argument and tries to convert that argument into a number. If the result is `NaN`, positive infinity (`Infinity`), or negative infinity (`-Infinity`), the `Number.isFinite()` function returns `false`; otherwise, it returns `true`. (False and true are known as Boolean values, discussed later in this lesson.)

```
Number.isFinite(21); // true
Number.isFinite("This is not a numeric value"); // false
Number.isFinite(Math.sqrt(-1)); // false
```

The `Number()` Function

The `Number()` function is your Swiss Army Knife for getting numerical values from other data types.

When you pass something to `Number()` as an argument, the function will do its best to return a numerical equivalent. If it can't, a value of `NaN` will be returned. Here are a few examples:

```
Number(true);            // returns 1
Number(false);           // returns 0
Number("666");           // returns 666
Number(021-555-3565);    // returns -4103
Number('horse');         // returns NaN
```

▼ TRY IT YOURSELF

The Unix Epoch

Here's a little fact that might get you out of having to attend any more dinner parties.

Unix time (sometimes called POSIX time) is a way of describing a point in time, and is based on the number of elapsed milliseconds since 00:00:00 (UTC) on Thursday, January 1, 1970. It's also sometimes referred to as the *Unix Epoch*, which I think sounds way cooler.

In the preceding lesson you learned about the `Date` object and how it can be used to create dates and times in JavaScript. So what happens when you pass a `Date` object to the `Number()` function?

Let's find out.

Open the JavaScript console in your browser of choice. Mine is Google Chrome, so I use Ctrl+Shift+J to open the console. If you then enter

```
var now = new Date();
```

at the prompt and have the console echo back the date you've just created, you'll get a response like mine in Figure 6.1.

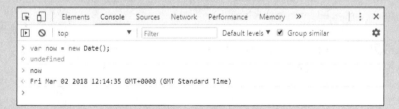

FIGURE 6.1
Creating a new `Date` object

Now you can test `Number()` by passing the newly minted `Date` object to it as an argument, as shown in Figure 6.2.

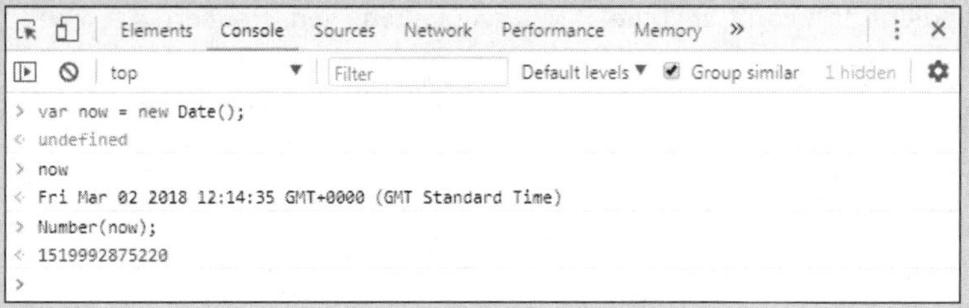

FIGURE 6.2
Using `Number()` on the new `Date` object

Hey, presto! `Number()` has carried out a conversion on the `Date` object and returned the number of milliseconds since the Unix Epoch.

Of course, you could pass any date to `Number()` and, provided the format can be interpreted, the function will return the corresponding number of milliseconds, as in the example shown in Figure 6.3.

```
Elements   Console   Sources   Network   Performance   Memory   »                    :   ×
top                     ▼   Filter              Default levels ▼  ☑ Group similar   2 hidden   ⚙
> var now = new Date();
< undefined
> now
< Fri Mar 02 2018 12:14:35 GMT+0000 (GMT Standard Time)
> Number(now);
< 1519992875220
> Number(new Date("2018-10-30"));
< 1540857600000
> |
```

FIGURE 6.3
Passing an arbitrary date to `Number()`

Such a value is generally referred to as a timestamp.

TIP
_____

Conversion from Timestamp to Date

You can convert a JavaScript timestamp back to a date simply by passing it as an argument to the `Date` object. In the console, enter the following:

```
> Number(new Date("2018-10-30"));
< 1540857600000
> new Date(1540857600000)
< Tue Oct 30 2018 00:00:00 GMT+0000 (GMT Standard Time)
```

Boolean Values

Data of the Boolean type can have one of only two values—`true` or `false`. Boolean variables are most often used to store the result of a logical operation in your code that returns a true/false or yes/no result:

```
var answer = confirm("Do you want to continue?"); // answer will contain
                                                   // true or false
```

CAUTION

Boolean `true` and `false`

When you want to assign a Boolean value of `true` or `false`, do NOT enclose the value in quotation marks; otherwise, the value will be interpreted as a string literal:

```
var success = false; // correct
var success = "false"; // incorrect
```

If you write code that expects Boolean values in computations, JavaScript automatically converts `true` to 1 and `false` to 0.

```
var answer = confirm("Do you want to continue?"); // answer will contain
                                                  // true or false
alert(answer * 1); // will display either 0 or 1
```

It works the other way too. JavaScript interprets any nonzero value as `true` and zero as `false`. JavaScript interprets all the following values as `false`:

- `Boolean false` (you don't say?)
- `undefined`
- `null`
- 0 (zero)
- NaN
- `""` (empty string)

The Negation Operator (`!`)

JavaScript interprets the `!` character, when placed before a Boolean variable, as "not," that is, "the opposite value." Take a look at this code snippet:

```
var success = false;
alert(!success); // alerts 'true'
```

In Lesson 10, "Controlling Program Flow," we'll use this and other operators to test the values of JavaScript variables and have programs make decisions based on the results.

The values `null` and `undefined`

JavaScript also has two keywords called *object literals*—`null` and `undefined`.

Normally, you assign the value `null` to something when you want it to have a valid but nonexistent value. For a numeric value, `null` is equivalent to zero, for a string it equates to the empty string (`""`), and for a Boolean value it means `false`.

Unlike `null`, `undefined` is not a keyword. It is a predefined global variable used to store the value of a variable whose name has been used in a statement but that does not have a value assigned to it. This means that it is not zero or `null`, but it is *undefined*—JavaScript does not recognize it.

TIP

Truthy and Falsy

The values `null` and `undefined` are often referred to as *falsy*, meaning "not exactly false, but can be interpreted as false." Values that JavaScript interprets as true are likewise referred to as *truthy*.

Summary

In this lesson you learned about the number data types supported by JavaScript.

You also read about the `Number` object and saw some examples of how to manipulate numerical data using this object's methods. You also found out about the `Number()` function for converting values into number type.

Finally, you learned about Boolean values and the negation operator.

Q&A

Q. What is the largest integer JavaScript can handle?

A. JavaScript can handle numbers up to 53 bits, that is, up to values of $2^{53} - 1$, or 9,007,199,254,740,991. Luckily, you don't have to memorize this number; JavaScript's `Number` object has a constant property `Number.MAX_SAFE_INTEGER` that you can use instead, if you need it in your script.

Q. Does the `Number` object have other constants as properties?

A. Yes, it has several, though most of them are unlikely to be necessary in most of your JavaScript programs. You can see them documented at various websites, for example, https://docs.microsoft.com/en-us/scripting/javascript/reference/number-constants-javascript.

Workshop

Quiz questions and exercises to test your understanding and to stretch your skills.

Quiz

1. When JavaScript tries to treat something non-numerical as a number but can't evaluate it numerically, it returns

   a. Zero

   b. Undefined

   c. NaN

2. The `parseFloat()` function

   a. Parses a string and returns a floating-point number

   b. Parses a floating-point number and returns an integer

   c. Parses a floating-point number and returns a string

3. What would the expression `isFinite(-1)` return?

   a. Error

   b. True

   c. False

4. When expecting a Boolean value, JavaScript interprets a value of −1 as

   a. True

   b. False

   c. NaN

5. If you try to use Boolean values in computations,

   a. JavaScript will return `NaN`.

   b. JavaScript will produce an error.

   c. JavaScript will interpret `true` as 1 and `false` as 0.

TIP

Register Your Book

Just a reminder for those of you reading these words in the print or e-book edition of this book: If you go to www.informit.com/register and register this book (using ISBN 978-0-672-33809-0), you can receive free access to an online Web Edition that not only contains the complete text of this book but also features an interactive version of this quiz.

Answers

1. c. `NaN`

2. a. Parses a string and returns a floating-point number.

3. b. `True`

4. a. `True`

5. c. JavaScript will interpret `true` as 1 and `false` as 0.

Exercise

Write a JavaScript function to format a number up to a given number of decimal places. For the purposes of this exercise, you can assume that both the number to be processed and that representing the number of decimal places will be passed in suitable formats and so do not need type-checking. (In a real-world program you'd want to check this. You might like to return to this exercise after completing the lessons in Parts I, "Your First Steps with JavaScript," and II, "Cooking with Code," to see whether you can improve on your solution.)

Working with Character Strings

What You'll Learn in This Lesson:

▶ How to use the `string` data type
▶ How to define a string
▶ How to manipulate strings using string methods
▶ How to use escape sequences
▶ How to use template strings

A string is a fundamental data type in JavaScript (as it is in many other programming languages) and is composed of a collection of letters, numerals, and symbols. In this lesson you learn about JavaScript strings and about some built-in methods for creating and handling values of this type.

You also find out about *escape sequences* in strings.

Strings

A string is a sequence of characters from within a given character set (for example, the ASCII or Unicode character sets) and is usually used to store text.

CAUTION

Strings and Numbers

JavaScript differentiates between data stored as a string and data stored as a number, even if the characters are identical. So a string containing a one and three zeros, `"1000"`, is different from the numerical value 1000.

In the previous lesson you read about some methods for converting between the two types. You may want to skip back to that lesson and refresh your memory.

You define a string by enclosing it in single or double quotation marks:

```
var myString = "This is a string";
```

Remember, though, that if you want to use double quote marks inside your string, you need to use single quote marks to enclose the string:

```
var myString = 'This is a "special" string';
```

The reverse is also true: if you have an apostrophe within your string, make sure you use double quotes to enclose the string. If you forget to do this, JavaScript will terminate the string before you intended it to do so and probably cause an error:

```
var myString = 'This is Phil's string'; // error: this string will terminate early
```

You can also get around this problem by escaping characters within your string. You learn about escape sequences in a moment.

You can define an empty string by using two quote marks with nothing between them:

```
var myString = "";
```

The `length` property

It's straightforward to get the length of a string in JavaScript. Simply take a look at the `length` property, which will return the number of characters the string contains:

```
var myString = "How long am I?";
alert(myString.length);  // alerts 14
```

The value of the `length` property is automatically updated by JavaScript as you manipulate string variables.

Note that length is a read-only value. If you try to reassign a value—for instance, in code or in the console—like this:

```
myString.length = 15;
```

the value will remain unchanged.

Escape Sequences

Some characters that you want to put in a string may not have associated keys on the keyboard or may be special characters that for other reasons can't occur in a string. Examples include the tab character, the new line character, and the single or double quotes that enclose the string itself. To use such a character in a string, it must be represented by the character preceded by a backslash (\ ), a combination that JavaScript interprets as the desired special character. Such a combination is known as an *escape sequence*.

Suppose that you wanted to enter some new line characters into a string, so that when the string is shown by a call to the `alert()` method, the message will be split into several lines:

```
var message = "IMPORTANT MESSAGE:\n\nError detected!\nPlease check your data";
alert(message);
```

The result of inserting these escape sequences is shown in Figure 7.1.

FIGURE 7.1
Using escape sequences in a string

The more common escape sequences are shown in Table 7.1.

TABLE 7.1 Some Common Escape Sequences

Escape Sequence	Character
\t	Tab
\n	New line; inserts a line break at the point where it appears in the string
\"	Double quote
\'	Single quote or apostrophe
\\	The backslash itself
\x99	Two-digit number specifying the hexadecimal value of an ASCII character
\u9999	Four-digit hexadecimal number specifying a Unicode character

String Methods

A full list of the properties and methods of the `string` object is beyond the scope of this lesson, but for now let's look at some of the important ones, listed in Table 7.2.

TABLE 7.2 Some Popular Methods of the `string` Object

Method	Description
concat	Joins strings and returns a copy of the joined string
indexOf	Returns the position of the first occurrence of a specified value in a string
lastIndexOf	Returns the position of the last occurrence of a specified value in a string
repeat	Returns a new string with a specified number of copies of the string it was called on
replace	Searches for a match between a substring and a string, and replaces the substring with a new substring

Method	Description
split	Splits a string into an array of substrings, and returns the new array
substr	Extracts a substring from a string, beginning at a specified start position, and through the specified number of characters
toLowerCase	Converts a string to lowercase letters
toUpperCase	Converts a string to uppercase letters

concat()

In earlier lessons you joined strings together using the + operator. This operation is known as *string concatenation*, and JavaScript strings have a concat() method offering additional capabilities:

```
var string1 = "The quick brown fox ";
var string2 = "jumps over the lazy dog";
var longString = string1.concat(string2);
```

TIP

A new string is returned by concat()

The strings that you concatenate with the concat() method are not altered by the operation. Instead, JavaScript returns a new string containing the concatenated content.

In JavaScript, strings are *immutable*; in other words, they cannot be changed. All you can do is make new strings based on mutations of those that already exist. Immutability doesn't just apply to strings; numbers in JavaScript are immutable too.

indexOf()

You can use indexOf() to find the first place where a particular substring of one or more characters occurs within a string. The method returns the index (the position) of the searched-for substring, or −1 if it isn't found anywhere in the string:

```
var string1 = "The quick brown fox ";
string1.indexOf('fox') // returns 16
string1.indexOf('dog') // returns −1
```

TIP

Strings Are Zero-indexed

Remember that the index of the first character in a string is 0, not 1.

lastIndexOf()

As you likely have guessed, lastIndexOf() works just the same way as indexOf(), but it finds the last occurrence of the substring, rather than the first.

repeat()

The repeat() method returns a new string composed of a specified number of copies of the string it was called on. The number of copies required is passed to the method as an argument:

```
var inStr = "lots and ";
var outStr = str.repeat(3); // outStr contains ' lots and lots and lots and '
```

replace()

The replace() method searches for a match between a substring and a string, and it returns a new string with the substring replaced by a new substring:

```
var string1 = "The quick brown fox ";
var string2 = string1.replace("brown", "orange"); // string2 is now "the quick orange fox"
```

split()

The split() method enables you to split a string into an array of substrings and return the new array:

```
var string1 = "The quick brown fox ";
var newArray = string1.split(" ")
```

TIP

split() Is an Array Method Too

You'll learn about arrays in the next lesson. Make a note to refer back to this method after you've read about arrays.

substr()

The substr() method takes one or two arguments.

The first is the starting index: substr() extracts the characters from a string, beginning at the starting index, for the specified number of characters, returning the new substring. The second parameter (number of characters) is optional, and if omitted, all the remaining string will be extracted:

```
var string1 = "The quick brown fox ";
var sub1 = string1.substr(4, 11); // extracts "quick brown"
var sub2 = string1.substr(4); // extracts "quick brown fox"
```

toLowerCase() and toUpperCase()

The toLowerCase() and toUpperCase() methods put the string into all lowercase or all uppercase:

```
var string1 = "The quick brown fox ";
var sub1 = string1.toLowerCase(); // sub1 contains "the quick brown fox "
var sub2 = string1.toUpperCase(); // sub2 contains "THE QUICK BROWN FOX "
```

▼ TRY IT YOURSELF

A Simple Spam Detector Function

Let's use two of these methods to write a simple function that detects the presence in a given string of a particular word. In the example, we'll use the word *fake* as our target word. The function should return a zero or positive value if it detects the word *fake* anywhere in a string passed in as a parameter; otherwise, it should return a negative number. Here's the "empty" function:

```
function detectSpam(input) {
}
```

You might use a function like this to examine email subject lines, for example, to detect spam email selling fake designer items. In a practical application, the code would be much more complex, but it's the string manipulation that's important here.

First, you need to convert the string to lowercase:

```
function detectSpam(input) {
    input = input.toLowerCase();
}
```

This step is necessary because you'll then use `indexOf()` to look for the word *fake*, and `indexOf()` differentiates between upper- and lowercase:

```
function detectSpam(input) {
    input = input.toLowerCase();
    return input.indexOf("fake");
}
```

Now enter the code in Listing 7.1 into your editor and save it as an HTML file.

LISTING 7.1 Spam Detector Function

```
<!DOCTYPE html>
<html>
<head>
    <title>Spam Detector</title>
</head>
<body>
    <script>
        function detectSpam(input) {
            input = input.toLowerCase();
            return input.indexOf("fake");
        }

        var mystring = prompt("Enter a string");
        alert(detectSpam(mystring));
```

```
        </script>
    </body>
</html>
```

Open the page in your browser, and enter a string into the prompt dialog, as depicted in Figure 7.2.

FIGURE 7.2
Entering a string

A new dialog will open, displaying the location in the input string where the word *fake* was found, or −1 if the word did not appear anywhere.

Figure 7.3 shows the target word being found at position 15, that is, the 16th character in the string.

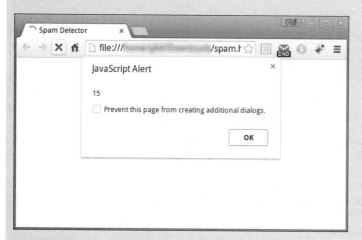

FIGURE 7.3
Output from spam detection script

Template Strings

Template strings provide help in constructing strings and are similar to string interpolation features in some other programming languages such as Perl and Python (among others).

```
var name = "John";
var course = "Mathematics III";
var myString = `Hello ${name}, welcome to ${course}.`;
```

You formulate the string by enclosing variable names within ${ ... } as in this example. The string will be built at runtime using the current values of the relevant variables.

Note that the template string *must* be enclosed between two instances of the backtick (`) character, not the standard apostrophe. A handy side effect of this is that you can use standard quotation marks within your string without having to escape them.

You can substitute more complex expressions too:

```
var total = 20;
var tax = 4;
msg = `Total is ${total} dollars (or ${total + tax} dollars, including tax)`;
alert(msg); // "Total is 20 dollars (or 24 dollars, including tax)"
```

Another cool feature of template strings is their ability to span multiple lines. For instance, you can write

```
var condition = "pressure";
var myString = `WARNING

The maximum safe ${condition} has been exceeded!`;
```

At runtime this string will be converted to

```
"WARNING\n\nThe maximum safe pressure has been exceeded!"
```

Summary

In this lesson you learned about JavaScript's string data type.

After learning how to define a string, you found out how to include special characters in your string using escape sequences. You then learned how to perform various manipulations on strings using JavaScript's string methods.

Finally, you read about template strings and how they can save you time and effort in populating strings with variable data.

Q&A

Q. Using the `replace()` method seems to change only one instance of a matching substring in my string. Is there a way to change all matching instances?

A. Yes. The `replace()` method can be used with a regular expression as the first parameter. It's beyond the scope of this lesson, but you'll learn about regular expressions in Lesson 19, "Matching Patterns Using Regular Expressions."

Q. Is there a maximum number of characters for a JavaScript string?

A. According to Mozilla.org, the latest ECMAScript 2016 (ed. 7) JavaScript standard established a maximum length of $2^{53} - 1$ elements (in other words, *huge*). Previously, no maximum length was specified. In practice the number is likely to depend on the specifics of your platform such as memory size and operating system. Unless you're doing something very, *very* strange in JavaScript, this isn't likely to ever be a problem!

Workshop

Quiz questions and exercises to test your understanding and to stretch your skills.

Quiz

1. What statement would return a new string created by appending one string called `string2` to another string called `string1`?

   a. `concat(string1) + concat(string2);`

   b. `string1.concat(string2);`

   c. `join(string1, string2);`

2. Which statement sets the value of the variable `paid` to Boolean `true`?

   a. `var paid = true;`

   b. `var paid = "true";`

   c. `var paid.true();`

3. For a string called `myString` containing the value `"stupid is as stupid does"`, which of the following would return a value of −1?

   a. `myString.indexOf("stupid");`

   b. `myString.lastIndexOf("stupid");`

   c. `myString.indexOf("is stupid");`

4. You define a string as follows:

```
var string1 = "Marry in haste, repent at leisure";
```

What value would be returned by the expression `string1.lastIndexOf("re")`?

  a. 16

  b. 31

  c. −1

5. What does the escape sequence `\n` represent?

  a. New line

  b. Negation

  c. Numeral

TIP

Register Your Book

Just a reminder for those of you reading these words in the print or e-book edition of this book: If you go to www.informit.com/register and register this book (using ISBN 978-0-672-33809-0), you can receive free access to an online Web Edition that not only contains the complete text of this book but also features an interactive version of this quiz.

Answers

  1. b. `string1.concat(string2);`

  2. a. `var paid = true;`

  3. c. `myString.indexOf("is stupid");`

  4. b. 31

  5. a. New line

Exercise

Write a JavaScript function to truncate a string if it is longer than 20 characters. The truncated string should then be terminated by an ellipsis sequence ("…"). Test your function in a simple HTML page.

Storing Data In Arrays

What You'll Learn in This Lesson:

▶ What we mean by the array data type

▶ How to declare and populate arrays

▶ How to use the common array methods

▶ How to manage array contents

▶ About JavaScript's three-dots notation

Sometimes it makes sense to store multiple variable values under a single variable name. JavaScript has the *array* data type to help you do this.

Arrays take the form of lists, in that they allow you to assign a list of values to a single variable name. The items that you place in an array don't have to all be of the same type. Arrays are particularly useful for containing data that is somehow logically related; you can add and delete items, and perform sorts or other manipulations while keeping everything under the umbrella of a single variable name.

In this lesson you see how JavaScript arrays are created and how the data stored in these arrays can be manipulated in code.

Arrays

An *array* is a type of object used for storing multiple values in a single variable. Each value has a numeric index that may contain data of any data type—Booleans, numbers, strings, functions, objects, and even other arrays. You can access any item in an array by referencing its numeric index, corresponding to the item's position within the array. It's normal to refer to the items in an array as the array *elements*.

Creating a New Array

The syntax used for creating an array will already be familiar to you; after all, an array is simply another object:

```
var myArray = new Array();
```

However, for arrays, there is a shorthand version—simply use square brackets ([]) like this:

```
var myArray = [];
```

Initializing an Array

You can optionally preload data into your array at the time it is created:

```
var myArray = ['Monday', 'Tuesday', 'Wednesday'];
```

Alternatively, elements can be added after the array has been created:

```
var myArray = [];
myArray[0] = 'Monday';
myArray[1] = 'Tuesday';
myArray[2] = 'Wednesday';
```

Note that you don't need to add elements in sequence. It would be just as valid to have populated the preceding array like this:

```
var myArray = [];
myArray[1] = 'Tuesday';
myArray[2] = 'Wednesday';
myArray[0] = 'Monday';
```

The `array.length` Property

All arrays have a `length` property that tells how many items the array contains. The `length` property is automatically updated when you add items to or remove items from the array. The following code returns the length of the preceding array:

```
myArray.length // returns 3
```

CAUTION

Array Length

The length is always 1 higher than the highest index, even if there are actually fewer items in the array. Suppose you add a new item to the preceding array:

```
myArray[50] = 'Ice cream day';
```

`myArray.length` now returns 51, even though the array has only four entries.

Array Methods

Like the other JavaScript objects that you've met so far, arrays have their own properties and methods. In this section you look at some of the more common array methods.

You might like to try out the snippets of sample code in your browser's JavaScript console to make sure you get the same results.

CAUTION

Array and String Properties and Methods Share Names

You may have noticed that strings (dealt with in the preceding lesson) and arrays both have a `length` property. You'll notice too that some of the array *methods* have the same names—and almost the same functions—as string methods.

Be aware of what data type you are working with; otherwise, your script might not function as you would like.

Table 8.1 describes some of the more commonly used methods of the array object.

TABLE 8.1   Some Useful Array Methods

Method	Description
concat	Joins multiple arrays
join	Joins all the array elements together into a string
toString	Returns the array as a string
indexOf	Searches the array for specific elements
lastIndexOf	Returns the last item in the array that matches the search criteria
slice	Returns a new array from the specified index and length
sort	Sorts the array alphabetically or by the supplied function
splice	Adds or deletes the specified index(es) to or from the array

concat()

You've already had experience with string concatenation, and JavaScript arrays have a `concat()` method too:

```
var myOtherArray = ['Thursday','Friday'];
var myWeek = myArray.concat(myOtherArray);
// myWeek will contain 'Monday', 'Tuesday', 'Wednesday', 'Thursday', 'Friday'
```

join()

To join all of an array's elements together into a single string, you can use the `join()` method:

```
var longDay = myArray.join(); // returns MondayTuesdayWednesday
```

Optionally, you can pass a string argument to this method; the passed string will then be inserted as a separator in the returned string:

```
var longDay = myArray.join("-"); // returns Monday-Tuesday-Wednesday
```

toString()

toString() is almost a special case of join(). It returns the array as a string with the elements separated by commas:

```
var longDay = myArray.toString(); // returns Monday,Tuesday,Wednesday
```

indexOf()

You can use indexOf() to find the first place where a particular element occurs in an array. The method returns the index of the searched-for element, or –1 if it isn't found anywhere in the array:

```
myArray.indexOf('Tuesday') // returns 1 (remember, arrays start with index 0)
myArray.indexOf('Sunday') // returns -1 to indicate that the element was not found
```

lastIndexOf()

As you might expect, lastIndexOf() works just the same way as indexOf(), but finds the last occurrence in the array of the search term, rather than the first occurrence.

slice()

When you need to create an array that is a subset of your starting array, you can use slice(), passing to it the starting index and finishing index of the elements you want to retrieve. Note that the array element at the finishing index is not included in the new array:

```
var myWeek = ['Monday', 'Tuesday', 'Wednesday', 'Thursday', 'Friday'];
var myShortWeek = myWeek.slice(1, 3);
// myShortWeek contains ['Tuesday', 'Wednesday']
```

You can pass negative values to slice() as values for the starting index and/or finishing index. JavaScript will interpret negative values as offsets from the end of the sequence:

```
var myWeek = ['Monday', 'Tuesday', 'Wednesday', 'Thursday', 'Friday'];
var myShortWeek = myWeek.slice(-3, 4);
// myShortWeek contains ["Wednesday", "Thursday"]

var myShortWeek = myWeek.slice(1, -2);
// myShortWeek contains ["Tuesday", "Wednesday"]
```

Note too that both arguments are optional. If the starting index is undefined, `slice()` begins from index 0, and if no finishing index is supplied, `slice()` extracts all elements through the end of the sequence.

sort()

You can use `sort()` to carry out an alphabetical sort:

```
myWeek.sort() // returns 'Friday', 'Monday', 'Thursday', 'Tuesday', 'Wednesday'
```

CAUTION

Sorting Numbers

Be aware that when you use `sort()` on an array containing numerical values, the numbers will be sorted alphabetically (that is, by the first digit):

```
var myArray = [14, 9, 31, 22, 5];
alert(myArray.sort());  // alerts 14,22,31,5,9
```

This result may not have been what you were expecting!

splice()

To add or delete specific items from the array, you can use `splice()`.

The syntax for this method is a little more complex than that of the previous examples:

```
array.splice(index, howmany, [new elements]);
```

The first element sets the location in the array where you want to perform the splice; the second element, how many items to remove (if set to 0, none are deleted); and thereafter, an optional list of any new elements to be inserted.

```
myWeek.splice(2,1,"holiday")
```

The preceding line of code moves to the array item with index 2 (`'Wednesday'`), removes one element (`'Wednesday'`), and inserts a new element (`'holiday'`); so `myWeek` now contains `'Monday'`, `'Tuesday'`, `'holiday'`, `'Thursday'`, `'Friday'`. The method returns any removed elements.

CAUTION

Take Care with `splice()`

Using `splice()` changes the original array! If you need to preserve the array for use elsewhere in your code, copy the array to a new variable before executing `splice()`.

▼ TRY IT YOURSELF

Array Manipulation

Let's put some of these methods to work. In your text editor, create the script in Listing 8.1 and save it as array.html.

LISTING 8.1   Array Manipulation

```
<!DOCTYPE html>
<html>
<head>
    <title>Strings and Arrays</title>
    <script>
        function wrangleArray() {
            var sentence = "JavaScript is a really cool language";
            var newSentence = "";
            //Write it out
            document.getElementById("div1").innerHTML = "<p>" + sentence + "</p>";
            //Convert to an array
            var words = sentence.split(" ");
            // Remove 'really' and 'cool', and add 'powerful' instead
            var message = words.splice(3,2,"powerful");
            // use an alert to say what words were removed
            alert('Removed words: ' + message);
            // Convert the array to a string, and write it out
            document.getElementById("div2").innerHTML = "<p>" + words.join(" ") + "</p>";
        }
    </script>
</head>
<body>
    <div id="div1"></div>
    <div id="div2"></div>
    <script>wrangleArray();</script>
</body>
</html>
```

As we work through this listing, you may want to refer to the definitions of the individual string and array methods given earlier in the lesson, and the discussion of `getElementById()` and `innerHTML` from Lesson 5, "Using DOM Objects and Built-in Objects."

Stepping through the function `wrangleArray()`, you first define a string:

```
var sentence = "JavaScript is a really cool language";
```

After writing it out to any empty `<div>` element using `innerHTML`, you apply the `split()` method to the string, passing to it a single space as an argument. The method returns an array of elements, created by splitting the string wherever a space occurs—that is, splits it into individual words. You store that array in the variable `words`.

You next apply the `splice()` array method to the `words` array, removing two words at array index 3, `"really"` and `"cool"`. Since the `splice()` method returns any deleted words, you can display these in an `alert()` dialog:

```
var message = words.splice(3,2,"powerful");
alert('Removed words: ' + message);
```

Finally, you apply the `join()` method to the array, once more collapsing it into a string. Since you supply a single space as the argument to `join()`, the individual words are once more separated by spaces. Finally, you output the revised sentence to a second `<div>` element by using `innerHTML`.

The `wrangleArray()` function is called by a small script in the body of the document:

```
<script>wrangleArray();</script>
```

The script operation is shown in Figure 8.1.

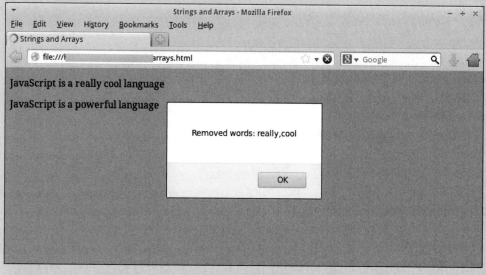

FIGURE 8.1
Output from array manipulation script

How to Iterate Through Arrays

Often you'll want to go through the items in an array, performing some process on each element in turn.

Later in Lesson 10, "Controlling Program Flow," you'll see how to use various types of loops. Many of them can also be used to loop through array contents, but here we limit ourselves to some techniques that are more specific to arrays.

Using `forEach()`

The `forEach()` array method accepts a function as an argument and applies it sequentially to every item in an array. Here's an example:

```
var myArray = [2, 3, 4, 5, 6];
function cube(x) {
    console.log(x*x*x);
}
myArray.forEach(cube);
```

Executing the `forEach()` method of the array applies the `cube()` function to each element in turn, logging the result to the JavaScript console. The result is shown in Figure 8.2.

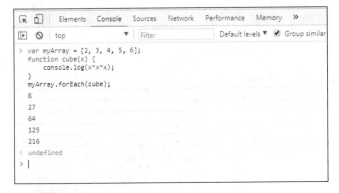

FIGURE 8.2
Using the `forEach()` array method

Using `map()`

There's another handy method, `map()`, which at first looks pretty similar to `forEach()` but has one significant difference.

The `forEach()` method doesn't actually return any value. It simply calls a particular function on each element in your array, as in the previous example. This function is allowed to change the values in the original array, if it's written to do so.

The `map()` method will similarly call a nominated function on every element in the array, but `map()` returns a new array of the same size as the original:

```
var myArray = [2, 3, 4, 5, 6];
function cube(x) {
```

```
    return (x*x*x);
}
var newArray = myArray.map(cube);    // newArray = [8, 27, 64, 125, 216]
```

It's important to realize that `map()` will always return a new array and is often useful where you want the original array to remain unaltered.

Accessing Arrays with `for-of`

In addition to the loops you'll see in later lessons, JavaScript also has a structure called `for-of`, which is intended specifically for looping through iterable structures such as arrays. The syntax is very simple:

```
for (var y of arr1) {
    ... do something ...
}
```

In this example, the values stored in the array `arr1` are sequentially assigned to variable `y`, which can then be processed in the statements between the curly braces. Let's look at an example using the same array and function used previously:

```
var myArray = [2, 3, 4, 5, 6];
function cube(x) {
    console.log(x*x*x);
}
for (var y of myArray) {
    cube(y);
}
```

Go ahead and give it a try in your JavaScript console. You should get a similar result to that shown in Figure 8.2.

The Three-Dots Operator

A recent addition to JavaScript is an operator taking the form of three periods written before the name of a variable, like this:

```
...myvar
```

You'll hear some people refer to it as the *spread operator*; others will refer to it as *rest parameters*. What you call it really refers more to what you are using it for, but its purpose is to help you *expand* the contents of an array (for example, into a list of arguments to pass to a function) or to *collapse* a list of values into an array.

That probably sounds quite confusing, so let's look at a few examples.

Combining Multiple Arrays

Suppose you have this array:

```
var array1 = ['apple', 'banana', 'pear'];
```

You want to declare another array that includes but extends `array1`. It would be straightforward to declare your new array like this:

```
var array2 = ['orange', 'cherry', 'fig'];
```

Then you would combine the two arrays with a method such as `concat()`, which you've already seen. But if you want to position the second array *at a specific point* in the first, you then have more work to do. Instead, you can simply do this:

```
var array2 = ['orange', ...array1, 'cherry', 'fig'];
```

When you examine `array2`, you'll find it now contains

```
['orange', 'apple', 'banana', 'pear', 'cherry', 'fig'];
```

Calling Functions with an Array of Arguments

You can use the same notation to divide an array into a list of arguments to pass to a function or method.

Let's suppose you want to find the minimum value in a numeric array. (In this case, we use the `min()` method of JavaScript's `Math` object, though the principle works in just the same way with any other function, including the ones you define yourself.)

```
var myArray = [91, 35, 17, 101, 29, 77];
alert(Math.min(...myArray));  // alerts 17
```

Collecting Values

Finally, let's see how the three-dots notation can be used to collect values into an array.

Suppose you declare an array like this:

```
var [a, b, ...c] = [1, 2, 3, 4, 5, 6, 7, 8, 9];
```

In this case, JavaScript will allocate values for a and b, and use variable c to form an array of those remaining, so that a=1, b=2, and c=[3, 4, 5, 6, 7, 8, 9].

Summary

An array is a convenient means of storing multiple values in a single variable.

In this lesson you learned about some of the methods of creating JavaScript array objects and manipulating them using the language's array methods.

Finally, you learned about three-dots notation and how it can be used to collapse data into arrays or expand data out of an array.

Q&A

Q. Does JavaScript allow associative arrays?

A. JavaScript does not directly support associative arrays (arrays with named indexes). However, there are ways to simulate their behavior by using objects. You'll see examples of this later in the book.

Q. Can I create a multidimensional array in JavaScript?

A. You can create an array of arrays, which amounts to the same thing:

```
var myArray = [[1,2], [3,4], [5,6]];

alert(myArray[1][0]); // alerts '3'
```

Workshop

Quiz questions and exercises to test your understanding and to stretch your skills.

Quiz

1. If the element with highest index in array `Foo` is `Foo[8]`, what value will be returned by `Foo.length`?

   a. 7

   b. 8

   c. 9

2. You have an array called `monthNames` containing the names of all the months of the year. How would you use `join()` to create a string name containing all these month names with a single space between names?

   a. `var names = monthNames.join();`

   b. `var names = monthNames.join(" ");`

   c. `var names = monthNames.join(\s);`

3. What value will be returned by `indexOf()` if it is passed a value that does not appear in the array to which it is applied?

   a. `null`

   b. `undefined`

   c. `−1`

4. What array method would you use to delete a particular index from an array?

   a. `indexOf()`

   b. `slice()`

   c. `splice()`

5. What is returned when the `toString()` method is used on an array?

   a. A single string composed of the array elements joined by commas

   b. A single string composed of the array elements joined by spaces

   c. A single string composed of the array elements joined with no separating characters

TIP
_____

Register Your Book

Just a reminder for those of you reading these words in the print or e-book edition of this book: If you go to www.informit.com/register and register this book (using ISBN 978-0-672-33809-0), you can receive free access to an online Web Edition that not only contains the complete text of this book but also features an interactive version of this quiz.
_____

Answers

1. c. `Foo.length` will return 9.

2. b. `var names = monthNames.join(" ");`

3. c. It will return −1.

4. c. `splice()`

5. a. A single string composed of the array elements joined by commas

Exercises

Review the array and string methods that share a method name. Familiarize yourself with how the syntax and operation change depending on whether these methods are applied to a string or an array.

Using the three-dots notation, write a function that takes as its argument an arbitrary number of numeric arrays and returns the sum of the elements from all the arrays. (For the purpose of this exercise, you can assume that type-checking of the input data is not required.)

Test your function in the JavaScript console.

Handling Events in JavaScript

What You'll Learn in This Lesson:

▶ What we mean by events

▶ What event handlers are and what they do

▶ The different ways of adding event handlers

▶ How to use the `event` object

▶ Event bubbling and capturing

Some JavaScript programs begin their execution at the first line of code and then carry on through, line by line, oblivious to anything else that may be happening until they complete. Often, though, we want our programs to react to the things that happen in their environment—to the user clicking on a page element, perhaps, or the loading of an image being completed. We call these occurrences *events*, and JavaScript is equipped to detect and act upon a long list of them.

Types of Events

It's easiest to parcel up the possible events into groups. The events you are perhaps most likely to deal with on a regular basis are mouse events, keyboard events, DOM object events, and form events. Tables 9.1 to 9.4 summarize the more commonly used events in each of these categories.

NOTE

Other Types of Events

Many other types of events are available in JavaScript, relating to activities such as drag and drop, clipboard use, printing, animation, and so on. You may see some of these events crop up in other lessons, even if they're not covered here. The basic principles are, of course, just the same.

TABLE 9.1 Mouse Events

Event	Occurs When...
onclick	The user clicks on an element
oncontextmenu	The user right-clicks on an element to open a context menu
ondblclick	The user double-clicks on an element
onmousedown	The user presses a mouse button over an element
onmouseenter	The pointer is moved onto an element
onmouseleave	The pointer is moved out of an element
onmousemove	The pointer is moving while it is over an element
onmouseover	The pointer is moved onto an element or onto one of its children

TABLE 9.2 Keyboard Events

Event	Occurs When...
onkeydown	The user is pressing a key
onkeypress	The user presses a key
onkeyup	The user releases a key

TABLE 9.3 DOM Object Events

Event	Occurs When...
onerror	An error occurs while loading an external file
onload	An object has loaded
onresize	The document view is resized
onscroll	An element's scrollbar is being scrolled

TABLE 9.4 Form Events

Event	Occurs When...
onblur	An element loses focus
onchange	The content, selection, or checked state has changed
onfocus	An element gets focus
onreset	A form is reset
onselect	The user selects some text
onsubmit	A form is submitted

TIP

Get a Complete List of Events

The complete list of events handled by JavaScript is huge, and I don't intend to cover all of them here. Instead, see www.w3schools.com/jsref/dom_obj_event.asp for a more complete list.

Event Handlers

So what do we mean when referring to an *event handler*? Put simply, an event handler is a piece of code that is executed when a specified event is detected by JavaScript. Here are a few possible examples:

- ▶ When the user's mouse hovers over the enter button, change the button's color.

- ▶ When the user presses the P key, pause the operation of the program.

- ▶ When the page finishes loading, make the menu elements visible.

There are several different ways to add event handlers to your programs. Let's look at each of them in turn, starting with the oldest and simplest.

Inline Event Handlers

When JavaScript was first introduced to web pages, event handlers were generally added inline to page elements. Inline event handlers usually take this form:

```
handlername = "JavaScript code"
```

They also are usually inserted in the opening tag of an HTML element. Let's look at an example:

```
<a href="https://www.w3.org/" onclick="alert('hello W3C!')">World Wide Web
Consortium (W3C)</a>
```

TIP

Different Strokes

Different event handlers work with various HTML tags. While `onclick` can be inserted into many HTML tags, handlers like `onload` work only with `<body>` and `<img>` elements.

Event Handlers as Properties of DOM Objects

This method of assigning event handlers works okay for trivial examples, but it has some major disadvantages. The main one is that it mixes up how things *look* (the presentation layer, as it's often called) with what things *do*. This can make your web pages a nightmare to maintain and update. You'll read more about assigning them in Lesson 22, "Good Coding Practice."

There's a better way to assign event handlers. Each DOM object has the events it can receive stored as properties of the object itself. Rather than hard-wiring the event handler to the code in the HTML markup, you can instead assign event handlers to these object properties programmatically.

Here's a simple example—first, in the HTML page:

```
<a href="https://www.w3.org/" id="a1">World Wide Web Consortium (W3C)</a>
```

Here's what it looks like in the JavaScript code:

```
var myLink = document.getElementById('a1');
myLink.onclick = function() {
    alert('hello W3C!');
}
```

In the preceding example, you select the element via its `id` value and then use an anonymous function to add the event handler code to the element. In fact, it would be equally valid (just a little more verbose) to add the event handler via a named function:

```
var myLink = document.getElementById('a1');
function sayHello() {
    alert('hello W3C!');
}
myLink.onclick = sayHello;
```

Adding event handlers this way leaves the HTML page neat and tidy by removing all the event handler code into the page's JavaScript. But there's a newer and even more flexible way to add event handlers—by using `addEventListener()`.

Using `addEventListener()`

The two methods we've already discussed work well enough, are supported in pretty much every modern browser, and are in use all over the Web. Even so, there are a few areas that could use some improvement.

The most important of these is highlighted when you want to add more than one event handler to an element. You may, for example, want to alert the user and also increment a counter each time a button is clicked. You could perhaps do this by coding a single event handler that calls both functions, but your code can rapidly become unwieldy and hard to maintain.

Modern browsers support a new, more flexible method called `addEventListener`. The `addEventListener` method can listen on any DOM node you specify (not just on page elements) and trigger code to be executed whenever a specified event occurs. You can listen for as many separate events as you like by adding multiple event listeners of this type. Here's the previous sample rewritten to use `addEventListener`:

```
var myLink = document.getElementById('a1');
function sayHello() {
    alert('hello W3C!');
}
myLink.addEventListener('click', sayHello);
```

Inside the `addEventListener()` function, you specify a first parameter, which is the name of the event for which you want to register this handler, and a second parameter specifying the handler function you want to run in response to the event being detected.

TIP

Callback Functions

A function passed into another function as an argument in this way, to later be invoked inside that other function, is often referred to as a *callback function*.

NOTE

`removeEventListener()`

There is a further function, `removeEventListener()`, that will delete a previously added listener. For example, to remove the listener set in the previous example, you use

```
myLink.removeEventListener('click', sayHello);
```

Calling `removeEventListener()` with parameters that don't match any currently registered listeners does not generate an error but has no effect.

Adding Multiple Listeners

Let's go back to our previous example:

```
var myLink = document.getElementById('a1');
function sayHello() {
    alert('hello W3C!');
}
myLink.onclick = sayHello;
```

Now imagine that you want to alert the user and also increment a counter each time the link is clicked. Suppose you had tried to add two event listeners this way:

```
myLink.onclick = sayHello;
myLink.onclick = updateCounter;
```

The second statement would effectively overwrite the previous line of code, leaving `updateCounter()` as the only function to be fired when the link is clicked. But instead you can use `addEventListener()`:

```
myLink.addEventListener('click', sayHello);
myLink.addEventListener('click', updateCounter);
```

This way, both event handlers would be executed.

TIP

Writing for Older Browsers

If you need to support old browsers (those prior to Internet Explorer 8), you may encounter problems. These older browsers use different event models from the current ones. If these browsers must be supported, one of the easier ways to deal with them is to use libraries such as jQuery, which are designed to eradicate cross-browser differences. We'll talk about this issue in Lesson 24, "Where to Go Next."

The event object

Sometimes it would be really useful if your event handler code could get to know more detailed information about the event that has been detected. For example, if a key has been pressed, then which one?

The DOM provides an `event` object that contains this type of information. In an event handler function, you might see a parameter (usually specified with a name such as `event` or simply `e`, though you can choose any name) that represents this `event` object. This `event` object is automatically passed to event handlers.

Suppose you have a form and have told the user to press the Escape key in a certain field to bring up help information:

```
myInputField = document.getElementById("form_input_1");
function myFunction(e) {
    var kc = e.keyCode;
    if (kc == 27) {
        alert ("Possible values for this field are: .... ");
    }
}
myInputField.addEventListener('onkeydown', myFunction);
```

In this example, the `event` object has the property `keyCode` that identifies which key has been pressed (the `keyCode` value of 27 identifies the Escape key, as I'm sure you guessed if you didn't already know!).

Preventing Default Behavior

The event object has a number of methods too. One of these is the preventDefault() method, which, as its name suggests, prevents the event from doing what it would normally do.

Consider one of our previous examples:

```
var myLink = document.getElementById('a1');
function sayHello() {
    alert('hello W3C!');
}
myLink.addEventListener('click', sayHello);
```

Suppose, for example, that you wanted to alter a message to inform users that they were not allowed to follow the link they had clicked. You might offer an alternative function like this:

```
function refuseAccess() {
    alert('Sorry, but you are not yet authorized to follow this link.');
}
myLink.addEventListener('click', refuseAccess);
```

Unfortunately, as soon as a user clears the alert message, the default action of the link will kick in. Having been clicked, the link will be followed!

However, you can prevent this outcome with a call to the preventDefault() method of the event object:

```
var myLink = document.getElementById('a1');
function refuseAccess(e) {
    alert('Sorry, but you are not yet authorized to follow this link.');
    e.preventDefault();
}
myLink.addEventListener('click', refuseAccess);
```

TRY IT YOURSELF ▼

Using preventDefault()

The simple HTML page in Listing 9.1 contains two essentially identical links to Google's search page. Using preventDefault(), the technique described in the preceding section is applied to just one of the two links.

LISTING 9.1 Preventing Default Action with preventDefault()

```
<!DOCTYPE html>
<html>
<head>
    <title>Preventing Default Action</title>
```

```
<script>
    window.onload = function() {
        var Go = document.getElementById('a1');
        var NoGo = document.getElementById('a2');
        function permitAccess() {
            alert('Go right ahead - have fun!');
        }
        function refuseAccess(e) {
            alert('Sorry, but you are not yet authorized to follow this link.');
            e.preventDefault();
        }
        Go.addEventListener('click', permitAccess);
        NoGo.addEventListener('click', refuseAccess);
    }
</script>
</head>
<body>
    <a href="https://www.google.com" target=_blank id="a1">Go to Google</a><br/>
    <a href="https://www.google.com" target=_blank id="a2">DO NOT go to Google</a>
</body>
</html>
```

Save the code from Listing 9.1 in a file named prevent.html and load it into your browser. Your page should look something like Figure 9.1.

FIGURE 9.1
A simple page to test using `preventDefault()`

Click on the Go to Google link. Notice that clicking on this link does not immediately take you to Google's page. Instead, the event listener detects the click event, and the `permitAccess()` function is executed. You should see something like the message shown in Figure 9.2.

FIGURE 9.2
The message alert generated by `permitAccess()`

Clear the alert by clicking on the OK button. The default action of the clicked link should now happen; Google's page should open (in a new tab, since the link specified `target=_blank`). You should see something like the page shown in Figure 9.3.

FIGURE 9.3
The default action of the link has now been executed.

▼ Okay, you can close that tab to return to the original tab. If you now click on the second link, DO NOT go to Google, the event listener for this link should execute the function `refuseAccess()`, alerting a different message, as shown in Figure 9.4.

FIGURE 9.4
The function `refuseAccess()` has been executed.

This time, however, when you clear the alert box by clicking OK, the `preventDefault()` method is executed, denying the default behavior of the clicked link. This time, the second tab containing Google's page doesn't open.

Event Bubbling and Capture

It's common for page elements to be nested one inside another, sometimes to many levels of depth.

Consider the situation where a link occurs within a `<span>` element, which is itself inside a `<div>`:

```
<div id="d1">
    <span id="sp1">
        <a href="https://www.google.com" id="a1">Google</a>
    </span>
</div>
```

It's quite possible to attach event listeners to the click events of both the link and its enclosing `<span>` and `<div>` elements. When the link is clicked, in what order should the event handlers fire?

The usual way for events to be handled in a situation like this is called *bubbling*. Events on the inner element are assumed to happen first and then "bubble up" through the enclosing elements, in this case via the `<span>` element and then the `<div>`. The event handlers would fire in that order.

You can, however, choose to change this arrangement using an optional third parameter with `addEventListener()`. This third parameter can take the Boolean value `true` or `false`. If you don't provide a third parameter, as in the examples so far, JavaScript will assume it has the default value of `false`, and bubbling will take place from the innermost element first, up to the outermost element last.

```
document.getElementById("a1").addEventListener('click', myFunction(), false);
```

By setting the third parameter to `true`, however, you can instead use the so-called *capture* method. Using capture, the event handler associated with the outermost element would fire first, and that associated with the innermost element, last.

Turning Off Bubbling and Capture

If you decide that an event has been fully processed, you can easily prevent it from doing any further bubbling or capturing, which may save your browser from using resources unnecessarily.

The `event` object that we discussed earlier in the lesson has a method called `stopPropagation()` that does exactly that—it prevents any further bubbling or capture. Here's the previous example of capturing a key press:

```
myInputField = document.getElementById("form_input_1");
function myFunction(e) {
    var kc = e.keyCode;
    if (kc == 27) {
        alert ("Possible values for this field are: .... ");
    }
}
myInputField.addEventListener('onkeydown', myFunction);
```

As it stands, this code would allow the `onkeydown` event to bubble up to enclosing elements; for instance, to the `<form>` element, which presumably contains `myInputField`. You can add one extra line to stop this from happening:

```
myInputField = document.getElementById("form_input_1");
function myFunction(e) {
    var kc = e.keyCode;
    e.stopPropagation(); // prevent further bubbling
```

```
    if (kc == 27) {
        alert ("Possible values for this field are: .... ");
    }
}
myInputField.addEventListener('onkeydown', myFunction);
```

After the line

```
e.stopPropagation(); // prevent further bubbling
```

has been executed, no further bubbling will take place for the event e.

TIP

Knowing Where an Event Began

Occasionally, one of your event handlers in a containing element may need to know in which nested element an event was initially detected. A property of the event object called target contains this information and isn't changed during the bubbling process.

Summary

In this lesson you learned about JavaScript events and event handlers.

You also learned various ways in which event listeners can be created to detect the occurrence of particular events and execute related event handler code.

Finally, you were introduced to the concepts of event propagation by means of bubbling and capture and how to deal with these actions in your JavaScript code.

Q&A

Q. How can I capture the screen location where a mouse event occurs?

A. There are a number of ways to find the position where a mouse event occurs by using similar but subtly different properties of the event object. For an event e, e.screenX and e.screenY return the number of pixels from (respectively) the left and top of the *screen*. The number of pixels from the left and top of the *browser window* are found in e.clientX and e.clientY, while e.pageX and e.pageY hold the number of pixels from the left and top of the *document*, irrespective of whether it has been scrolled.

Q. Clicking the mouse seems to produce mousedown, mouseup, and click events. In what order do these fire?

A. The mousedown and then mouseup events both occur before the click event is fired.

Q. **How can I detect whether a user is holding down the Alt, Shift, or Control keys when another key is pressed?**

A. Several Boolean attributes return `true` when a so-called *modifier key* is held down when another key is pressed. They are

`ctrlKey`   The Control key is held down.

`shiftKey`   The Shift key is held down.

`altKey`   The Alt key is held down.

`metaKey`   The Meta key is held down.

Q. **How do I remove an event that I added using an anonymous function?**

A. You cannot easily do so. You shouldn't use anonymous functions as parameters in `addEventListener()` if you might want to remove the listener later, because `removeEventListener()` needs a reference to the function name. Use a named function instead.

Workshop

Quiz questions and exercises to test your understanding and to stretch your skills.

Quiz

1. Which of the following is the correct event handler to detect a mouse click on a link?

   a. `onmouseup`

   b. `onlink`

   c. `onclick`

2. During bubbling, nested elements fire an event

   a. All together

   b. From innermost to outermost

   c. From outermost to innermost

3. To turn on capture mode instead of bubbling, what should be the third parameter given to `addEventListener`?

   a. `true`

   b. `capture`

   c. `stopPropagation`

4. Adding multiple event listeners to the same DOM object is most easily and effectively carried out using

   a. Inline event listeners

   b. The `event` object

   c. The `addEventListener()` function

5. The `addEventListener()` function can add event listeners to

   a. Only HTML page elements

   b. Any DOM object capable of receiving events

   c. Only the `event` object

TIP
_____

Register Your Book

Just a reminder for those of you reading these words in the print or e-book edition of this book: If you go to www.informit.com/register and register this book (using ISBN 978-0-672-33809-0), you can receive free access to an online Web Edition that not only contains the complete text of this book but also features an interactive version of this quiz.
_____

Answers

1. c. `onclick`

2. b. from innermost to outermost

3. a. `true`

4. c. The `addEventListener()` function

5. b. Any DOM object capable of receiving events

Exercises

Design a simple HTML page with some nested elements, and write an associated script that demonstrates bubbling by adding log statements to the JavaScript console in the order that events fire, after an initial `click` event is detected in the innermost nested element.

Modify your script to instead demonstrate capture.

Controlling Program Flow

What You'll Learn in This Lesson:

▶ Using conditional statements
▶ Comparing values with comparison operators
▶ Applying logical operators
▶ Writing loops and control structures
▶ Setting timers in JavaScript

In previous lessons you took a quick trip through the data types that JavaScript variables can contain. To create anything but the simplest scripts, though, you're going to need your code to make decisions based on those values. In this lesson we examine ways to recognize particular conditions and have our program act in a prescribed way as a result.

Conditional Statements

Conditional statements, as the name implies, are used to detect particular conditions arising in the values of the variables you are using in your script. JavaScript supports various such conditional statements, as outlined in the following sections.

The `if()` Statement

In the preceding lesson we discussed Boolean variables, which can take one of only two values—`true` or `false`.

JavaScript has several ways to test such values, the simplest of which is the `if` statement. It has the following general form:

```
if(this condition is true) then do this.
```

Let's look at a trivial example:

```
var message = "";
var bool = true;
if(bool) message = "The test condition evaluated to TRUE";
```

First, you declare a variable `message` and assign an empty string to it as a value. You then declare a new variable, `bool`, which you set to the Boolean value of `true`. The third statement tests the value of the variable `bool` to see whether it is true; if so (as in this case), the value of the variable `message` is set to a new string. Had you assigned a value of `false` to `bool` in the second line, the test condition would not have been fulfilled, and the instruction to assign a new value to `message` would have been ignored, leaving the variable `message` containing the empty string.

Remember, we said that the general form of an `if` statement is

```
if(this condition is true) then do this.
```

In the case of a Boolean value, as in this example, we have replaced the condition with the variable itself; since its value can only be `true` or `false`, the contents of the parentheses passed back to `if` accordingly evaluate to `true` or `false`.

You can test for the Boolean value `false` by using the negation character (`!`):

```
if(!bool) message = "The value of bool is FALSE";
```

Clearly, for `!bool` to evaluate to `true`, `bool` must be of value `false`.

Comparison Operators

The `if()` statement is not limited to testing the value of a Boolean variable; instead, you can enter a condition in the form of an expression into the parentheses of the `if` statement, and JavaScript will evaluate the expression to determine whether it is true or false:

```
var message = "";
var temperature = 60;
if(temperature < 64) message = "Turn on the heating!";
```

The less-than operator (`<`) is one of a range of comparison operators available in JavaScript. Some of the comparison operators are listed in Table 10.1.

TABLE 10.1 JavaScript Comparison Operators

Operator	Meaning
==	Is equal to
===	Is equal to in both value and type
!=	Is not equal to
>	Is greater than
<	Is less than
>=	Is greater than or equal to
<=	Is less than or equal to

Extending the Spam Detector

In Lesson 7, "Working with Character Strings," you developed a simple function to detect the word *fake* in a given input string.

Now you can further develop that function using the `if()` statement.

Here's the function from Lesson 7:

```
function detectSpam(input) {
    input = input.toLowerCase();
    return input.indexOf("fake");
}
```

The function, you'll recall, currently returns a number corresponding with the location in the input string where the word *fake* has been located.

Let's modify the function to instead return `true` or `false` depending on whether the target word was found:

```
if(input.indexOf("fake") < 0) {
    return false;
}
return true;
```

Now you can see that, if the condition

```
input.indexOf("fake") < 0
```

is met, the function will terminate, returning `false`; otherwise, execution will continue to the next line after the `if()` block, and the function will terminate, returning `true`.

Listing 10.1 shows the modified code in a complete HTML file. Create this file in your editor.

LISTING 10.1   Spam Detector Function

```
<!DOCTYPE html>
<html>
<head>
    <title>Spam Detector</title>
</head>
<body>
    <script>
        function detectSpam(input) {
            input = input.toLowerCase();
            if(input.indexOf("fake") < 0) {
                return false;
            }
```

```
        return true;
        }

        var mystring = prompt("Enter a string");
        alert(detectSpam(mystring));
    </script>
</body>
</html>
```

Now let's see how the program performs when given the same string used in Lesson 7, as shown in Figure 10.1.

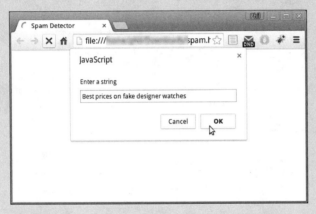

FIGURE 10.1
Entering a string

As you can see in Figure 10.2, the alert dialog now simply reports `true`, rather than showing the location in the string where the target word was found. Reload the file in the browser and try it again with a string that doesn't contain the word *fake* to confirm that the detector returns `false`.

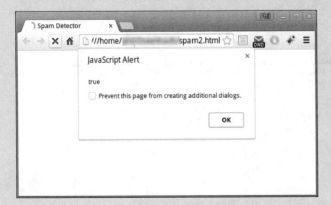

FIGURE 10.2
The spam detector reports `true`

How to Test for Equality

In the previous example, how could you test to see whether the temperature *exactly equals* 64 degrees? Remember that you use the equal sign (=) to *assign* a value to a variable, so this code won't work as might be expected:

```
if(temperature = 64) ....
```

Were you to use this statement, the expression within the parentheses would be evaluated by JavaScript and the variable `temperature` would be *assigned* the value of 64. If this value assignment terminates successfully—and why shouldn't it?—then the value assignment would return a value of `true` back to the `if()` statement, and the rest of the statement would therefore be executed. This isn't the behavior you want at all.

Instead, to test for equality, you must use a double equal sign (==):

```
if(temperature == 64) message = "64 degrees and holding!";
```

CAUTION

Testing Two Items

If you need to test whether two items are equal **both in value and in type**, JavaScript has an operator, ===, to perform this test. For example:

```
var x = 2; // assign a numeric value
if(x == "2") ... // true, as the string "2" is interpreted
if(x === "2") ...// false, a string is not numeric
```

This operation can be useful when testing to see whether a returned value is actually `false`, or just a value that is falsy (can be **interpreted** as `false`):

```
var x = 0; // assign a value of zero
if(!x) ... // evaluates to true
if(x === false)..// evaluates to false
```

More About `if()`

The previous examples carry out only a single statement when the test condition is met. What if you want to do more than this—for instance, carry out several statements?

To achieve this, you simply enclose in curly braces ({ }) all the code statements that you want to execute if the condition is fulfilled:

```
if(temperature < 64) {
    message = "Turn on the heating!";
    heatingStatus = "on";
    // ... more statements can be added here
}
```

You can also add a clause to the `if` statement that contains code you want to execute if the condition is *not* fulfilled. To achieve this, you use the `else` construct:

```
if(temperature < 64) {
    message = "Turn on the heating!";
    heatingStatus = "on";
    // ... more statements can be added here
} else {
    message = "Temperature is high enough";
    heatingStatus = "off";
    // ... more statements can be added here too
}
```

TIP

A Shorter Syntax

There exists a shorthand form of the syntax for the `if()` statement:

```
(condition is true)? [do if true] : [do if false];
```

Here's an example:

```
errorMessage = count + ((count == 1)? " error ":" errors ") + "found.";
```

In this example, if the number of errors stored in the variable `count` is exactly 1, the message variable will contain

```
1 error found.
```

If the value in `count` is 0 or a number greater than 1, the message variable will contain a string such as

```
3 errors found.
```

How to Test Multiple Conditions

You can use "nested" combinations of `if` and `else` to test multiple conditions before deciding how to act.

Let's return to the heating system example and have it switch on the cooling fan if the temperature is too high:

```
if(temperature < 64) {
    message = "Turn on the heating!";
    heatingStatus = "on";
    fanStatus = "off";
} else if(temperature > 72){
    message = "Turn on the fan!";
    heatingStatus = "off";
    fanStatus = "on";
```

```
} else {
    message = "Temperature is OK";
    heatingStatus = "off";
    fanStatus = "off";
}
```

The `switch` Statement

When you're testing for a range of different possible outcomes of the same conditional statement, a concise syntax you can use is that of JavaScript's `switch` statement:

```
switch(color) {
    case "red" :
        message = "Stop!";
        break;
    case "yellow" :
        message = "Pass with caution";
        break;
    case "green" :
        message = "Come on through";
        break;
    default :
        message = "Traffic light out of service. Pass only with great care";
}
```

The keyword `switch` has in parentheses the name of the variable to be tested.

The tests themselves are listed within the braces, { and }. Each `case` statement (with its value in quotation marks) is followed by a colon and then the list of actions to be executed if that case has been matched. There can be any number of code statements in each section.

Note the `break` statement after each case. This jumps you to the end of the `switch` statement after having executed the code for a matching case. If `break` is omitted, it's possible that more than one case will have its code executed.

The optional `default` case has its code executed if none of the specified cases were matched.

Logical Operators

Sometimes you want to test a combination of criteria to determine whether a test condition has been met, and doing so with `if ... else` or `switch` statements becomes unwieldy.

Let's return once more to the temperature control program. JavaScript allows you to combine conditions using logical AND (`&&`) and logical OR (`||`). Here's one way:

```
if(temperature >= 64 && temperature <= 72) {
    message = "The temperature is OK";
```

```
} else {
    message = "The temperature is out of range!";
}
```

You can read the preceding condition as "If the temperature is greater than or equal to 64 AND the temperature is less than or equal to 72."

You can achieve exactly the same functionality using OR instead of AND:

```
if(temperature < 64 || temperature > 72) {
    message = "The temperature is out of range!";
} else {
    message = "The temperature is OK";
}
```

This example reverses the way to carry out the test; the conditional statement is now fulfilled when the temperature is *out of* range and can be read as "If the temperature is less than 64 OR greater than 72."

Loops and Control Structures

The `if` statement can be thought of as a *junction* in program execution. Depending on the result of the test performed on the data, the program may go down one route or another with its execution of statements.

On many occasions, though, you might want to execute some operation a number of times before continuing with the rest of the program. If the number of repeats is fixed, you could perhaps achieve this with multiple `if` statements and incrementing counter variables, though the code would be messy and hard to read. But what if you don't know how many times you need to repeat the piece of code because the number of repeats depends on, for example, the changing value of a variable?

JavaScript has various built-in loop structures that allow you to achieve such goals.

while

The syntax of the `while` statement is very much like the syntax for the `if` statement:

```
while(this condition is true) {
    carry out these statements ...
}
```

The `while` statement *works* just like `if` too. The only difference is that, after completing the conditional statements, `while` goes back and tests the condition again. All the time the condition keeps coming up `true`, `while` keeps right on executing the conditional code. Here's an example:

```
var count = 10;
var sum = 0;
while(count > 0) {
    sum = sum + count;
    count--;
}
alert(sum);
```

Each time `while` evaluates the condition as `true`, the statements in the curly braces are executed over and over, adding the current value of `count` to the variable `sum` on each trip around the loop.

When `count` has been decremented to zero, the condition fails and the loop stops; program operation then continues from after the closing brace. By this time, the variable `sum` has a value of

`10 + 9 + 8 + 7 + 6 + 5 + 4 + 3 + 2 + 1 = 55`

do...while

The `do...while` structure is similar in operation to `while`, but with one important difference. Here's the syntax:

```
do {
    ... these statements ...
} while(this condition is true)
```

The only real difference here is that, since the `while` clause appears *after* the braces, the list of conditional statements is executed once *before* the `while` clause is evaluated. The statements in a `do...while` clause will therefore always be executed at least once.

for

The `for` loop is another loop similar in operation to `while`, but with a more comprehensive syntax. With the `for` loop, you can specify an initial condition, a test condition (to end the loop), and a means of changing a counter variable for each pass through the loop, all in one statement. Have a look at the syntax:

```
for(x=0; x<10; x++) {
    ... execute these statements ...
}
```

You can interpret this as follows:

> For `x` initially set to zero, and while `x` is less than 10, and incrementing `x` by 1 on each pass through the loop, carry out the conditional statements.

Let's rewrite the example we gave when looking at the `while` loop, but this time using a `for` loop:

```
var count;
var sum = 0;
for(count = 10; count > 0; count--) {
    sum = sum + count;
}
```

If the counter variable has not previously been declared, it is often convenient to declare it with the `var` keyword within the `for` statement instead of outside:

```
var sum = 0;
for(var count = 10; count > 0; count--) {
    sum = sum + count;
}
alert(sum);
```

As in the previous example, after the loop terminates, the variable `sum` has a value of

```
10 + 9 + 8 + 7 + 6 + 5 + 4 + 3 + 2 + 1 = 55
```

Leaving a Loop with `break`

The `break` command works within a loop pretty much as it does in a `switch` statement: it kicks you out of the loop and returns operation to the line of code immediately after the closing brace.

Here's an example:

```
var count = 10;
var sum = 0;
while(count > 0) {
    sum = sum + count;
    if(sum > 42) break;
    count--;
}
alert(sum);
```

You saw previously that, without the break instruction, the value of `sum` evolved like this:

```
10 + 9 + 8 + 7 + 6 + 5 + 4 + 3 + 2 + 1 = 55
```

Now, you find that when the value of `sum` reaches

```
10 + 9 + 8 + 7 + 6 + 5 = 45
```

the conditional clause of the `if(sum > 42)` statement will come up `true` and cause the loop to terminate due to the `break` command.

CAUTION

Beware of Infinite Loops

Beware of accidentally creating an infinite loop. Here's a loop used earlier:

```
while(count > 0) {
    sum = sum + count;
    count--;
}
```

Imagine, for example, that you omitted the line
```
count--;
```

Now every time `while` tests the variable `count`, it finds it to be greater than zero, and the loop never ends. An infinite loop can stop the browser from responding, cause a JavaScript error, or cause the browser to crash.

Looping Through Objects with `for . . . in`

The `for . . . in` loop is a special sort of loop intended for stepping through the properties of an object. Let's see it in action applied to an array object in Listing 10.2.

LISTING 10.2   The `for . . . in` **Loop**

```
<!DOCTYPE html>
<html>
<head>
    <title>Loops and Control</title>
</head>
<body>
    <script>
        var days = ['Sun','Mon','Tue','Wed','Thu','Fri','Sat'];
        var message = "";
        for (i in days) {
            message += 'Day ' + i + ' is ' + days[i] + '\n';
        }
        alert(message);
    </script>
</body>
</html>
```

In this sort of loop, you don't need to worry about maintaining a loop counter or devising a test to see when the loop should complete. The loop will occur once for every property of the supplied object (in this example, once for every array item) and then terminate.

The result of running this example is shown in Figure 10.3.

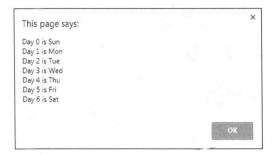

FIGURE 10.3
Result of running the `for . . . in` loop

NOTE

Using `for . . . in` On Other Objects

You'll recall that an array is one type of JavaScript object.

You can use the `for . . . in` loop to investigate the properties of any object, whether it's a DOM object, a JavaScript built-in object, or one you've created yourself (as you'll be doing in Lesson 11, "Introducing Object-Oriented Programming").

How to Set and Use Timers

In some situations you'll want to program a specific delay into the execution of your JavaScript code. This type of delay is especially common when writing user interface routines; for instance, you may want to display a message for a short period before removing it.

To help you, JavaScript provides two useful methods: `setTimeout()` and `setInterval()`.

NOTE

Timer Methods

`setTimeout()` and `clearTimeout()` are both methods of the HTML DOM `window` object.

`setTimeout()`

The `setTimeout(action, delay)` method calls the function (or evaluates the expression) passed in its first argument after the number of milliseconds specified in its second argument. You can use it, for example, to display an element in a given configuration for a fixed period of time:

```
<div id="id1">I'm about to disappear!</div>
```

Let's suppose your page contains the preceding `<div>` element. If you put the following code into a `<script>` element in the page `<head>` section, the function `hide()` will be executed 3 seconds after the page finishes loading, making the `<div>` element invisible:

```
function hide(elementId) {
    document.getElementById(elementId).style.display = 'none';
}
window.onload = function() {
    setTimeout("hide('id1')", 3000);
}
```

The `setTimeout()` method returns a value. If later you want to cancel the timer function, you can refer to it by passing that returned value to the `clearTimeout()` method:

```
var timer1 = setTimeout("hide('id1')", 3000);
clearTimeout(timer1);
```

setInterval()

The `setInterval(action, delay)` method works similarly to `setTimeout()`, but instead of imposing a single delay before executing the statement passed to it as its first argument, it executes it repeatedly, with a delay between executions corresponding to the number of milliseconds specified in the second argument.

Like `setTimeout()`, `setInterval()` returns a value that you can later pass to the `clearInterval()` method to stop the timer:

```
var timer1 = setInterval("updateClock()", 1000);
clearInterval(timer1);
```

Summary

In this lesson you learned about testing conditions and controlling program flow based on the values of variables, and how to write various kinds of program loops controlled by conditions.

You also learned about using timers in your programs.

Q&A

Q. Is there any particular reason why I should use one sort of loop over another?

A. It's true that there is usually more than one type of loop that will solve any particular programming problem. You can use the one you feel most comfortable with, though it's usually good practice to use whichever loop makes the most sense (in conjunction with your chosen variable names) in the context of what your code sets out to do.

Q. **Is there a way to stop the current trip around a loop and move straight to the next iteration?**

A. Yes, you can use the `continue` command. It works pretty much like `break`, but instead of canceling the loop and continuing code execution from after the closing brace, `continue` cancels only the current trip around the loop and moves on to the next one.

Workshop

Quiz questions and exercises to test your understanding and to stretch your skills.

Quiz

1. How is "greater than or equal to" expressed in JavaScript?

   a. `>`

   b. `>=`

   c. `>==`

2. What command forces the cancellation of a loop and moves code operation to the statement after the closing brace?

   a. `break;`

   b. `loop;`

   c. `close;`

3. Which of the following is likely to cause an infinite loop to occur?

   a. The wrong sort of loop has been used.

   b. The condition to terminate the loop is never met.

   c. There are too many statements in the loop.

4. If no specified case is matched in a switch statement,

   a. An error will be generated.

   b. The optional default case will execute, if one is present.

   c. The obligatory default case is executed.

5. The statements in a `do ... while` clause

   a. Will always be executed at least once

   b. May be executed zero or more times

   c. Will continue to be executed until a break statement is encountered

Answers

1. b. JavaScript interprets >= as "greater than or equal to."

2. a. The `break` command ends loop execution.

3. b. An infinite loop occurs if the condition to terminate the loop is never met.

4. b. The optional default case will execute, if one is present.

5. a. The statements in a `do . . . while` clause will always be executed at least once.

Exercises

In Lesson 5, "Using DOM Objects and Built-in Objects," you learned how to get the current day of the week. Write a program using a `switch` statement to output a different message to the user, depending on what day it is today.

Modify Listing 10.2 to list the months of the year rather than the days of the week. How can you modify the code to list the months starting with January as Month 1 rather than Month 0?

LESSON 11
Introducing Object-Oriented Programming

What You'll Learn in This Lesson:

▶ What object-oriented programming is

▶ Two ways to create objects

▶ How to instantiate an object

▶ How to extend and inherit objects using `prototype`

▶ How to access object methods and properties

As your programs become more complex, you need to use coding techniques that help you maintain control and ensure that your code remains efficient, readable, and maintainable. In this lesson you learn the basics of object-oriented programming (OOP), an important technique for writing clear and reliable code that you can reuse over and over.

What Is Object-Oriented Programming?

The code examples to date have been so-called *procedural* programming. Procedural programming is characterized by having data stored in variables, which are operated on by lists of instructions. Each instruction (or list of instructions, such as a function) can create, destroy, or modify the data, yet the data always remains somehow "separate" from the program code.

In object-oriented programming, the program instructions and the data on which they operate are more intertwined. OOP is a way of conceptualizing a program's data into discrete "things" referred to as *objects*—each having its own *properties* (data) and *methods* (instructions).

Suppose, for example, you wanted to write a script to help manage a car rental business. You might design a general-purpose object called `Car`. The `Car` object would have certain properties (`color`, `year`, `odometerReading`, and `make`) and perhaps a few methods (such as a method `setOdometer(newMiles)` to update the `odometerReading` property to the current figure `newMiles`).

For each car in the rental fleet, you would create an *instance* of the `Car` object.

NOTE

Objects and Instances

An instance of an object is an existing example of an object based on a specific design blueprint. For example, the general object template `Car` might have a specific instance where a `Car` object has been created with specific data identifying it as a "blue 2016 Ford" and another instance described as a "yellow 2014 Nissan." In most discussions of object-oriented programming, such a blueprint is referred to as a *class*. Until recently, JavaScript did not have a keyword `class`, but this syntax has now been added to the language. You'll learn about it in the next lesson.

Writing OOP code offers several advantages over procedural methods:

▶ **Code reuse:** First, OOP enables you to reuse your code in a variety of scripts. You could achieve this with regular functions, but it would soon become difficult to keep track of all the variables that needed to be passed, their scope, and meaning. For objects, in contrast, you only need to document the properties and methods for each object. Providing they adhere to these rules, other programs—and even other programmers—can easily use your object definitions.

▶ **Encapsulation:** You can define the way objects interact with other parts of your scripts by carefully controlling the properties and methods that the rest of the program can "see." The *internal* workings of the object can be hidden away, forcing code external to the object to access that object's data only through the documented interfaces that the object offers.

▶ **Inheritance:** Often when coding you will have a need for some code that is nearly, but not quite, the same as something that's been coded before—maybe even something already coded in the same application. Using *inheritance*, you can create new objects based on the design of previously defined objects, optionally with additions or modifications to their methods and properties; the new object *inherits* properties and methods from the old.

In the previous lessons you often used objects—either those built into JavaScript or those that make up the DOM. However, you can also create your own objects, with their own properties and functions, to use in your programs.

NOTE

Object Oriented Languages

Some programming languages such as C++ and Smalltalk lean heavily toward OOP, and are often referred to as *object-oriented languages*.

JavaScript is not one of these languages, but it does support enough of the essentials to allow you to write useful OOP code. We could easily fill a whole book with theory and practice of OOP, but we just look at the basics here.

Object Creation

JavaScript offers several ways to create an object. Let's look first at how to declare a *direct instance* of an object; later we create an object by using a *constructor function*.

Creating a Direct Instance

JavaScript has a built-in object simply called `Object` that you can use as a kind of blank canvas for creating your own objects:

```
myNewObject = new Object();
```

Okay, you now have a brand new object, `myNewObject`. For the moment, it doesn't actually do anything because it doesn't have any properties or methods. You can begin to rectify that by adding a property:

```
myNewObject.info = 'I am a shiny new object';
```

Now your object owns a property—in this case a text string containing some information about the object and called `info`. You can also easily add a method to the object, by first defining a function, and then attaching it to `myNewObject` as one of the object's methods:

```
function myFunc() {
    alert(this.info);
}
myNewObject.showInfo = myFunc;
```

CAUTION

Function Names

Notice that you use just the name of the function here without the parentheses. You do so because you are trying to assign to method `myNewObject.showInfo` the **definition** of the function `myFunc()`. Had you used the code

```
myNewObject.showInfo = myFunc();
```

you would have been asking JavaScript to **execute** `myFunc()` and assign its **return value** to `myNewObject.showInfo`.

To call the new method, you can simply use the now-familiar dot notation:

```
myNewObject.showInfo();
```

Using the `this` Keyword

Note the use of the `this` keyword in the previous function definition. You may recall that you used such a keyword in Lesson 2, "Writing Simple Scripts," and Lesson 3, "Introducing Functions." In those previous examples, you used `this` in an inline event handler:

```
<img src="tick.gif" alt="tick" onmouseover="this.src='tick2.gif';" />
```

When used in that way, `this` refers to the HTML element itself—in the preceding case the `<img>` element. When you use `this` inside a function (or method), the keyword `this` refers to the function's *parent* object.

Upon the first declaration of the function `myFunc()`, its parent is the global object—that is, the `window` object. The `window` object does not have a property called `info`, so if you were to call the `myFunc()` function directly, an error would occur.

However, you can go on to create a method called `showInfo` of `myNewObject` and assign `myFunc()` to that method:

```
myNewObject.showInfo = myFunc;
```

In the context of the `showInfo()` method, `myNewObject` is the parent object, so `this.info` refers to the property `myNewObject.info`.

Let's see if we can clarify this a little with the code in Listing 11.1.

LISTING 11.1   Creating an Object

```
<!DOCTYPE html>
<html>
<head>
    <title>Object Oriented Programming</title>
    <script>
        myNewObject = new Object();
        myNewObject.info = 'I am a shiny new object';
        function myFunc(){
            alert(this.info);
        }
        myNewObject.showInfo = myFunc;
    </script>
</head>
<body>

<input type="button" value="Good showInfo Call" onclick="myNewObject.showInfo()" />
    <input type="button" value="myFunc Call" onclick="myFunc()" />
    <input type="button" value="Bad showInfo Call" onclick="showInfo()" />
</body>
</html>
```

Notice that in the <head> section of the page, you create the object myNewObject and assign it the property info and the method showInfo, as described earlier.

Loading this page into your browser, you are confronted with three buttons.

Clicking on the first button makes a call to the showInfo method of the newly created object:

```
<input type="button" value="Good showInfo Call" onclick="myNewObject.showInfo()" />
```

As you would hope, the value of the info property is passed to the alert() dialog, as shown in Figure 11.1.

FIGURE 11.1
The info property is correctly called

The second button attempts to make a call directly to the myFunc() function:

```
<input type="button" value="myFunc Call" onclick="myFunc()" />
```

Because myFunc() is a method of the global object (having been defined without reference to any other object as parent), it attempts to pass to the alert() dialog the value of a nonexistent property window.info, with the result shown in Figure 11.2.

FIGURE 11.2
The global object has no property called info

Finally, your third button attempts to call showInfo without reference to its parent object:

```
<input type="button" value="Bad showInfo Call" onclick="showInfo()" />
```

Because the method does not exist outside the object myNewObject, JavaScript reports an error, as shown in Figure 11.3.

The JavaScript Console

We'll talk more about dealing with JavaScript errors using your browser's JavaScript Console or Error Console in Lesson 23, "Debugging Your Code."

FIGURE 11.3
JavaScript reports that `showInfo` is not defined

Using Anonymous Functions

There is a more convenient and elegant way to assign a value to your object's `showInfo` method, without having to create a separate, named function and then later assign it by name to the required method. Instead of this code:

```
function myFunc() {
    alert(this.info);
}
myNewObject.showInfo = myFunc;
```

you could simply have written the following:

```
myNewObject.showInfo = function() {
    alert(this.info);
}
```

Because you haven't needed to give a name to your function prior to assigning it, this technique is referred to as using an *anonymous function*.

By using similar assignment statements, you can add as many properties and methods as you need to your instantiated object.

TIP

Later You'll Meet JSON

JavaScript offers a further way to create a direct instance of an object; the technique uses JavaScript Object Notation (JSON). It isn't covered here, because we'll explore JSON in detail in Lesson 14, "Meet JSON."

Using a Constructor Function

Directly creating an instance of an object is fine if you think you'll need only one object of that type. Unfortunately, if you need to create another instance of the same type of object, you'll have to go through the same process again—creating the object, adding properties, defining methods, and so on.

TIP

Singleton Objects

An object with only one global instance is sometimes called a *singleton* object. These objects are useful sometimes; for example, a user of your program might have only one associated `userProfile` object, perhaps containing his username, URL of last page viewed, and similar properties.

A better way to create objects that will have multiple instances is to use an *object constructor function*. An object constructor function creates a kind of "template" from which further objects can be instantiated.

Let's look at the following code. Instead of using `new Object()`, you first declare a function, `myObjectType()`, and in its definition, you can add properties and methods using the `this` keyword:

```
function myObjectType(){
    this.info = 'I am a shiny new object';
    this.showInfo = function(){
        alert(this.info); // show the value of the property info
    }
    this.setInfo = function (newInfo) {
        this.info = newInfo; // overwrite the value of the property info
    }
}
```

In the preceding code you added a single property, info, and two methods: showInfo, which simply displays the value currently stored in the info property, and setInfo. The setInfo method takes an argument, newInfo, and uses its value to overwrite the value of the info property.

Instantiating an Object

You can now create as many instances as you want of this object type. All will have the properties and methods defined in the myObjectType() function. Creating an object instance is known as *instantiating* an object.

Having defined your constructor function, you can create an instance of your object simply by using the constructor function:

```
var myNewObject = new myObjectType();
```

NOTE

This syntax is identical to using new Object(), except that you use your purpose-designed object type in place of JavaScript's general-purpose Object().

In doing so, you instantiate the object complete with the properties and methods defined in the constructor function.

Now you can call its methods and examine its properties:

```
var x = myNewObject.info // x now contains 'I am a shiny new object'
myNewObject.showInfo(); // alerts 'I am a shiny new object'
myNewObject.setInfo("Here is some new information"); // overwrites the info property
```

Creating multiple instances is as simple as calling the constructor function as many times as you need to:

```
var myNewObject1 = new myObjectType();
var myNewObject2 = new myObjectType();
```

Let's see this in action. The code in Listing 11.2 defines an object constructor function the same as the one described previously.

LISTING 11.2   Creating Objects with a Constructor Function

```
<!DOCTYPE html>
<html>
<head>
    <title>Object Oriented Programming</title>
    <script>
```

```
        function myObjectType(){
            this.info = 'I am a shiny new object';
            this.showInfo = function(){
                alert(this.info);
            }
            this.setInfo = function (newInfo) {
                this.info = newInfo;
            }
        }
        var myNewObject1 = new myObjectType();
        var myNewObject2 = new myObjectType();
    </script>
</head>
<body>
    <input type="button" value="Show Info 1" onclick="myNewObject1.showInfo()" />
    <input type="button" value="Show Info 2" onclick="myNewObject2.showInfo()" />
    <input type="button" value="Change info of object2" onclick="myNewObject2.
setInfo('New Information!')" />
</body>
</html>
```

Here, two instances of the object are instantiated; clearly, both objects are initially identical. You can examine the value stored in the info property for each object by clicking on one of the buttons labeled Show Info 1 or Show Info 2.

A third button calls the setInfo method of object myNewObject2, passing a new string literal as an argument to the method. This overwrites the value stored in the info property of object myNewObject2, but of course leaves myNewObject unchanged. The revised values can be checked by once again using Show Info 1 and Show Info 2.

Using Constructor Function Arguments

There is nothing to stop you from customizing your objects at the time of instantiation, by passing one or more arguments to the constructor function. In the following code, the definition of the constructor function includes one argument, personName, which is assigned to the name property by the constructor function. As you instantiate two objects, you pass a name as an argument to the constructor function for each instance.

```
function Person(personName){
    this.name = personName;
    this.info = 'I am called ' + this.name;
    this.showInfo = function(){
        alert(this.info);
    }
}
var person1 = new Person('Adam');
var person2 = new Person('Eve');
```

TIP

Multiple Arguments

You can define the constructor function to accept as many or as few arguments as you want:

```
function Car(Color, Year, Make, Miles) {
    this.color = Color;
    this.year = Year;
    this.make = Make;
    this.odometerReading = Miles;
    this.setOdometer = function(newMiles) {
        this.odometerReading = newMiles;
    }
}
var car1 = new Car("blue", "2016", "Ford", 79500);
var car2 = new Car("yellow", "2014", "Nissan", 56350);
car1.setOdometer(82450);
```

Extending and Inheriting Objects Using `prototype`

A major advantage of using objects is the capability to reuse already written code in a new context. JavaScript provides a means to modify objects to include new methods and/or properties or even to create brand-new objects based on ones that already exist.

These techniques are known, respectively, as *extending* and *inheriting* objects.

Extending Objects

What if you want to extend your objects with new methods and properties after the objects have already been instantiated? You can do so using the keyword `prototype`. The `prototype` object allows you to quickly add a property or method that is then available for all instances of the object.

▼ TRY IT YOURSELF

Extend an Object Using `prototype`

Let's extend the `Person` object of the previous example with a new method, `sayHello`:

```
Person.prototype.sayHello = function() {
    alert(this.name + " says hello");
}
```

Create a new HTML file in your editor, and enter the code from Listing 11.3.

LISTING 11.3   Adding a New Method with `prototype`

```
<!DOCTYPE html>
<html>
<head>
<title>Object Oriented Programming</title>
    <script>
        function Person(personName){
            this.name = personName;
            this.info = 'This person is called ' + this.name;
            this.showInfo = function(){
                alert(this.info);
            }
        }
        var person1 = new Person('Adam');
        var person2 = new Person('Eve');
        Person.prototype.sayHello = function() {
            alert(this.name + " says hello");
        }
    </script>
</head>
<body>
    <input type="button" value="Show Info on Adam" onclick="person1.showInfo()" />
    <input type="button" value="Show Info on Eve" onclick="person2.showInfo()" />
    <input type="button" value="Say Hello Adam" onclick="person1.sayHello()" />
    <input type="button" value="Say Hello Eve" onclick="person2.sayHello()" />
</body>
</html>
```

Let's walk through this code and see what's happening.

First, you define a constructor function that takes a single argument, `personName`. Within the constructor, two properties, `name` and `info`, and one method, `showInfo`, are defined.

You create two objects, instantiating each with a different `name` property. Having created these two Person objects, you then decide to add a further method, `sayHello`, to the `Person` object definition. You do so using the `prototype` keyword.

Load the HTML file into your browser. Clicking on the four buttons visible on the page shows that the initially defined `showInfo` method is still intact, but the new `sayHello` method operates too, and is available for both of the existing instances of the object type.

Inheriting Objects

Inheritance is the capability to create one object type from another; the new object type inherits the properties and methods of the old, as well as optionally having further properties and methods of its own. This capability can save you a lot of work because you can first devise "generic" classes of objects and then refine them into more specific classes by inheritance.

JavaScript uses the `prototype` keyword to emulate inheritance too.

Because `object.prototype` is used to add new methods and properties, you can utilize it to add ALL the methods and properties of an existing constructor function to your new object.

Let's define another simple object:

```
function Pet() {
    this.animal = "";
    this.name = "";
    this.setAnimal = function(newAnimal) {
        this.animal = newAnimal;
    }
    this.setName = function(newName) {
        this.name = newName;
    }
}
```

A `Pet` object has properties that contain the type of animal and the name of the pet, and methods to set these values:

```
var myCat = new Pet();
myCat.setAnimal = "cat";
myCat.setName = "Sylvester";
```

Now suppose you want to create an object specifically for dogs. Rather than starting from scratch, you want to inherit the `Dog` object from `Pet` but add an additional property, `breed`, and an additional method, `setBreed`.

First, let's create the `Dog` constructor function and in it define the new property and method:

```
function Dog() {
    this.breed = "";
    this.setBreed = function(newBreed) {
        this.breed = newBreed;
    }
}
```

Having added the new property, `breed`, and the new method, `setBreed`, you can now additionally inherit all the properties and methods of `Pet`. You do so using the `prototype` keyword:

```
Dog.prototype = new Pet();
```

You can now access the properties and methods of `Pet` in addition to those of `Dog`:

```
var myDog = new Dog();
myDog.setName("Alan");
myDog.setBreed("Greyhound");
alert(myDog.name + " is a " + myDog.breed);
```

TRY IT YOURSELF ▼

Extending JavaScript's Own Objects

`Prototype` can also be used to extend JavaScript's built-in objects. You can implement the `String.prototype.backwards` method, for instance, that will return a reversed version of any string you supply, as in Listing 11.4.

LISTING 11.4 Extending the `String` Object

```
<!DOCTYPE html>
<html>
<head>
    <title>Object Oriented Programming</title>
    <script>
        String.prototype.backwards = function(){
            var out = '';
            for(var i = this.length-1; i >= 0; i--){
                out += this.substr(i, 1);
            }
            return out;
        }
    </script>
</head>
<body>
    <script>
        var inString = prompt("Enter your test string:");
        document.write(inString.backwards());
    </script>
</body>
</html>
```

Save the code in Listing 11.4 as an HTML file and open it in your browser. The script uses a `prompt()` dialog to invite you to enter a string and then shows the string reversed on the page.

Let's see how the code works:

```
String.prototype.backwards = function(){
    var out = '';
    for(var i = this.length-1; i >= 0; i--){
```

```
            out += this.substr(i, 1);
        }
        return out;
    }
}
```

First, you declare a new variable, `out`, within the anonymous function that you are creating. This variable will hold the reversed string.

You then begin a loop, starting at the end of the input string (remember that JavaScript string character indexing starts at 0, not 1, so you need to begin at `this.length - 1`) and decrementing one character at a time. As you loop backwards through the string, you add characters one at a time to your output string stored in `out`.

When you reach the beginning of the input string, the reversed string is returned. The result is shown in Figure 11.4.

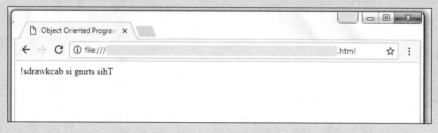

FIGURE 11.4
Method to reverse a string

Encapsulation

Encapsulation is the name given to OOP's capability to hide data and instructions inside an object. How this is achieved varies from language to language, but in JavaScript any variables declared inside the constructor function are available only from within the object; they are invisible from outside. The same is true of any function declared inside the constructor function.

Such variables and functions become accessible to the outside world only when they are assigned with the `this` keyword; they then become properties and methods of the object.

Let's look at an example:

```
function Box(width, length, height) {
    function volume(a,b,c) {
        return a*b*c;
    }
    this.boxVolume = volume(width, length, height);
}
```

```
var crate = new Box(5,4,3);
alert("Volume = " + crate.boxVolume); // works correctly
alert(volume(5,4,3)); // fails as function volume() is invisible
```

In the preceding example, the `function volume(a,b,c)` cannot be called from any place outside the constructor function because it has not been assigned to an object method by using `this`. However, the property `crate.boxVolume` *is* available outside the constructor function; even though it uses the function `volume()` to calculate its value, it only does so inside the constructor function.

If you don't "register" methods and properties using `this`, they are not available outside. Such methods and properties are referred to as *private*.

Summary

In this lesson you learned about object-oriented programming (OOP) in JavaScript, starting with the basic concepts behind OOP and how it can help your code development, especially for more complex applications.

You learned a way to directly instantiate an object and add properties and methods to it. You then learned to create an object constructor function, from which you can instantiate multiple similar objects.

You also learned about the `prototype` keyword and how it can be used to extend objects or create new objects via inheritance.

Q&A

Q. **Should I always write object-oriented code?**

A. It's a matter of personal preference. Some coders prefer to always think in terms of objects, methods, and properties, and they write all their code with those principles in mind. Others feel that, particularly for smaller and simpler programs, the level of abstraction provided by OOP is too much, and that procedural coding is okay.

Q. **How would I use my objects in other programs?**

A. An object's constructor function is quite a portable entity. If you link into your page a JavaScript file containing an object constructor function, you have the means to create objects and use their properties and methods throughout your code.

Workshop

Quiz questions and exercises to test your understanding and to stretch your skills.

Quiz

1. What is a new object created from a constructor function known as?

    a. An instance of the object

    b. A method of the object

    c. A prototype

2. What is deriving new objects by using the design of currently existing objects known as?

    a. Encapsulation

    b. Inheritance

    c. Instantiation

3. Which of the following is a valid way to create a direct instance of an object?

    a. `myObject.create();`

    b. `myObject = new Object;`

    c. `myObject = new Object();`

4. What is the OOP mechanism for restricting outside access to some of an object's properties and methods known as?

    a. Encapsulation

    b. Inheritance

    c. Instantiation

5. What is a function that was declared without a named identifier to refer to it known as?

    a. A method

    b. A constructor function

    c. An anonymous function

TIP

Register Your Book

Just a reminder for those of you reading these words in the print or e-book edition of this book: If you go to www.informit.com/register and register this book (using ISBN 978-0-672-33809-0), you can receive free access to an online Web Edition that not only contains the complete text of this book but also features an interactive version of this quiz.

Answers

1. a. A new object created from a constructor function is known as an instance.

2. b. New objects are derived from existing ones through inheritance.

3. c. `myObject = new Object();`

4. a. The OOP mechanism for restricting outside access to some of an object's properties and methods is known as encapsulation.

5. c. A function that was declared without a named identifier to refer to it is known as an anonymous function.

Exercises

Write a constructor function for a `Card` object with properties of `suit` (diamonds, hearts, spades, or clubs) and `face` (ace, 2, 3 ... king). Add methods to set the values of `suit` and `face`.

Can you include a `shuffle` method to set the `suit` and `face` properties to represent a random card from the deck? (Hint: Use the `Math.random()` method described in Lesson 5, "Using DOM Objects and Built-in Objects.")

Extend JavaScript's `Date` object using the `prototype` keyword to add a new method, `getYesterday()`, that returns the name of the previous day to that represented by the `Date` object.

LESSON 12
Learning More About Objects

What You'll Learn in This Lesson:

▶ About JavaScript's recently introduced `class` syntax
▶ How to use `get` and `set`
▶ About the `symbol` data type
▶ Inheritance using `extends` and `super`
▶ Feature detection using objects and `typeof`

In Lesson 11, "Introducing Object-Oriented Programming," you learned that object-oriented programming (OOP) is a style of programming that bundles code into objects, each with properties and methods.

JavaScript was not designed from the get-go as an object-oriented language. It does, however, have the capability to work as one, as you saw in the preceding lesson, though until recently the required syntax has been rather different from the approach used in most other languages.

Recent additions to JavaScript have narrowed the gap, and programmers coming to JavaScript from other languages should now find the transition more straightforward.

In this lesson you learn about some new features of the JavaScript language relating to OOP. You also see how objects can be used to determine the capabilities of a user's platform and have code adapt accordingly.

Classes

Most languages that support OOP take a different approach to object creation to the one used in JavaScript.

Programmers using such languages are generally accustomed to dealing with the concept of classes. A class acts as a template or blueprint for the creation of objects. New classes can be created that inherit features from other classes and serve as blueprints for objects created to this inherited design, creating subclass relationships in a hierarchical system.

JavaScript instead has always had a prototypal system of inheritance, in which a prototype is a functioning instance of an object, and objects inherit directly from such parent objects.

To build a bridge between these concepts, JavaScript has recently seen the introduction of a `class` keyword. Let's see how it works using the `Pet` object from Lesson 11. Here's a reminder of the code used there:

```
function Pet() {
    this.animal = "";
    this.name = "";
    this.setAnimal = function(newAnimal) {
        this.animal = newAnimal;
    }
    this.setName = function(newName) {
        this.name = newName;
    }
}
var myCat = new Pet();
myCat.setAnimal = "cat";
myCat.setName = "Sylvester";
```

Now let's look at how you might create a similar object using the `class` keyword. Here's the equivalent code using the newer syntax:

```
class Pet {
    constructor(animal, name) {
        this.animal = animal,
        this.name = name
    }
    setAnimal(newAnimal) {
        this.animal = newAnimal;
    }
    setName(newName) {
        this.name = newName;
    }
}
var myCat = new Pet();
myCat.setAnimal("cat");
myCat.setName("Sylvester");
```

The new version is a little more concise and easy to read. In particular, there's no need for so many `function` keywords.

NOTE

Syntactic Sugar

This new syntax does not add anything to JavaScript that wasn't possible before. It's merely so-called syntactic sugar—a clearer, handier syntax that's easier to understand and use, especially for those arriving from other OOP environments.

This version also has a function called `constructor`. This is the function that's run when you create an object using the `new` keyword. In the preceding example, you could just as easily have set the values for `name` and `animal` directly in the object definition, using the constructor function:

```
var myCat = new Pet("cat", "Sylvester");
```

Constructor functions are useful places to write any code you might need in the setup and initialization of a new object.

NOTE

Constructors Require `new`

Unlike a regular function, a class constructor can't be called without using the `new` keyword; otherwise, an error will be generated:

```
> var MyCat = Pet(); // Uncaught TypeError: Class constructor Pet cannot be invoked
                     // without 'new'
```

Instead, always use a constructor function with `new` as in the preceding example.

With the new class syntax comes another feature from other OOP environments—*getters* and *setters*.

Using Getters and Setters

By using `get` and `set`, you can run specific code on the reading (in the case of `get`) or writing (using `set`) of an object's property. You might use `set`, for example, to check the validity of some data being used to set the value of a property or use `get` to return a computed or specially formatted value.

If `get` and `set` are defined for an object, they are called invisibly when you access the object's properties and methods via the normal dot notation. Suppose, for example, your object `obj` had the following getter defined on it:

```
get name() {
    return this.name.toUpperCase();
}
```

Then the code of the getter would be executed when the value of `name` is accessed:

```
obj.name = "Sandy";
console.log(obj.name);  // logs "SANDY" to the console
```

The same principle applies when setting a property's value: if a setter has been created using the `set` keyword, it will be called in the background when any attempt is made to change the value of an object property.

To demonstrate this, let's return to the Pet class. Suppose, for example, that you wanted to have your code capitalize only the first letter of any new value supplied as a pet's name. You can do that with a setter:

```
class Pet {
    constructor(animal, name) {
        this.animal = animal,
        this.name = name
    }
    setAnimal(newAnimal) {
        this.animal = newAnimal;
    }
    setName(newName) {
        this.name = newName;
    }
    get name() {
        return this._name;
    }
    set name(n) {
        // set first character to uppercase, the rest to lowercase
        n = n.charAt(0).toUpperCase() + n.slice(1).toLowerCase();
        this._name = n;
    }
}
```

Notice that in the getter and setter, the property name is now prefixed with an underscore character to make _name. Using the underscore is necessary to prevent a condition in the JavaScript interpreter that would eventually cause the program to halt with a stack overflow, since without this precaution get would be called repeatedly, thus forming an infinite loop. Essentially, you are hiding the private, internal property value _name, while allowing the name property to be accessed from outside.

Let's see what happens now when you create and modify an instance of the Pet class using this line:

```
var myCat = new Pet("cat", "sylvester");
```

Look at the console output in Figure 12.1.

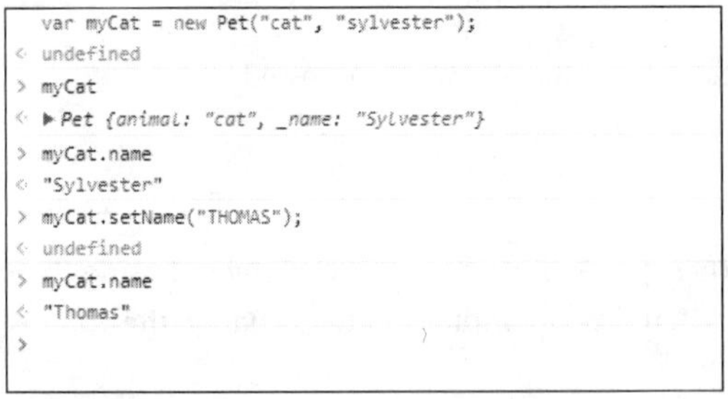

```
  var myCat = new Pet("cat", "sylvester");
< undefined
> myCat
< ▶ Pet {animal: "cat", _name: "Sylvester"}
> myCat.name
< "Sylvester"
> myCat.setName("THOMAS");
< undefined
> myCat.name
< "Thomas"
>
```

FIGURE 12.1
Using getters and setters

Getters and setters are a convenient way to automatically run code on the reading and writing of an object property. Using them, you can disallow direct value assignments to object properties and instead control all value assignments via a setter method, keeping the actual object property private.

CAUTION

Privacy Is Relative

Remember that such object properties are not truly private. Your code—or somebody else's—could still access the value of `myCat._name` directly. If you need a more secure private property, a better approach might be to use the symbol data type, which we look at next.

Symbols

Since JavaScript was first implemented in the 1990s, there have been six primitive data types. Every value in your JavaScript program was `undefined`, `null`, a boolean, a number, a string, or an object.

Now there's a new kid on the block, in the form of the recently introduced *symbol* data type.

A symbol is unlike any of the other data types. Once created, a symbol is guaranteed to be unique; this makes it handy for naming object properties that can't later be overwritten or otherwise corrupted by somebody else's code.

Creating a Symbol

The syntax used to create a symbol uses the `Symbol()` function:

```
var mySymbol = Symbol();
```

Optionally, you can specify a string between the parentheses:

```
var mySymbol = Symbol('A description of mySymbol');
```

The string simply acts as a description, which can be helpful for debugging. When you write the symbol using `console.log()` or convert it to a string using `.toString()`, it's the description that you see returned (since the symbol itself has no literal form).

Using Symbol-Keyed Properties

Because of their uniqueness, symbols are a good choice for creating object properties that are safe from name collisions.

```
var myname = Symbol('nickname of pet');
myCat[myname] = 'Sylvester';
```

Strings and integers are not unique values, so using a string as a property name runs the risk that the same name could also be in use elsewhere in the programs. Using a symbol means you can be more confident about the value being supplied.

NOTE
_____

Use Square Brackets for Symbol-Keyed Properties

Like array elements, symbol-keyed properties can't be accessed using dot syntax. They must be accessed using square brackets as in the preceding example.
_____

Object Inheritance

You saw in Lesson 11 how to implement inheritance using prototypes. To refresh your memory, here's an example:

```
function Dog() {
    this.breed = "";
    this.setBreed = function(newBreed) {
        this.breed = newBreed;
    }
}

Dog.prototype = new Pet();

var myDog = new Dog();
myDog.setName("Alan");
myDog.setBreed("Greyhound");
alert(myDog.name + " is a " + myDog.breed);
```

Using the `class` syntax, you can now perform inheritance in a way more familiar to OOP programmers from other languages—by using `extends` and `super`.

Using `extends` and `super`

Here's how you might create a new object with inheritance using `extends` and `super`:

```
class Dog extends Pet {
    constructor(name, breed) {
        super(name);
        this.breed = breed;
    }
}
var myDog = new Dog("Alan", "greyhound");
alert(myDog.name + " is a " + myDog.breed);
```

See how the `extends` keyword is used to create a class as a child of another class, while the `super` keyword enables you to call the parent object whose features are being inherited and use any logic, getters, or setters it might contain. Note that if a constructor is not defined on a child class, the `super` class constructor will be invoked by default.

Here the `super` keyword is used in the constructor, allowing you to call the constructor of a parent class and inherit all its properties.

In truth, this is just syntactic sugar: everything using classes can be rewritten in functions and prototypes, just like you learned in the previous lesson. However, it's much more compatible with other popular languages and somewhat easier to read.

Feature Detection

Let's round off our journey through objects by taking a look at how their detection can help us write robust and elegant code.

Back in the dark days before the W3C DOM evolved to its current state, JavaScript developers were forced into horrible code contortions to try to cope with browsers' different DOM implementations. It was not uncommon for scripts to be written almost as two or more separate programs, the version to be executed only being decided after an attempt to detect the browser in use.

As you saw in your work with the `navigator` object in Lesson 5, "Using DOM Objects and Built-in Objects," browser detection is a tricky business. The `navigator` object contains information that can be misleading at best (and sometimes downright incorrect). Also, when a new browser or version is introduced with new capabilities and features, your browser-detecting code is usually broken once again.

Thankfully, a much better way to write cross-browser code has emerged, based on objects. Instead of attempting browser detection, it's a much better idea to have JavaScript examine whether the particular feature you need is supported. You can do this by testing for the availability of a specific object, method, or property. In many cases it's sufficient to try to use the object, method, or property in question and detect the value JavaScript returns.

Here's an example of testing for browser support of the `document.getElementById()` method, which you've already met. While `getElementById()` has been supported by all new browsers for some time now, very early browsers do not support this method. You can test for the availability of the `getElementById()` method (or any similar method or property) by using `if()`:

```
if(document.getElementById) {
    myElement = document.getElementById(id);
} else {
    // do something else
}
```

If `document.getElementById` is not available, the `if()` conditional statement will switch code operation to avoid using that method.

Another, related method uses the `typeof` operator to check whether a JavaScript function exists before calling it:

```
if(typeof document.getElementById == 'function') {
    // you can use getElementById()
} else {
    // do something else
}
```

A number of possible values can be returned by `typeof`, as listed in Table 11.1.

TABLE 11.1 Values Returned by `typeof`

Evaluates to	Operand is
`"number"`	A number
`"string"`	A string
`"boolean"`	A Boolean
`"object"`	An object
`"function"`	A function
`null`	Null
`undefined`	Not defined

You can use this technique to check for the existence not only of DOM and built-in objects, methods, and properties, but also those created within your scripts.

Note that at no point in this exercise have you tried to determine what browser your user has; you simply want to know whether it supports the objects, properties, or methods you are about to try to use. Not only is such *feature detection* much more accurate and elegant than so-called *browser sniffing* (trying to infer the browser in use by interpreting properties of the `navigator` object), but it's also much more future proof; the introduction of new browsers or browser versions won't break anything in your code's operation.

▼ TRY IT YOURSELF

Using Feature Detection

Let's use feature detection to examine your browser's support of the `symbol` data type.

This data type is supported in the current versions of nearly every browser, so if you've upgraded to the latest stable version of your favorite browser (and you have, right?), you should find it supported. The most common exception is Microsoft's Internet Explorer (the forerunner to the current and much more standards-compliant Edge browser), which didn't support symbols.

Any browser that knows how to deal with symbols will offer the `Symbol()` function used to create them, so performing a `typeof` test on this function will return a value of `function`. Any other result implies that the browser has no symbol support.

Let's look at the code in Listing 12.1. The anonymous function assigned to the `window.onload` handler performs the test:

```
if(typeof Symbol == 'function') {
  out = 'Your browser supports Symbols';
} else {
  out = 'Your browser has no Symbol support - upgrade!! (returned ' + typeof
  ➥ Symbol + ')';
}
```

Note that, in the case of failure, the actual value returned by `typeof` is displayed to the user to add a little more information.

LISTING 12.1   Using Feature Detection

```
<!DOCTYPE html>
<html>
<head>
  <title>Feature Detection</title>
  <script>
    window.onload = function () {
      if(typeof Symbol == 'function') {
        out = 'Your browser supports Symbols';
      } else {
        out = 'Your browser has no Symbol support - upgrade!! (returned ' + typeof
        ➥ Symbol + ')';
      }
      document.getElementById('div1').innerHTML = out;
    }
  </script>
</head>
<body>
  <div id="div1"></div>
</body>
</html>
```

The result I obtained from Google Chrome is shown in Figure 12.2. Clearly, this browser has support for the `Symbol()` function.

FIGURE 12.2
Google's Chrome browser has Symbol support

Microsoft Internet Explorer, as expected, provided a somewhat different result, as shown in Figure 12.3. Here, the `typeof` test returned a value of `undefined`, indicating that the browser has no `Symbol()` function available.

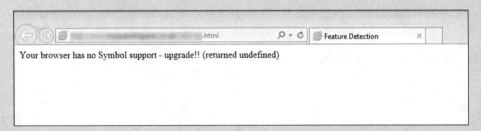

FIGURE 12.3
Microsoft's IE11 under Windows has no Symbol support

Save the code in Listing 12.1 into a file called detection.html and load it in your browser. How does your browser fare on supporting symbols?

Summary

In this lesson you learned about the recently introduced `class` keyword and how it can be used as an alternative way of defining objects in JavaScript.

Next, you learned about JavaScript's recently introduced symbol data type.

You also found out how to implement inheritance using the `extends` and `super` keywords.

Finally, you looked at the use of the `typeof` operator and how it can be used to detect browser support for given JavaScript objects, properties, and methods.

Q&A

Q. Does it matter where in my code I declare a class definition?

A. Yes. You first need to declare your class and then access it; otherwise, code like the following will throw a reference error:

```
var p = new Pet(); // Reference Error thrown
class Pet { … }
```

Instead, you need to declare the class first:

```
class Pet { … }
var p = new Pet();
```

This code will work.

Q. Am I allowed multiple constructor functions in a class?

A. No. There can be only one method named "constructor" in a class. A syntax error will be thrown if the class contains more than one occurrence of a constructor method.

Workshop

Quiz questions and exercises to test your understanding and to stretch your skills.

Quiz

1. Which of the following has the correct syntax to create a new object `myObject` using a class called `Person`?

   a. `var myObject = Person();`

   b. `var myObject.Person();`

   c. `var myObject = new Person();`

2. Which of the following statements about symbols is incorrect?

   a. Symbol is a JavaScript primitive data type.

   b. The `Symbol()` function cannot accept an argument.

   c. Every symbol created has a unique value.

3. What does the keyword `super` refer to?

   a. The parent class of the class being defined

   b. The child class of the class being defined

   c. Neither of the above

4. What would the expression `typeof window.alert` return?

   a. `"object"`

   b. `undefined`

   c. `"Function"`

5. Which of the following will never be returned by `typeof`?

   a. `"float"`

   b. `"boolean"`

   c. `"string"`

TIP
_____

Register Your Book

Just a reminder for those of you reading these words in the print or e-book edition of this book: If you go to www.informit.com/register and register this book (using ISBN 978-0-672-33809-0), you can receive free access to an online Web Edition that not only contains the complete text of this book but also features an interactive version of this quiz.

Answers

1. c. `var myObject = new Person();`

2. b. The `Symbol()` function cannot accept an argument. (This is untrue. The function can accept a string that acts as a description of the Symbol.)

3. a. The parent class of the class being defined

4. c. `"Function"`

5. a. `"float"`

Exercise

Go back to Lesson 11 and review Listing 11.3. Rewrite the program in that listing using the `class` syntax described in this lesson and try it out. (Hint: After defining the class `Person`, use `extends` and `super` to define a subclass that includes the extra method `sayHello()`.) Do you get the same result as in Lesson 11?

Scripting with the DOM

What You'll Learn in This Lesson:

▶ The concept of nodes

▶ The different types of nodes

▶ How to use `nodeName`, `nodeType`, and `nodeValue`

▶ How to use the `childNodes` collection

▶ How to select elements with `getElementsByTagName()`

▶ How to use Mozilla's DOM Inspector

▶ How to create new elements

▶ Ways to add, edit, and remove child nodes

▶ Ways to dynamically load JavaScript files

▶ How to change element attributes

You've already learned about the W3C DOM and, in the code examples in previous lessons, you used various DOM objects, properties, and methods.

In this lesson you begin exploring how JavaScript can directly interact with the DOM. In particular, you learn some new ways to navigate around the DOM, selecting particular DOM objects that represent parts of the page's HTML contents. You see how to create new elements; how to add, edit, and remove nodes of the DOM tree; and how to manipulate elements' attributes.

DOM Nodes

Part I, "Your First Steps with JavaScript," introduced you to the W3C Document Object Model (DOM) as a hierarchical tree of parent-child relationships that together form a model of the current web page. By using appropriate methods, you can navigate to any part of the DOM and retrieve details about it.

You probably recall that the top-level object in the DOM hierarchy is the `window` object and that one of its children is the `document` object. In this lesson we mainly deal with the `document` object and its properties and methods.

Let's look at the simple web page in Listing 13.1.

LISTING 13.1   A Simple Web Page

```
<!DOCTYPE html>
<html>
<head>
    <title>To-Do List</title>
</head>
<body>
    <h1>Things To Do</h1>
    <ol id="toDoList">
        <li>Mow the lawn</li>
        <li>Clean the windows</li>
        <li>Answer your email</li>
    </ol>

    <p id="toDoNotes">Make sure all these are completed by 8pm so you can watch the
game on TV!</p>
</body>
</html>
```

Figure 13.1 shows the page displayed in Mozilla Firefox.

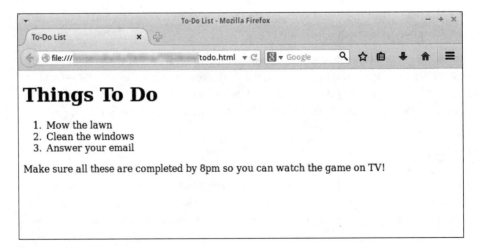

FIGURE 13.1
A simple web page displayed in Firefox

When page loading has completed, the browser has a full, hierarchical DOM representation of this page available for you to examine. Figure 13.2 shows a simplified version of how part of that representation might look.

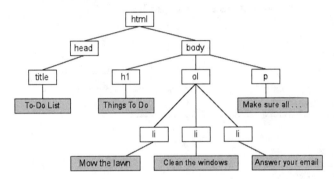

FIGURE 13.2
The DOM's tree model of the page

Look at how the tree diagram of Figure 13.2 relates to the code in Listing 13.1.

The <html> element contains all the other markup of the page. It is the *parent* element to two immediate *child* elements, the <head> and <body> elements. These two elements are *siblings*, because they share a parent. They are also parents themselves; the <head> element has one child element, <title>, and the <body> element three children: the <h1> heading, the ordered list <ol>, and a paragraph, <p>. Of these three siblings, only <ol> has children, those being three <li> list item elements. Various of these elements of the tree contain text, represented in the gray boxes in Figure 13.2.

The DOM is constructed as a hierarchy of such relationships. The boxes that make up the junctions and terminating points of the tree diagram are known as *nodes*.

Types of Nodes

Figure 13.2 shows various *element nodes*, each of which represents an HTML element such as a paragraph element, <p>, along with some *text nodes*, representing the text content of such page elements.

TIP

Text Nodes and Element Nodes

Where they exist, text nodes are always contained within element nodes. However, not every element node contains a text node.

There are a number of other node types, representing such information as each element's attributes, HTML comments, and other information relevant to the page. Many node types can, of course, contain other nodes as children.

Each different type of node has an associated number known as its `nodeType` property. The `nodeType` properties for the various types of nodes are listed in Table 13.1.

TIP

Node Types 1, 2, and 3

You'll likely do most of your work using node types 1, 2, and 3, as you manipulate page elements, their attributes, and the text that those elements contain.

TABLE 13.1 `nodeType` **Values**

nodeType	Type of Node
1	Element
2	Attribute
3	Text (including whitespace)
4	CDATA section
5	Entity reference
6	Entity
7	Processing instruction
8	HTML comment
9	Document
10	Document type (DTD)
11	Document fragment
12	Notation

The `childNodes` Property

A useful DOM property for each node is a collection of its immediate children. This array-like list is called `childNodes`, and it enables you to access information about the children of any DOM node.

The `childNodes` collection is a so-called *NodeList*, in which the items are numerically indexed. A collection looks and (for the most part) behaves like an array: you can refer to its members like those of an array, and you can iterate through them like you would for an array. However, there are a few array methods you can't use, such as `push()` and `pop()`. For all the examples here, you can treat the collection like you would a regular array.

A node list is a live collection, which means that any changes to the collection to which it refers are immediately reflected in the list; you don't have to fetch it again when changes occur.

Using the `childNodes` Property

You can use the collection returned by the `childNodes` property to examine the ordered list element `<ol>` that appears in Listing 13.1. For this example, you write a small function to read the child nodes of the `<ol>` element and return the total number present in the list.

First, you can retrieve the `<ol>` element via its ID:

```
var olElement = document.getElementById("toDoList");
```

The child nodes of the `<ol>` element will now be contained in the object:

```
olElement.childNodes
```

You want to select only the `<li>` elements in the list, so you step through the `childNodes` collection, counting just those nodes for which `nodeType == 1` (that is, those corresponding to HTML elements), ignoring anything else contained in the ordered list element such as comments and whitespace. Remember, you can treat the collection pretty much like an array; here you use the `length` property as you would for an array:

```
var count = 0;
for (var i=0; i < olElement.childNodes.length; i++) {
  if(olElement.childNodes[i].nodeType == 1) count++;
}
```

CAUTION

Be Careful With Whitespace

The browser generally ignores whitespace (such as the space and tab characters) in HTML code when rendering the page. However, the presence of whitespace within a page element—for example, within your ordered list element—will in many browsers create a child node of type text (`nodeType == 3`) within the element. This makes simply using `childNodes.length` a risky business.

Let's cook up a little function to carry out this task when the page has loaded and output the result with an alert dialog:

```
function countListItems() {
    var olElement = document.getElementById("toDoList");
    var count = 0;
    for (var i=0; i < olElement.childNodes.length; i++) {
        if(olElement.childNodes[i].nodeType == 1) count++;
    }
    alert("The ordered list contains " + count + " items");
}
window.onload = countListItems;
```

Create a new HTML page in your editor and enter the code in Listing 13.1. Incorporate the preceding JavaScript code into a `<script>` element in the page head; then load the page into the browser.

Figure 13.3 shows the result of loading the page in Mozilla Firefox.

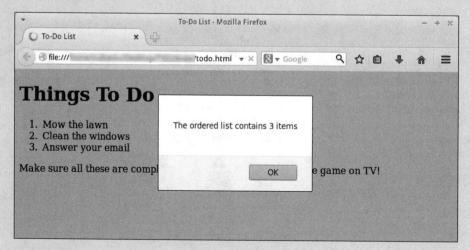

FIGURE 13.3
Using the `childNodes` array

firstChild **and** lastChild

There is a handy shorthand for selecting the first and last elements in the `childNodes` array.

`firstChild` is, unsurprisingly, the first element in the `childNodes` array. Using `firstChild` is equivalent to using `childNodes[0]`.

To access the last element in the collection, you gain a big advantage by using `lastChild`. To access this element, you would otherwise have to do something like this:

```
var lastChildNode = myElement.childNodes[myElement.childNodes.length - 1];
```

That's pretty ugly. Instead, you can simply use

```
var lastChildNode = myElement.lastChild;
```

The `parentNode` Property

The `parentNode` property, unsurprisingly, returns the parent node of the node to which it's applied. In the previous example, you used

```
var lastChildNode = myElement.lastChild;
```

Using `parentNode` you can go one step back up the tree. The line

```
var parentElement = lastChildNode.parentNode;
```

would return the parent element of `lastChildNode`, which is, of course, the object `myElement`.

`nextSibling` and `previousSibling`

Sibling nodes are nodes that share a parent node. When applied to a specified parent node, these read-only properties return the next and previous sibling nodes, respectively, or `null` if there is no such node.

```
var olElement = document.getElementById("toDoList");
var firstOne = olElement.firstChild;
var nextOne = firstOne.nextSibling;
```

Using `nodeValue`

In addition to `nodeType`, the DOM offers the property `nodeValue` to return the value stored in a node. You generally want to use this property to return the text stored in a text node.

Let's suppose that instead of counting the list items in the previous example, you wanted to extract the text contained in the <p> element of the page. To do this, you need to access the relevant <p> node, find the text node that it contains, and then use `nodeValue` to return the information:

```
var text = '';
var pElement = document.getElementById("toDoNotes");
```

```
for (var i=0; i < pElement.childNodes.length; i++) {
    if(pElement.childNodes[i].nodeType == 3) {
        text += pElement.childNodes[i].nodeValue;
    }
}
alert("The paragraph says:\n\n" + text );
```

Using nodeName

The nodeName property returns the name of the specified node as a string value. The values returned by the nodeName value are summarized in Table 13.2. The nodeName property is read-only; you can't change its value.

Where nodeName returns an element name, it does so without the surrounding < and > that you would use in HTML source code:

```
var pElement = document.getElementById("toDoNotes");
alert(pElement.nodeName); // alerts 'P'
```

TABLE 13.2 Values Returned by the nodeName Property

nodeType	Type of Node	nodeName
1	Element	Element (tag) name
2	Attribute	Attribute name
3	Text	The string "#text"

Selecting Elements with getElementsByTagName()

You already know how to access an individual page element using the document object's getElementById() method. Another method of the document object, getElementsBy TagName(), allows you to build an array populated with all the occurrences of a particular tag.

Like getElementById(), the getElementsByTagName() method accepts a single argument. However, in this case it's not the element ID but the required tag name that is passed to the method as an argument.

CAUTION

Element and Elements

Make careful note of the spelling. *Elements* (plural) is used in getElementsByTagName(), whereas *Element* (singular) is used in getElementById().

As an example, suppose you wanted to work with all the `<div>` elements in a particular document. You can populate a variable with an array-like collection called `myDivs` by using

```
var myDivs = document.getElementsByTagName("div");
```

TIP

Returning a Single Element

Even if there is only one element with the specified tag name, `getElementsByTagName()` still returns a collection, although it will contain only one item.

You don't have to use `getElementsByTagName()` on the entire document. It can be applied to any individual object and return a collection of elements with the given tag name contained within that object.

TRY IT YOURSELF ▼

Using `getElementsByTagName()`

Earlier you wrote a function to count the list items (`<li>`) inside an ordered list (`<ol>`) element:

```
function countListItems() {
    var olElement = document.getElementById("toDoList");
    var count = 0;
    for (var i=0; i < olElement.childNodes.length; i++) {
        if(olElement.childNodes[i].nodeType == 1) count++;
    }
    alert("The ordered list contains " + count + " items");
}
```

You used the `childNodes` array to get all the child nodes and then selected those corresponding to elements by testing for `nodeType == 1`.

You can easily implement the same function by using `getElementsByTagName()`.

You start the same way by selecting the `<ol>` element based on its `id`:

```
var olElement = document.getElementById("toDoList");
```

▼

Now you can create an array called `listItems` and populate it with all the `<li>` elements contained in your `<ol>` object `olElement`:

```
var listItems = olElement.getElementsByTagName("li");
```

All that remains is to display how many items are in the array:

```
alert("The ordered list contains " + listItems.length + " items");
```

Listing 13.2 contains the complete code for the page, including the revised function `countListItems()`.

LISTING 13.2   Using `getElementsByTagName()`

```
<!DOCTYPE html>
<html>
<head>
    <title>To-Do List</title>
    <script>
        function countListItems() {
            var olElement = document.getElementById("toDoList");
            var listItems = olElement.getElementsByTagName("li");
            alert("The ordered list contains " + listItems.length + " items");
        }
        window.onload = countListItems;
    </script>
</head>
<body>
    <h1>Things To Do</h1>
    <ol id="toDoList">
        <li>Mow the lawn</li>
        <li>Clean the windows</li>
        <li>Answer your email</li>
    </ol>

    <p id="toDoNotes">Make sure all these are completed by 8pm so you can watch the
game on TV!</p>
</body>
</html>
```

Save this listing as an HTML file and load it into your browser. Check that the result is the same as in Figure 13.3.

Getting Elements by Class Name

A further useful method for getting a collection of elements is `document.getElementsBy ClassName()`.

As you can work out from the method name, this method returns all the page elements having a particular value of the `class` attribute. However, this capability was not supported in Internet Explorer until IE9.

How to Read an Element's Attributes

HTML elements often contain a number of attributes with associated values:

```
<div id="id1" title="report">Here is some text.</div>
```

The attributes are always placed within the opening tag, each attribute being of the form `attribute=value`. The attributes themselves are child nodes of the element node in which they appear, as depicted in Figure 13.4.

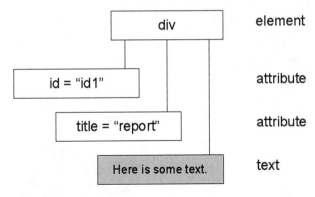

FIGURE 13.4
Attribute nodes

Having navigated to the element node of interest, you can read the value of any of its attributes using the `getAttribute()` method:

```
var myNode = document.getElementById("id1");
alert(myNode.getAttribute("title"));
```

The previous code snippet would display "report" within the `alert` dialog. If you try to retrieve the value of a nonexistent attribute, `getAttribute()` will return `null`. You can use this fact to efficiently test whether an element node has a particular attribute defined:

```
if(myNode.getAttribute("title")) {
    ... do something ...
}
```

The `if()` condition will only be met if `getAttribute()` returns a non-null value, since JavaScript interprets `null` as a "falsy" value (not Boolean `false`, but considered as such).

CAUTION

The `attributes` Property

There also exists a property simply called `attributes` that contains an array of all of a node's attributes.

In theory you can access the attributes as `name=value` pairs in the order they appear in the HTML code, by using a numerical key; so `attributes[0].name` would be `id` and `attributes[1].value` would be `'report'`. However, its implementation in Internet Explorer and some versions of Firefox is buggy. It's safer to use `getAttribute()` instead.

Mozilla's DOM Inspector

One of the easiest ways to view node information is to use the DOM Inspector available for Mozilla Firefox. If you use Firefox, you may find the DOM Inspector already installed, though since Firefox 3 it's been available as a separate add-on. You can download it from https://addons.mozilla.org/en-US/firefox/addon/dom-inspector-6622/.

Once it is installed, you can open the DOM Inspector for any page you have loaded in the browser by pressing Ctrl+Shft+I. The window that opens is shown in Figure 13.5, displaying the DOM representation of the web page in Listing 13.1.

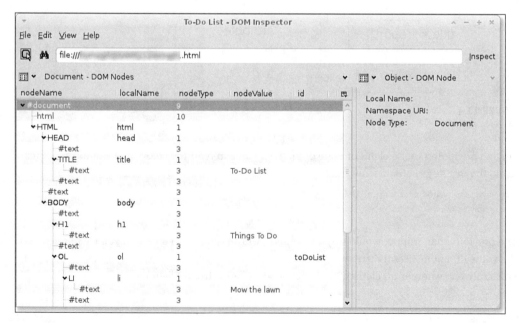

FIGURE 13.5
Mozilla's DOM Inspector

A DOM node is selected from the tree structure in the left-hand display pane, and details about it can be examined in the right-hand pane. As well as the viewer for the DOM tree, other viewers are included for viewing CSS rules, style sheets, computed style, JavaScript objects, and more.

The interface can seem a little daunting at first, but it's well worth exploring the program's capabilities.

You Change the DOM, Not the Source Code

When you amend the DOM using the methods described in this lesson, you change the way a page appears in the browser. Bear in mind, though, that you're not changing the document itself. If you ask your browser to display the source code of the page, you won't see any changes there.

The reason is that the browser is actually displaying the current DOM representation of the document. Change that, and you change what appears onscreen.

Creating New Nodes

Adding new nodes to the DOM tree is a two-stage process:

1. Create a new node. Once created, the node is initially in a kind of "limbo"; it exists, but it's not actually located anywhere in the DOM tree and therefore doesn't appear on the visible page in the browser window.

2. Add the new node to the tree, in the desired location. At this point it becomes part of the visible page.

Let's look at some of the methods of the `document` object that are available for creating nodes.

createElement()

You can call on the `createElement()` method to create new HTML elements having any of the standard HTML element types—paragraphs, spans, tables, lists, and so on.

Let's suppose you've decided to create a new <div> element for your document. To do so, you simply need to pass the relevant `nodeName` value—in this case "div"—to the `createElement()` method:

```
var newDiv = document.createElement("div");
```

The new <div> element now exists but currently has no contents, no attributes, and no location in the DOM tree. You see how to solve these issues shortly.

createTextNode()

Many of the HTML elements in your page need some content in the form of text. The createTextNode() method takes care of that. It works pretty much like createElement(), except that the argument it accepts is not a nodeName value, but a string containing the desired text content of the element:

```
var newTextNode = document.createTextNode("Here is some text content.");
```

As with createElement(), the newly created node is not yet located in the DOM tree; JavaScript has it stored in the newTextNode variable while it waits for you to place it in its required position.

cloneNode()

There's no point in reinventing the wheel. If you already have a node in your document that's just like the new one you want to create, you can use cloneNode() to do so.

Unlike createElement() and createTextNode(), cloneNode() takes a single argument—a Boolean value of true or false.

Passing true to the cloneNode() function tells JavaScript that you want to clone not only the node, but all of its child nodes:

```
var myDiv = document.getElementById("id1");
var newDiv = myDiv.cloneNode(true);
```

This example asks JavaScript to clone the element's child nodes too; for example, any text that myDiv contained (which would be contained in a child text node of the element) will be faithfully reproduced in the new <div> element.

If you call

```
var newDiv = myDiv.cloneNode(false);
```

then the new <div> element will be identical to the original, except that it will have no child nodes. It will, for instance, have any attributes belonging to the original element (provided that the original node was an element node, of course).

CAUTION

Take Care with the id Attribute

Remember that the id of an element is one of its attributes.

When you clone a node, remember to then change the id of your new element, since id values must be unique within a document.

As with new nodes created by `createElement()` and `createTextNode()`, the new node created by `cloneNode()` is initially floating in space; it does not yet have a place in the DOM tree.

You see how to achieve that next.

Manipulating Child Nodes

The new nodes you've created aren't yet of any practical value, because they don't yet appear anywhere in the DOM. A few methods of the `document` object are specifically designed for placing nodes in the DOM tree, and they are described in the following sections.

appendChild()

Perhaps the simplest way of all to attach a new node to the DOM is to append it as a child node to a node that already exists somewhere in the document. Doing so is just a matter of locating the required parent node and calling the `appendChild()` method:

```
var newText = document.createTextNode("Here is some text content.");
var myDiv = document.getElementById("id1");
myDiv.appendChild(newText);
```

In the preceding code snippet, a new text node has been created and added as a child node to the currently existing `<div>` element having an `id` of `id1`.

TIP

An Appended Node Becomes the Last Child Node

Remember that `appendChild()` always adds a child node after the last child node already present, so the newly appended node becomes the new `lastChild` of the parent node.

Of course, `appendChild()` works equally well with all types of nodes, not just text nodes. Suppose you needed to add another `<div>` element within the parent `<div>` element:

```
var newDiv = document.createElement("div");
var myDiv = document.getElementById("id1");
myDiv.appendChild(newDiv);
```

Your originally existing `<div>` element now contains a further `<div>` element as its last child; if the parent `<div>` element already contained some text content in the form of a child text node, then the parent `div` (as represented in the newly modified DOM, not in the source code) would now have the following form:

```
<div id="id1">
    Original text contained in text node
    <div></div>
</div>
```

insertBefore()

Whereas appendChild() always adds a child element to the end of the list of children, with insertBefore() you can specify a child element and insert the new node immediately before it.

The method takes two arguments: the new node and the child before which it should be placed. Let's suppose that your page contains the following HTML snippet:

```
<div id="id1">
    <p id="para1">This paragraph contains some text.</p>
    <p id="para2">Here's some more text.</p>
</div>
```

To insert a new paragraph between the two that are currently in place, first create the new paragraph:

```
var newPara = document.createElement("p");
```

Identify the parent node and the child node before which you want to make the insertion:

```
var myDiv = document.getElementById("id1");
var para2 = document.getElementById("para2");
```

Then pass these two as arguments to insertBefore():

```
myDiv.insertBefore(newPara, para2);
```

replaceChild()

You can use replaceChild() when you want to replace a current child node of a specific parent element with another node. The method takes two arguments—a reference to the new child element followed by a reference to the old one.

▼ TRY IT YOURSELF

Replacing Child Elements

Let's look at the code in Listing 13.3.

LISTING 13.3   Replacing Child Elements

```
<!DOCTYPE html>
<html>
<head>
    <title>Replace Page Element</title>
</head>
<body>
    <div id="id1">
        <p id="para1">Welcome to my web page.</p>
```

```
        <p id="para2">Please take a look around.</p>
        <input id="btn" value="Replace Element" type="button" />
    </div>
</body>
</html>
```

Suppose that you wanted to use the DOM to remove the first paragraph in the `<div>` and replace it instead with an `<h2>` heading as follows:

```
<h2>Welcome!</h2>
```

To do so, you first create the new node representing the `<h2>` heading:

```
var newH2 = document.createElement("h2");
```

This new element needs to contain a text node for the heading text. You can either create it and add it now, or do it later after you've added your new `<h2>` element to the DOM. Let's do it now:

```
var newH2Text = document.createTextNode("Welcome!");
newH2.appendChild(newH2Text);
```

Now you can swap out the unwanted child node of the `<div>` element and replace it with the new one:

```
var myDiv = document.getElementById("id1");
var oldP = document.getElementById("para1");
myDiv.replaceChild(newH2, oldP);
```

Finally, you need to add an `onclick` event handler to the button element, so that when the button is clicked, your element replacement function is executed. You do that with an anonymous function assigned to the `window.onload` method:

```
window.onload = function() {
    document.getElementById("btn").onclick = replaceHeading;
}
```

Listing 13.4 shows the code for the page with the JavaScript added.

LISTING 13.4 The Completed Code to Replace Child Elements

```
<!DOCTYPE html>
<html>
<head>
    <title>Replace Page Element</title>
    <script>
        function replaceHeading() {
            var newH2 = document.createElement("h2");
            var newH2Text = document.createTextNode("Welcome!");
```

```
            newH2.appendChild(newH2Text);
            var myDiv = document.getElementById("id1");
            var oldP = document.getElementById("para1");
            myDiv.replaceChild(newH2, oldP);
        }
        window.onload = function() {
            document.getElementById("btn").onclick = replaceHeading;
        }
    </script>
</head>
<body>
    <div id="id1">
        <p id="para1">Welcome to my web page.</p>
        <p id="para2">Please take a look around.</p>
        <input id="btn" value="Replace Element" type="button" />
    </div>
</body>
</html>
```

Create a new HTML file with your editor and insert the code listed in Listing 13.4. On loading the page into your browser, you should see the two single-line paragraphs of text with the button beneath. If all has gone according to plan, clicking the button should swap the first <p> element for your <h2> heading, as depicted in Figure 13.6.

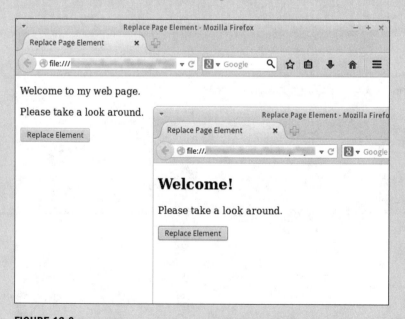

FIGURE 13.6
The element-replacement script in action

removeChild()

There is a DOM method specifically provided for removing child nodes from the DOM tree.

Referring once more to Listing 13.3, if you wanted to remove the <p> element with id="para2", you can just use

```
var myDiv = document.getElementById("id1");
var myPara = document.getElementById("para2");
myDiv.removeChild(myPara);
```

TIP

The parentNode Property

If you don't have a handy reference to the element's parent, just use the parentNode property:

```
myPara.parentNode.removeChild(myPara);
```

The return value from the removeChild() method contains a reference to the removed node. If you need to, you can use it to further process the child node that has just been removed:

```
var removedItem = myDiv.removeChild(myPara);
alert('Item with id ' + removedItem.getAttribute("id") + ' has been removed.');
```

Editing Element Attributes

Earlier in this lesson you saw how to read element attributes using the getAttribute() method.

There is a corresponding method named setAttribute() to allow you to create attributes for element nodes and assign values to those attributes. The method takes two arguments; unsurprisingly, these are the attribute to be added and the value it should have.

In the following example, the title attribute is added to a <p> element and assigned the value "Opening Paragraph":

```
var myPara = document.getElementById("para1");
myPara.setAttribute("title", "Opening paragraph");
```

Setting the value of an attribute that already exists effectively overwrites the value of that attribute. You can use that knowledge to effectively edit existing attribute values:

```
var myPara = document.getElementById("para1");
myPara.setAttribute("title", "Opening paragraph"); // set 'title' attribute
myPara.setAttribute("title", "New title"); // overwrite 'title' attribute
```

Dynamically Loading JavaScript Files

On occasion you'll want to load JavaScript code on the fly to a page that's already loaded in the browser. You can use `createElement()` to dynamically create a new `<script>` element containing the required code and then add this element to the page's DOM:

```
var scr = document.createElement("script");
scr.setAttribute("src", "newScript.js");
document.head.appendChild(scr);
```

Remember that the `appendChild()` method places the new child node after the last child currently present, so the new `<script>` element will go right at the end of the `<head>` section of the page.

Take note, though, that if you dynamically load JavaScript source files using this method, the JavaScript code contained in those files will not be available to your page until the external file has finished loading.

You would be well advised to have your program check that this is so before attempting to use the additional code.

Nearly all modern browsers implement an `onload` event when the script has downloaded. This works just like the `window.onload` event you've already met, but instead of firing when the main page has finished loading, it does so when the external resource (in this case a JavaScript source file) is fully downloaded and available for use:

```
src.onload = function() {
    ... things to do when new source code is downloaded ...
}
```

▼ TRY IT YOURSELF

A Dynamically Created Menu

In this exercise you're going to use the techniques learned in this lesson to create page menus on the fly.

The sample HTML page has a top-level `<h1>` heading, followed by a number of short articles each consisting of an `<h2>` heading followed by some paragraphs of text. This is similar to a format you might see in a blog, a news page, or the output from an RSS reader, among other examples.

What you are going to do is employ DOM methods to automatically generate a menu at the page head, having links that allow the user to jump to any of the articles on the page. The HTML file is shown in Listing 13.5. Create your own HTML file based on this script. Feel free to use your own content for the headings and text, so long as the section titles are contained in `<h2>` elements.

LISTING 13.5   HTML File for Dynamic Menu Creation   ▼

```html
<!DOCTYPE html>
<html>
<head>
    <meta charset="utf-8" />
    <title>Scripting the DOM</title>
    <script src="menu.js"></script>
    <script>window.onload = makeMenu;</script>
</head>
<body>
    <h1>The Extremadura Region of Western Spain</h1>
    <h2>Geography Of The Region</h2>
    <p>The autonomous community of Extremadura is in western Spain alongside the
Portuguese border. It borders the Spanish regions of Castilla y Leon, Castilla La
Mancha and Andalucía as well as Portugal (to the West). Covering over 40,000 square
kilometers it has two provinces: Cáceres in the North and Badajoz in the South.</p>
    <h2>Where To Stay</h2>
    <p>There is a wide range of accommodation throughout Extremadura including
small inns and guest houses ('Hostals') or think about renting a 'casa rural'
(country house)if you are traveling in a group.</p>
    <h2>Climate</h2>
    <p>Generally Mediterranean, except for the north, where it is continental.
Generally known for its extremes, including very hot and dry summers with frequent
droughts, and its long and mild winters.</p>
    <h2>What To See</h2>
    <p>Extremadura hosts major events all year round including theater, music,
cinema, literature and folklore. Spectacular venues include castles, medieval town
squares and historic centers. There are special summer theater festivals in the
Mérida, Cáceres, Alcántara and Alburquerque.</p>
    <h2>Gastronomy</h2>
    <p>The quality of Extremaduran food arises from the fine quality of the local
ingredients. In addition to free-range lamb and beef, fabulous cheeses, red and
white wines, olive oil, honey and paprika, Extremadura is particularly renowned for
Iberian ham. The 'pata negra' (blackfoot) pigs are fed on acorns in the cork-oak
forests, the key to producing the world's best ham and cured sausages.</p>
</body>
</html>
```

The page is shown in Figure 13.7.

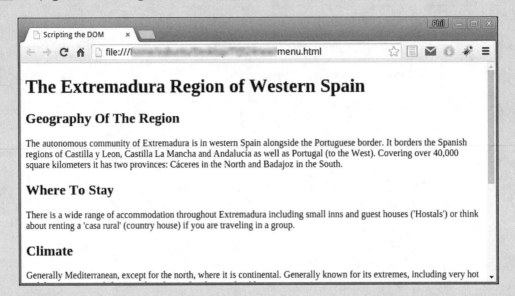

FIGURE 13.7
Page that is to have a dynamically created menu

The first thing to do is make a collection of all the `<h2>` elements from the page. These will form the items in your menu. For each of these headings, make a link to an anchor element that you place right next to the corresponding `<h2>` element.

The menu links will be arranged as links in an unordered list (`<ul>`) element. This list will be placed in a `<div>` container that you insert at the page head.

First, get the collection of `<h2>` elements:

```
var h2s = document.getElementsByTagName("h2");
```

Next, you need to create the `<div>` container to hold your menu; inside that `<div>`, there'll be a `<ul>` list element to contain the menu items:

```
var menu = document.createElement("div");
var menuUl = document.createElement("ul");
menu.appendChild(menuUl);
```

Now you can cycle through the collection of `<h2>` headings:

```
for(var i = 0; i < h2s.length; i++) {
    ... do things for each heading ...
}
```

For each heading you find in the document, you have a number of tasks to perform:

▶ Collect the content of the heading's child text node, which forms the text of the heading:

```
var itemText = h2s[i].childNodes[0].nodeValue;
```

▶ Create a new list item (`<li>`) element for the menu:

```
var menuLi = document.createElement("li");
```

▶ Add that `<li>` element to the menu:

```
menuUl.appendChild(menuLi);
```

▶ Each list item must contain a link to an anchor located next to the heading to which the menu item points:

```
var menuLiA = document.createElement("a");
menuLiA = menuLi.appendChild(menuLiA);
```

▶ Set an appropriate `href` attribute of the link (remember that variable i increments as you count through the headings in the array). These links will have the form

```
<a href="#itemX">[Title Text]</a>
```

where X is the index number of the menu item:

```
menuLiA.setAttribute("href", "#item" + i);
```

▶ Create a matching anchor element just before each `<h2>` heading. The anchor elements have the form

```
<a name="itemX">
```

so you need to add the `name` attribute, and locate the link just before the associated heading:

```
var anc = document.createElement("a");
anc.setAttribute("name", "item" + i);
document.body.insertBefore(anc, h2s[i]);
```

When all that has been completed for each `<h2>` heading, you can add your new menu to the page:

```
document.body.insertBefore(menu, document.body.firstChild);
```

The content of the JavaScript source file menu.js is shown in Listing 13.6. The code has been incorporated into a function named `makeMenu()` that is called by the `window.onload` event handler, building your menu as soon as the page has loaded and the DOM is therefore available.

▼ **LISTING 13.6**   JavaScript Code for menu.js

```javascript
function makeMenu() {
    // get all the H2 heading elements
    var h2s = document.getElementsByTagName("h2");
    // create a new page element for the menu
    var menu = document.createElement("div");
    // create a UL element and append to the menu div
    var menuUl = document.createElement("ul");
    menu.appendChild(menuUl);
    // cycle through h2 headings
    for(var i = 0; i < h2s.length; i++) {
        // get text node of h2 element
        var itemText = h2s[i].childNodes[0].nodeValue;
        // add a list item
        var menuLi = document.createElement("li");
        // add it to the menu list
        menuUl.appendChild(menuLi);
        // the list item contains a link
        var menuLiA = document.createElement("a");
        menuLiA = menuLi.appendChild(menuLiA);
        // set the href of the link
        menuLiA.setAttribute("href", "#item" + i);
        // set the text of the link
        var menuText = document.createTextNode(itemText);
        menuLiA.appendChild(menuText);
        // create matching anchor element
        var anc = document.createElement("a");
        anc.setAttribute("name", "item" + i);
        // add anchor before the heading
        document.body.insertBefore(anc, h2s[i]);
    }
    // add menu to the top of the page
    document.body.insertBefore(menu, document.body.firstChild);
}
```

Figure 13.8 shows the script in action.

By examining the modified DOM using your browser tools, you can see the additional DOM elements added to the page to form the menu and the anchors. Figure 13.9 shows how this is displayed in Google Chromium's Developer Tools, highlighting the additional elements.

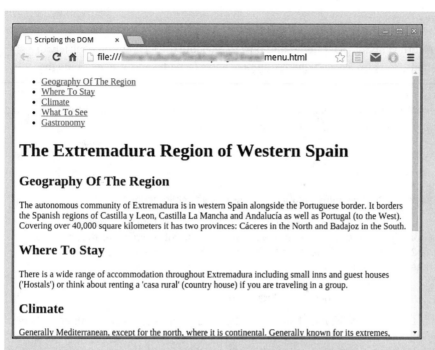

FIGURE 13.8
The automatic menu script in action

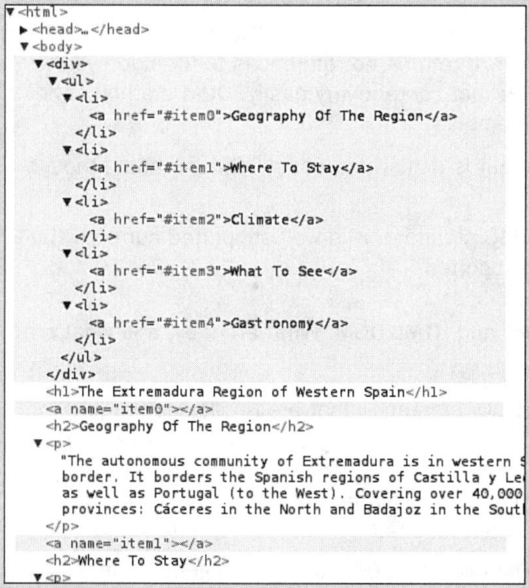

FIGURE 13.9
The additional DOM elements

Summary

In this lesson you learned about DOM nodes and how to navigate the DOM using a variety of node-related methods. You also learned about using Mozilla's DOM Inspector to examine the DOM of your page.

In addition, you learned how to create new nodes to add to the DOM and how to edit page content dynamically by adding, editing, and removing DOM nodes.

Q&A

Q. Is there a quick way to determine whether a node has any child nodes?

A. Yes, you can use the `hasChildNodes()` method. This method returns a Boolean value of `true` if the node has one or more child nodes, or `false` if not. Remember that attribute nodes and text nodes cannot have child nodes, so the method will always return `false` if applied to these types of nodes.

Q. Is Mozilla's DOM Inspector the only tool of its type?

A. Not at all. Just about every browser has some DOM inspection tools built into the developer tools. However, Mozilla's DOM Inspector gives a particularly clear view of the DOM hierarchy and the parameters of individual nodes; that's why I presented it here.

Q. Is it better to use the DOM to insert and retrieve HTML, or `innerHTML`?

A. Each has its advantages and disadvantages. To insert a chunk of HTML into a document, using `innerHTML` is quick and easy. However, it returns no references to the code you've inserted, so you can't carry out operations on that content very easily. DOM methods offer finer-grained control for manipulating page elements.

Wherever you use `innerHTML`, the same result is achievable using DOM methods, though usually with a little more code.

Remember, too, that `innerHTML` is not a W3C standard. It is well supported currently, but there's no guarantee that it will always be supported.

Q. I've seen references on the Web to DOM Core and HTML DOM. What are they, and what are the differences between them?

A. The DOM Core describes a basic nucleus of DOM methods that are applicable not just to HTML pages but also pages written in any similar markup language—XML, for example. HTML DOM is a larger collection of additional methods relating specifically to HTML pages. They do offer some shorthand ways of carrying out certain tasks, at the expense of making your code a little less portable to non-HTML applications.

The examples in this book generally use DOM Core methods to be more general. In Listing 13.6, for example, I used the statement

```
menuLiA.setAttribute("href", "#item" + i);
```

I could equally have used the HTML DOM statement

```
menuLiA.href = "#item" + i;
```

which is a little shorter.

Workshop

Quiz questions and exercises to test your understanding and to stretch your skills.

Quiz

1. Which of the following is NOT a type of node?

   a. Element

   b. Attribute

   c. Array

2. The `getElementsByTagName()` method returns

   a. An array-like collection of element objects

   b. An array-like collection of `nodeType` values

   c. An array-like collection of tag names

3. In some browsers the whitespace within a page element will cause the creation of

   a. A text node

   b. A JavaScript error

   c. An attribute node

4. What could you use to create a new `<span>` element?

   a. `document.createElement("span");`

   b. `document.createElement(span);`

   c. `document.appendChild("span");`

5. What could you use to copy a node, including all of its child nodes?

   a. `cloneNode(false);`

   b. `copyNode();`

   c. `cloneNode(true);`

6. What could you use to set the `alt` attribute of an `<img>` element to "Company Logo"?

   a. `setAttribute(alt, "Company Logo");`

   b. `setAttribute("alt", "Company Logo");`

   c. `setAttribute(alt = "Company Logo");`

TIP
Register Your Book

Just a reminder for those of you reading these words in the print or e-book edition of this book: If you go to www.informit.com/register and register this book (using ISBN 978-0-672-33809-0), you can receive free access to an online Web Edition that not only contains the complete text of this book but also features an interactive version of this quiz.

Answers

1. c. An array is not a type of node.

2. a. An array-like collection of element objects is returned.

3. a. Whitespace within an element usually creates a text node as a child node of the element.

4. a. Use `document.createElement("span");`.

5. c. Use `cloneNode(true);`.

6. b. Use `setAttribute("alt", "Company Logo");`.

Exercises

If you have Firefox, download and install the DOM Inspector and familiarize yourself with its interface. Use the program to investigate the DOM of some of your favorite web pages.

Having used the `insertBefore()` method, you might reasonably expect that there would be an `insertAfter()` method available. Unfortunately, that's not so. Can you write an `insertAfter()` function to do this task? Use similar arguments to `insertBefore()`; that is, `insertAfter(newNode, targetNode)`.

(Hint: Use `insertBefore()` and the `nextSibling` property.)

LESSON 14
Meet JSON

What You'll Learn in This Lesson:

- ▶ What JSON is
- ▶ How to simulate associative arrays
- ▶ About JSON and objects
- ▶ How to access JSON data
- ▶ Data serialization with JSON
- ▶ How to keep JSON secure

In an earlier lesson you saw how to directly instantiate an object using the `new Object()` syntax. In this lesson you learn about JavaScript Object Notation (JSON), which, as its name implies, offers another way to create object instances, and which can also act as a general-purpose data exchange syntax.

NOTE

JSON Home Page

The official home of JSON is at http://json.org/, which also has links to a wide variety of JSON resources on the Web.

What Is JSON?

JSON (pronounced "Jason") is a simple and compact notation for JavaScript objects. Once expressed in JSON, objects can easily be converted to strings to be stored and transmitted (across networks or between applications, for instance).

However, the real beauty of JSON is that an object expressed in JSON is really just expressed in normal JavaScript code. You therefore take advantage of "automatic" parsing in JavaScript; you can just have JavaScript interpret the contents of a JSON string as code, with no extra parsers or converters.

JSON Syntax

JSON data is expressed as a sequence of parameter and value pairs, each pair using a colon character to separate parameter from value. These `"parameter"`:`"value"` pairs are themselves separated by commas:

```
"param1":"value1", "param2":"value2", "param3":"value3"
```

Finally, the whole sequence is enclosed between curly braces to form a JSON object representing your data:

```
var jsonObject = {
 "param1":"value1",
 "param2":"value2",
 "param3":"value3"
}
```

The object `jsonObject` defined here uses a subset of standard JavaScript notation; it's just a little piece of valid JavaScript code.

Objects written using JSON notation can have properties and methods accessed directly using the usual dot notation:

```
alert(jsonObject.param1); // alerts 'value1'
```

More generally, though, JSON is a general-purpose syntax for exchanging data in a string format. Not only objects, but ANY data that can be expressed as a series of `parameter`:`value` pairs can be expressed in JSON notation. It is then easy to convert the JSON object into a string by a process known as *serialization*; serialized data is convenient for storage or transmission around networks. You see how to serialize a JSON object later in this lesson.

NOTE

JSON and XML

As a general-purpose data exchange syntax, JSON can be used somewhat like XML, though JSON can be simpler for humans to read. Also, the parsing of large XML files can be a slow process, whereas JSON gives your script a JavaScript object, ready to use.

JSON has gathered momentum recently because it offers several important advantages. JSON is

- ▶ Easy to read for both people and computers

- ▶ Simple in concept; a JSON object is nothing more than a series of `parameter`:`value` pairs enclosed by curly braces

- ▶ Largely self-documenting

- ▶ Fast to create and parse

- ▶ A subset of JavaScript, meaning that no special interpreters or other additional packages are necessary

A number of leading online services and APIs including Flickr, Twitter, and several services from Google and Yahoo! now offer data encoded using JSON notation.

NOTE

JSON Support in Flickr

See www.flickr.com/services/api/response.json.html for details of how Flickr supports JSON.

How to Access JSON Data

To recover the data encoded into the JSON string, you need to somehow convert the string back to JavaScript code. This is usually referred to as *deserializing* the string.

Using `eval()`

Only more recent browsers have native support for JSON syntax (we talk about using native browser support in just a moment). However, since JSON syntax is a subset of JavaScript, the JavaScript function `eval()` can be used to convert a JSON string into a JavaScript object.

NOTE

Understanding `eval()`

The JavaScript `eval()` function evaluates or executes whatever is passed as an argument. If the argument is an expression, `eval()` evaluates the expression; for example,

```
var x = eval(4 * 3); // x=12
```

If the argument is composed of one or more JavaScript statements, `eval()` executes those statements:

```
eval("a=1; b=2; document.write(a+b);"); // writes 3 to the page
```

The `eval()` function uses the JavaScript interpreter to parse the JSON text and produce a JavaScript object:

```
var myObject = eval ('(' + jsonObjectString + ')');
```

You can then use the JavaScript object in your script:

```
var user = '{"username" : "philb1234","location" : "Spain","height" : 1.80}';
var myObject = eval ('(' + user + ')');
alert(myObject.username);
```

CAUTION

Using Parentheses

The string must be enclosed in parentheses like this to avoid falling foul of an ambiguity in the JavaScript syntax.

Using Native Browser Support

All recent browsers offer native support for JSON, making the use of `eval()` unnecessary.

NOTE

Browser Support for JSON

Browsers natively supporting JSON include

- ▶ Firefox (Mozilla) 3.5+
- ▶ Internet Explorer 8+
- ▶ Microsoft Edge
- ▶ Google Chrome
- ▶ Opera 10+
- ▶ Safari 4+

Browsers with native JSON support create a JavaScript object called JSON to manage JSON encoding and decoding. The JSON object has two methods—`stringify()` and `parse()`.

Using JSON.parse()

You can interpret a JSON string using the method `JSON.parse()`, which takes a string containing a JSON-serialized object and breaks it up, creating an object with properties corresponding to the `"parameter":"value"` pairs found in the string:

```
var Mary = '{ "height":1.9, "age":36, "eyeColor":"brown" }';
var myObject = JSON.parse(Mary);
var out = "";
for (i in myObject) {
 out += i + " = " + myObject[i] + "\n";
}
alert(out);
```

You can see the result in Figure 14.1.

FIGURE 14.1
Using `JSON.parse()`

Data Serialization with JSON

In the context of data storage and transmission, *serialization* is the name given to the process of converting data into a format that can be stored or transmitted across a network and recovered later into the same format as the original.

In the case of JSON, a string is the chosen format of the serialized data. To serialize your JSON object (for instance, to send it across a network connection), you need to express it as a string. You may also hear this process referred to as "flattening an object."

In later browsers, those having JSON support, you can simply use the `JSON.stringify()` method.

Using `JSON.stringify()`

You can create a JSON-encoded string of an object using the `JSON.stringify()` method.

Let's create a simple object and add some properties:

```
var Dan = new Object();
Dan.height = 1.85;
Dan.age = 41;
Dan.eyeColor = "blue";
```

Now you can serialize the object using `JSON.stringify`:

```
alert( JSON.stringify(Dan) );
```

The serialized object is shown in Figure 14.2.

FIGURE 14.2
Using `JSON.stringify()`

▼ TRY IT YOURSELF

Parsing a JSON String

Create an HTML file using your editor, and enter the code in Listing 14.1.

LISTING 14.1   Parsing a JSON String

```
<!DOCTYPE html>
<html>
<head>
    <title>Parsing JSON</title>
    <script>
        function jsonParse() {
            var inString = prompt("Enter JSON object");
            var out = "";
            myObject = JSON.parse(inString);
            for (i in myObject) {
                out += "Property: " + i + " = " + myObject[i] + '\n';
            }
        alert(out);
        }
    </script>
</head>
<body onload="jsonParse()">
</body>
</html>
```

The function `jsonParse()` is called when the page finishes loading, by using the `onload` event handler of the `window` object attached to the `<body>` element of the page.

The first line of code inside the function invites you to enter a string corresponding to a JSON object:

```
var inString = prompt("Enter JSON object");
```

Type it carefully, remembering to enclose any strings in quotation marks, as in Figure 14.3.

FIGURE 14.3
Entering a JSON string

The script then declares an empty string variable called `out`, which later holds the output message:

```
var out = "";
```

The `JSON.parse()` method is then used to create an object based on the input string:

```
myObject = JSON.parse(inString);
```

You can now build your output message string by looping around the object methods:

```
for (i in myObject) {
    out += "Property: " + i + " = " + myObject[i] + '\n';
}
```

Finally, display the result:

```
alert(out);
```

The output message should look like the one in Figure 14.4.

FIGURE 14.4
The object created by parsing a JSON string

Reload the page and retry the script with a different number of `"parameter":"value"` pairs.

JSON Data Types

The parameter part of each `parameter:value` pair must follow a few simple grammatical rules:

- ▶ It must not be a JavaScript reserved keyword.
- ▶ It must not start with a number.
- ▶ It must not include any special characters except the underscore or dollar sign.

The values in JSON objects can contain any of the following data types:

- ▶ Number
- ▶ String

- ▶ Boolean

- ▶ Array

- ▶ Object

- ▶ null (empty)

CAUTION

Unsupported Data Types

JavaScript syntax has several data types that are not included in the JSON standard, including Date, Error, Math, and Function. These data types must be represented as some other data format, with the encoding and decoding programs following the same encoding and decoding rules.

How to Simulate Associative Arrays

In Lesson 8, "Storing Data in Arrays," we discussed the JavaScript array object and looked at its various properties and methods.

You may recall that the elements in JavaScript arrays have unique numeric identifiers:

```
var myArray = [];
myArray[0] = 'Monday';
myArray[1] = 'Tuesday';
myArray[2] = 'Wednesday';
```

In many other programming languages, you can use textual keys to make the arrays more descriptive:

```
myArray["startDay"] = "Monday";
```

Unfortunately, JavaScript does not directly support such so-called *associative* arrays.

However, by using objects, you can easily go some way toward simulating their behavior. Using JSON notation makes the code easy to read and understand:

```
var conference = { "startDay" : "Monday",
 "nextDay" : "Tuesday",
 "endDay" : "Wednesday"
}
```

You can now access the object properties as if the object were an associative array:

```
alert(conference["startDay"]); // outputs "Monday"
```

Using Square Brackets

This approach using JSON notation works because the two syntaxes

```
object["property"]
```

and

```
object.property
```

are equivalent in JavaScript.

This Is Not a True Associative Array

Remember that this example is not really an associative array, although it looks like one. If you loop through the object, you will get, in addition to these three properties, any methods that have been assigned to the object.

How to Create Objects with JSON

You also might recall from Lesson 8 that one convenient way to express an array is with square brackets:

```
var categories = ["news", "sport", "films", "music", "comedy"];
```

JSON provides a somewhat similar shorthand for defining JavaScript objects.

JSON is Language Independent

Although it was developed for describing JavaScript objects, JSON is independent of any language or platform. JSON libraries and tools exist for many programming languages, including Java, PHP, C, and others.

Properties

As you've already seen, to express an object in JSON notation, you enclose the object in curly braces, rather than square ones, and list object properties as "property":"value" pairs:

```
var user = {
 "username" : "philb1234",
 "location" : "Spain",
 "height" : 1.80
}
```

TIP

Creating an Empty Object

You may recall that using the statement

```
var myObject = new Object();
```

creates an "empty" instance of an object with no properties or methods. The equivalent in JSON notation, unsurprisingly, is

```
var myObject = {};
```

The object properties are immediately available to access in the usual fashion:

```
var name = user.username; // variable 'name' contains 'philb1234'
```

Methods

You can add methods this way too, by using anonymous functions within the object definition:

```
var user = {
 "username" : "philb1234",
 "location" : "Spain",
 "height" : 1.80,
 "setName":function(newName){
     this.username=newName;
 }
}
```

Then you can call the `setName` method in the usual way:

```
var newname = prompt("Enter a new username:");
user.setName(newname);
```

CAUTION

JSON Does Not Natively Support Methods

While adding methods in this manner works fine in a JavaScript context, it is not permitted when using JSON as a general-purpose data interchange format. Functions declared this way will not be parsed correctly in a browser using native JSON parsing, though `eval()` will work. However, if you simply need to instantiate objects for use within your own script, you can add methods this way.

See the following section on JSON security.

Arrays

Property values themselves can be JavaScript arrays:

```
var bookListObject = {
 "booklist": ["Foundation",
     "Dune",
```

```
    "Eon",
    "2001 A Space Odyssey",
    "Stranger In A Strange Land"]
}
```

In the preceding example, the object has a property named `booklist`, the value of which is an array. You can access the individual items in the array by passing the required array key (remember that the array keys begin at zero):

```
var book = bookListObject.booklist[2]; // variable book has value "Eon"
```

The preceding line of code assigns to the variable `book` the second item in the `booklist` array object, which is a property of the object named `bookListObject`.

Objects

The JSON object can even incorporate other *objects*. By making the array elements themselves JSON-encoded objects, you can access them using dot notation.

In the following sample code, the value associated with the property `booklist` is an array of JSON objects. Each JSON object has two `"parameter":"value"` pairs, holding the title and author, respectively, of the book in question.

After retrieving the array of books, as in the previous example, you can easily access the `title` and `author` properties:

```
var bookListObject = {
 "booklist": [{"title":"Foundation", "author":"Isaac Asimov"},
 {"title":"Dune", "author":"Frank Herbert"},
 {"title":"Eon", "author":"Greg Bear"},
 {"title":"2001 A Space Odyssey", "author":"Arthur C. Clarke"},
 {"title":"Stranger In A Strange Land", "author":"Robert A. Heinlein"}]
 }
//show the author of the third book
alert(bookListObject.booklist[2].author); // displays "Greg Bear"
```

TRY IT YOURSELF ▼

Manipulating JSON Objects

Let's take the previous JSON object `bookListObject` and construct a user message that lists the books and authors in an easily read format. Create an HTML file and enter the code from Listing 14.2. Your JSON object is identical to the one in the previous example, but this time you're going to access the array of books and step through it with a loop, building a message string by appending the books and authors as you go. Finally, you'll display the book information to the user.

▼ **LISTING 14.2   Handling JSON Multilevel Objects**

```
<!DOCTYPE html>
<html>
<head>
    <title>Understanding JSON</title>
    <script>
        var booklistObject = {
            "booklist": [{"title":"Foundation", "author":"Isaac Asimov"},
            {"title":"Dune", "author":"Frank Herbert"},
            {"title":"Eon", "author":"Greg Bear"},
            {"title":"2001 A Space Odyssey", "author":"Arthur C. Clarke"},
            {"title":"Stranger In A Strange Land", "author":"Robert A. Heinlein"}]
        }

        // a variable to hold our user message
        var out = "";

        // get the array
        var books = booklistObject.booklist;

        //Loop through array, getting the books one by one
        for(var i=0; i<books.length; i++) {
            var booknumber = i+1;
            out += "Book " + booknumber +
            " is: '" + books[i].title +
            "' by " + books[i].author +
            "\n";
        }
    </script>
</head>
<body onload="alert(out)">
</body>
</html>
```

After designing the JSON object, you declare a variable and assign an empty string. This variable will hold the output message as you build it:

```
var out = "";
```

Now you extract the array of books, assigning this array to a new variable, `books`, to avoid a lot of repetitive typing later:

```
var books = booklistString.booklist;
```

Afterward, you simply need to loop through the books array, reading the `title` and `author` properties of each book object, and constructing a string to append to your output message:

```
for(var i=0; i<books.length; i++) {
 var booknumber = i+1; // array keys start at zero!
 out += "Book " + booknumber +
 " is: '" + books[i].title +
 "' by " + books[i].author +
 "\n";
}
```

Finally, show your message to the user:

```
alert(out);
```

The result of running this script is shown in Figure 14.5.

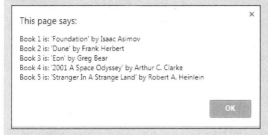

FIGURE 14.5
Your book information is displayed to the user

JSON Security

JavaScript's `eval()` function can execute any JavaScript command. This capability could represent a potential security problem, especially when you're working with JSON data from untrusted sources.

It is safer to use a browser with a native JSON parser to convert a JSON string into a JavaScript object. A JSON parser will recognize only JSON text and will not execute script commands. Native JSON parsers are generally faster than using `eval()` too.

Native JSON support is implemented in the newer browsers and in the latest ECMAScript (JavaScript) standard.

Summary

In this lesson you learned about JSON notation, a simple data interchange syntax that can also be used to create instances of JavaScript objects.

You learned how to use the native JSON support of modern browsers to serialize objects into JSON strings and parse JSON strings into JavaScript objects.

Q&A

Q. Where can I read the official JSON documentation?

A. The JSON syntax is formally described in RFC 4627. You can read it at www.ietf.org/rfc/rfc4627. There is also a good deal of information at the official home of JSON, http://json.org/.

Q. How can I find out whether my browser supports JSON natively?

A. You can check for the existence of the JSON object using the `typeof` operator, as described in Lesson 11, "Introducing Object-Oriented Programming."

```
if(typeof JSON == 'object') {
    // you have JSON support, go ahead!
} else {
    // find another way to work, e.g. using eval()
}
```

Of course, you must be sure that your script hasn't defined its own object called JSON; otherwise, this approach won't work as expected.

Workshop

Quiz questions and exercises to test your understanding and to stretch your skills.

Quiz

1. JSON is an acronym standing for

   a. JavaScript Object Notation

   b. Java String Object Notation

   c. JavaScript Serial Object Notation

2. Which of these can you do with JSON?

    a. Create a constructor function.

    b. Parse XML data.

    c. Directly instantiate an object.

3. What character is normally used to enclose the series of `parameter:value` pairs in a JSON object?

    a. Curly braces, `{}`

    b. Square braces, `[]`

    c. Parentheses, `()`

4. The `JSON.parse()` method

    a. Creates an object by interpreting a JSON string

    b. Creates a JSON-encoded string from a JavaScript object

    c. Neither of the above

5. The `JSON.stringify()` method

    a. Creates an object by interpreting a JSON string

    b. Creates a JSON-encoded string from a JavaScript object

    c. Neither of the above

TIP

Register Your Book

Just a reminder for those of you reading these words in the print or e-book edition of this book: If you go to www.informit.com/register and register this book (using ISBN 978-0-672-33809-0), you can receive free access to an online Web Edition that not only contains the complete text of this book but also features an interactive version of this quiz.

Answers

1. a. JavaScript Object Notation

2. c. Directly instantiate an object

3. a. Curly braces, `{}`

4. a. Creates an object by interpreting a JSON string

5. b. Creates a JSON-encoded string from a JavaScript object

Exercises

Load your file containing Listing 14.1 back into your browser. Try entering some JSON strings using arrays as property values, for example:

```
{"days":["Mon","Tue","Wed"] }
```

How does the program react? Is its behavior as you would expect?

Instantiate an object using the `new Object()` syntax you learned in Lesson 11 and add some properties with values of type `array`. Use the `stringify()` method to turn the object into a JSON string and display it.

LESSON 15
Programming HTML with JavaScript

What You'll Learn in This Lesson:

▶ About the recently introduced HTML5 markup tags

▶ How to handle video and audio

▶ How to use the `<canvas>` element

▶ How to drag and drop in HTML5

▶ How to work with local storage

▶ How to interface with the local file system

The previous version of HTML, HTML 4.01, has been around since 1999.

The XML-based version of HTML, XHTML, had been the subject of various W3C efforts, the latest having been moves toward XHTML2. In 2009 the W3C announced that XHTML2 was to be dumped in favor of diverting resources to a new version of HTML, HTML5.

TIP

HTML5

Note how it's written: HTML5. There's no space between the L and the 5.

This latest incarnation of HTML concentrates on developing HTML as a front end for web applications, extending the markup language via semantically rich elements, introducing some new attributes, and adding the possibility to use brand-new APIs in conjunction with JavaScript.

The HTML5 standard was finalized as the new standard for HTML in the fall of 2014, and the major browsers now support most of the later HTML5 elements and APIs.

In this lesson you learn how to control some of these powerful features with JavaScript.

Markup for HTML5

Even HTML pages that are well formed are more difficult to read and interpret than they could be, because the markup contains very little semantic information.

Page sections such as sidebars, headers and footers, and navigation elements are all contained in general-purpose page elements such as `div` elements, and only identifiable by the ID and class names invented by the page's developer.

HTML5 adds new elements to more easily identify each of these, and more, types of content. Some of the additional tags are listed in Table 15.1.

TABLE 15.1 Some HTML5 Tags

Tag	Description
`<section>`	Sections of pages
`<header>`	The header of a page
`<footer>`	The footer of a page
`<nav>`	The navigation on a page
`<article>`	The article or primary content on a page
`<aside>`	Extra content, such as a sidebar on a page
`<figure>`	Images that annotate an article
`<figcaption>`	A caption for a `<figure>` element
`<summary>`	A visible heading for a `<details>` element

Some Important Elements

While HTML5 introduces a wide variety of interesting capabilities, this section concentrates on the recently introduced tags that help ease some long-standing difficulties.

Controlling Video Playback with `<video>`

Video on the Web is extremely popular. However, the methods for implementing video are generally proprietary, reproduction happening via plug-ins such as Flash, Windows Media, and Apple QuickTime. Markup that works for embedding these elements in one browser doesn't always work in the others.

HTML5 contains a `<video>` element, the aim of which is to enable the embedding of any and all video formats.

Using the `<video>` tag, you can implement your favorite QuickTime movie like this:

```
<video src="video.mov" />
```

So far there has been much debate about which video formats (codecs) should be supported by the video element; at the time of writing, the search continues for a codec that requires no special licensing terms, though WebM (/www.webmproject.org/) is currently looking like the favorite. For the time being, quoting multiple sources gets around the problem and avoids the need for browser sniffing; there are currently three widely supported video formats—MP4, WebM, and Ogg.

```
<video id="vid1" width="400" height="300" controls="controls">
    <source src="movie.mp4" type="video/mp4" />
    <source src="movie.ogg" type="video/ogg" />
    <source src="movie.webm" type="video/webm" />
    <p>Video tag not supported.</p>
</video>
```

It is also a good practice to include height and width attributes for the `<video>` element. If height and width are not set, the browser doesn't know how much screen space to reserve, resulting in the page layout changing as the video loads.

You are also recommended to place some suitable text between the `<video>` and `</video>` tags to display in browsers that don't support the `<video>` tag.

Some important properties of the `<video>` tag are listed in Table 15.2.

TABLE 15.2 Some Attributes of the `<video>` Element

Attribute	Description
`loop`	Play in a loop
`autoplay`	Start video on load
`controls`	Display playback controls for playback (how they look is browser dependent)
`ended`	Return Boolean `true` if playback has finished (read-only)
`paused`	Return Boolean `true` if playback is paused (read-only)
`poster`	Set an optional image that will be displayed while the movie is loading
`volume`	Set audio volume from 0 (silent) to 1 (maximum)

Note that the appearance of the controls added using the `controls` property will depend on the browser in use, as shown in Figure 15.1.

FIGURE 15.1
The appearance of controls varies between browsers

You can access these properties in the same way as any other JavaScript or DOM object. For the previous video definition, you might use

```
var myVideo = document.getElementById("vid1").volume += 0.1;
```

to marginally increase the volume, or

```
if(document.getElementById("vid1").paused) {
    alert(message);
}
```

to pass a message to the user indicating that video playback is currently paused.

TIP

Video Element Reference

You can find a comprehensive reference to these tags and their properties and methods at https://html.spec.whatwg.org/multipage/media.html#the-video-element.

Testing Format Support with `canPlayType()`

You can check for support for a particular codec using the JavaScript method

```
media.canPlayType(type)
```

In the preceding example, `type` is a string containing the media type, for example, `"video/webm"`. This method must return an empty string if the browser knows it cannot play the content. The method might also return `"probably"` if the browser is confident it can support the format, or `"maybe"` otherwise.

Controlling Playback

Playback can also be controlled programmatically using the `pause()` and `play()` commands, as in the following code snippet:

```
var myVideo = document.getElementById("vid1").play();
var myVideo = document.getElementById("vid1").pause();
```

Playing Sound with the `<audio>` Tag

Pretty much everything stated previously about the `<video>` tag applies equally well to the `<audio>` tag. The simple way to use the `<audio>` tag is like this:

```
<audio src="song.mp3"></audio>
```

You can add further attributes to achieve more control over playback, such as `loop` and `autoplay`:

```
<audio src="song.mp3" autoplay loop></audio>
```

TIP

Use `loop` and `autoplay` sparingly

Don't abuse `loop` and `autoplay`, or you may find that many of your site visitors don't return!

As with the earlier examples for video files, you can include alternative formats to help ensure that a user's browser will find one that it can play, as in the following code:

```
<audio controls="controls">
    <source src="song.ogg" type="audio/ogg" />
    <source src="song.mp3" type="audio/mpeg" />
    <p>Your browser does not support the audio element.</p>
</audio>
```

MP3, WAV, and Ogg are typically supported file formats for the `<audio>` element. Controlling an audio file in JavaScript uses the same methods as for the `<video>` tag.

To add and play an audio file via JavaScript, you can treat it just like any other JavaScript or DOM object:

```
var soundElement = document.createElement('audio');
soundElement.setAttribute('src', 'sound.ogg');
soundElement.play();
soundElement.pause();
```

The `<audio>` and `<video>` tags have many valuable properties that you can access via JavaScript. Here are a few useful ones, the meaning of which will be immediately apparent:

```
mediaElement.duration
mediaElement.currentTime
mediaElement.playbackRate
mediaElement.muted
```

For example, to move to a point 45 seconds into a song, you might use

```
soundElement.currentTime = 45;
```

Drawing on the Page with `<canvas>`

The new `<canvas>` tag gives you just that: a rectangular space in your page where you can draw shapes and graphics, as well as load and display image files and control their display via JavaScript. The many practical uses for the element include dynamic charts, JavaScript/HTML games, and instructional animations.

Using the `<canvas>` tag simply allows you to define a region by setting its `width` and `height` parameters; everything else related to creating the graphical content is done via JavaScript. There is an extensive set of drawing methods known as the Canvas 2D API.

▼ TRY IT YOURSELF

Moving a Ball Using `<canvas>`

Here you're going to make a simple animation in a `<canvas>` element—just a red disc (to represent a ball) moving in a circle on the page.

The only HTML markup required in the body of the page is the `<canvas>` element itself:

```
<canvas id="canvas1" width="400" height="300"></canvas>
```

All the drawing and animation will be done in JavaScript.

TIP

Default Canvas Size

If you don't set `width` and `height` parameters, the canvas defaults to 300 pixels wide by 150 pixels high.

You first need to specify the rendering context. At the time of writing, 2D is the only widely supported context, though a 3D context is under development:

```
context = canvas1.getContext('2d');
```

The only primitive shapes supported by `<canvas>` are rectangles:

```
fillRect(x,y,width,height); //draw a filled rectangle
strokeRect(x,y,width,height); //draw an outlined rectangle
clearRect(x,y,width,height); // clear the rectangle
```

All other shapes must be created by using one or more path-drawing functions. Since you want to draw a colored disc, that's what you need here.

Several different path-drawing functions are offered by <canvas>.

Move to x, y without drawing anything:

```
moveTo(x, y)
```

Draw a line from the current location to x, y:

```
lineTo(x, y)
```

Draw a circular arc of radius r, having circle center x, y, from startAngle to endAngle.

```
arc(x, y, r, startAngle, endAngle, anti)
```

Setting the last parameter to Boolean true makes the arc draw counterclockwise instead of the default clockwise.

To create shapes using these basic commands, you need some additional methods:

```
object.beginPath();
object.closePath(); //complete a partial shape
object.stroke(); //draw an outlined shape
object.fill(); //draw a filled shape
```

TIP

Close Shapes Automatically with `fill`

If you use the `fill` method, an open shape will be closed automatically without you having to use `closePath()`.

To make the ball you're going to generate a filled circle, let's make it red, of radius 15, and centered on canvas coordinates 50, 50:

```
context.beginPath();
context.fillStyle="#ff0000";
context.arc(50, 50, 15, 0, Math.PI*2, true);
context.closePath();
```

To animate the ball, you need to alter the x and y coordinates of the ball center using a timer. Take a look at the animate() function:

```
function animate() {
    context.clearRect(0,0, 400,300);
    counter++;
```

```
x += 20 * Math.sin(counter);
y += 20 * Math.cos(counter);
paint();
}
```

This function is called repeatedly via the `setInterval()` method. Each time it's called, the canvas is cleared by using the `clearRect()` method across the full size of the `<canvas>` element. The variable counter is incremented on each loop, and its new value is then used to redefine the position of the disc's center.

The complete code is shown in Listing 15.1.

LISTING 15.1   Moving a Ball Using `<canvas>`

```html
<!DOCTYPE HTML>
<html>
<head>
    <title>HTML5 canvas</title>
    <script>
        var context;
        var x=50;
        var y=50;
        var counter = 0;
        function paint() {
            context.beginPath();
            context.fillStyle="#ff0000";
            context.arc(x, y, 15, 0, Math.PI*2, false);
            context.closePath();
            context.fill();
        }
        function animate() {
            context.clearRect(0,0, 400,300);
            counter++;
            x += 20 * Math.sin(counter);
            y += 20 * Math.cos(counter);
            paint();
        }
        window.onload = function() {
            context= canvas1.getContext('2d');
            setInterval(animate, 100);
        }
    </script>
</head>
```

```
<body>
    <canvas id="canvas1" width="400" height="300">
        <p>Your browser doesn't support the canvas element.</p>
    </canvas>
</body>
</html>
```

Create this file and load it into your browser. If your browser supports the `<canvas>` element, you should see a red disc following a circular route on the page, as in Figure 15.2.

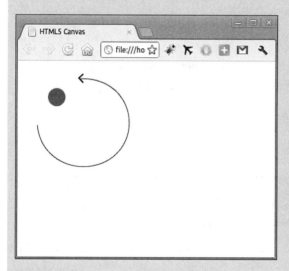

FIGURE 15.2
An animation using `<canvas>`

Drag and Drop

Drag and drop is a part of the HTML5 standard. Just about any element can be made draggable.

To make an element draggable, all that's required is to set its `draggable` attribute to `true`:

```
<img draggable="true" />
```

Dragging something, though, isn't much use by itself. To employ a draggable object to achieve something useful, you will probably want to be able to drop it somewhere.

To define where an object can be dropped and to control the dragging and dropping process, you need to write event listeners to detect and control the various parts of the drag-and-drop process.

There are a few different events you can utilize to control your drag and drop:

▶ `dragstart`

▶ `drag`

▶ `dragenter`

▶ `dragleave`

▶ `dragover`

▶ `drop`

▶ `dragend`

To control your drag and drop, you need to define a source element (where the drag starts), the data payload (what it is you're dragging), and a drop target (an area to catch the dropped item).

TIP

Not All Page Elements Accept Drops

Not all items can be drop targets; an `<img>`, for example, cannot accept drops.

The `dataTransfer` property contains a piece of data sent in a drag action. The value of `dataTransfer` is usually set in the `dragstart` event and read/handled in the `drop` event.

Calling `setData(format, data)` or `getData(format, data)` will (respectively) set or read this piece of data.

▼ TRY IT YOURSELF

Drag and Drop in HTML5

In this example you build a demonstrator for the HTML5 drag-and-drop interface.

Fire up your editor and create a file containing the code shown in Listing 15.2.

LISTING 15.2 HTML5 Drag and Drop

```
<!DOCTYPE HTML>
<html>
<head>
    <title>HTML5 Drag and Drop</title>
    <style>
        body {background-color: #ddd; font-family: arial, verdana, sans-serif;}
        #drop1 {width: 200px;height: 200px;border: 1px solid black;background-
        ➥color:white}
```

```
        #drag1 {width: 50px;height: 50px;}
    </style>
    <script>
        function allowDrop(ev) {
            ev.preventDefault();
        }

        function drag(ev) {
            ev.dataTransfer.setData("Text",ev.target.id);
        }

        function drop(ev) {
            var data = ev.dataTransfer.getData("Text");
            ev.target.appendChild(document.getElementById(data));
            ev.preventDefault();
        }

        window.onload = function() {
            var dragged = document.getElementById("drag1");
            var drophere = document.getElementById("drop1");
            dragged.ondragstart = drag;
            drophere.ondragover = allowDrop;
            drophere.ondrop = drop;
        }
    </script>
</head>
<body>
    <div id="drop1" ></div>
    <p>Drag the image below into the box above:</p>
    <img id="drag1" src="drag.gif" draggable="true" />
</body>
</html>
```

To get the party started, you define a couple of HTML elements on your page. The `<div>` element with ID of `drop1` is the target area for catching the drop, and the image with ID of `drag1` is to become your draggable item.

Three important functions are defined in the code. Each of these functions is passed the current event to process. Behind the scenes, `ev.target` changes automatically for each type of event, depending on where you are in the drag-and-drop process:

▶ A function named `drag(ev)` is executed when the drag starts. This function sets the value of the `dataTransfer` property for the drag to the ID of the dragged object:

```
function drag(ev) {
  ev.dataTransfer.setData("Text",ev.target.id);
}
```

▶ Another function named `allowDrop(ev)` is executed when the drag passes over the intended drop area. All that this function must achieve is to prevent the drop area's default behavior from taking place (as the default behavior prevents dropping):

```
function allowDrop(ev) {
 ev.preventDefault();
}
```

▶ Finally, a function named `drop(ev)` is executed when the dragged item is dropped. In this function, the value of the `dataTransfer` property is read to determine the ID of the dragged object; then that object is appended as a child object to the drop area object. Once again, the default operation needs to be prevented from taking place:

```
function drop(ev) {
 var data = ev.dataTransfer.getData("Text");
 ev.target.appendChild(document.getElementById(data));
 ev.preventDefault();
}
```

The loaded page should look something like the one shown in Figure 15.3. Dragging the small image and dropping it over the white drop area, you should see it "dock" into the `<div>` element, as shown in the figure.

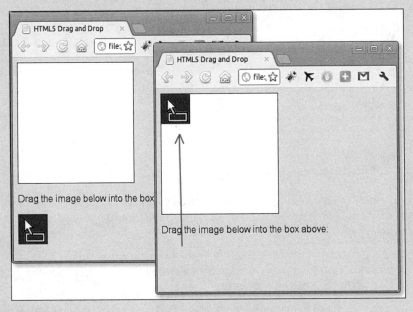

FIGURE 15.3
HTML5 drag and drop

Local Storage

HTML5 pages can store even large amounts of data within the user's browser, without any negative effect on the website's performance. Web storage is more secure and faster than doing this via cookies. As when using cookies, the data is stored in key/value pairs, and a web page can only access the data it has itself stored.

The two new objects for storing data locally in the browser are

▶ `localStorage`: Stores data with no expiration date

▶ `sessionStorage`: Stores data just for the current session

If you're unsure about your browser's support for local storage, once again you can use feature detection:

```
if(typeof(Storage)!=="undefined") {
    ... both objects are available ...
}
```

To store a value, you can invoke the `setItem` method, passing to it a key and a value:

```
localStorage.setItem("key", "value");
```

Alternatively, you can use the `localStorage` object like an associative array:

```
localStorage["key"] = "value";
```

Retrieving the values can use either of these methods too:

```
alert(localStorage.getItem("key"));
```

or

```
alert(localStorage["key"]);
```

How to Work with Local Files

At last HTML provides a standard way to interact with the user's local files, using HTML5's File API specification. There are several ways to access external files:

▶ `File` provides information including name, size, and MIME type, and gives a reference to the file handle.

▶ `FileList` is an array-like sequence of `File` objects.

▶ The `FileReader` interface uses `File` and `FileList` to asynchronously read a file. You can check on read progress, catch any errors, and find out when a file is completely loaded.

Checking for Browser Support

Once more, you can check whether your browser supports the File API by using the usual feature-detection method:

```
if (window.File && window.FileReader && window.FileList) {
    // we're good
}
```

▼ TRY IT YOURSELF

Interacting with the Local File System

In this example you modify the previous drag-and-drop example to allow a list of files to be dragged into a web page from the local file system. To do so, you use the `FileList` data structure.

Take a look at the modified `drop(ev)` function:

```
function drop(ev) {
    var files = ev.dataTransfer.files;
    for (var i = 0; i < files.length; i++) {
        var f = files[i];
        var pnode = document.createElement("p");
        var tnode = document.createTextNode(f.name + " (" + f.type + ") " + f.size
        ➥+ " bytes");
        pnode.appendChild(tnode);
        ev.target.appendChild(pnode);
    }
    ev.preventDefault();
}
```

Here the array-like `FileList` containing information about the dragged files is extracted from the `dataTransfer` object:

```
var files = ev.dataTransfer.files;
```

Then each file is processed in turn by iterating through them individually:

```
for (var i = 0; i < files.length; i++) {
    var f = files[i];
    ...statements to process each file ...
}
```

The complete listing is shown in Listing 15.3.

LISTING 15.3   Interacting with the Local File System

```
<!DOCTYPE html>
<html>
<head>
    <title>HTML5 Local Files</title>
    <style>
```

```
        body {background-color: #ddd; font-family: arial, verdana, sans-serif;}
        #drop1 {
            width: 400px;
            height: 200px;
            border: 1px solid black;
            background-color: white;
            padding: 10px;
        }
    </style>
    <script>
        function allowDrop(ev) {
            ev.preventDefault();
        }

        function drop(ev) {
            var files = ev.dataTransfer.files;
            for (var i = 0; i < files.length; i++) {
                var f = files[i]
                var pnode = document.createElement("p");

                var tnode = document.createTextNode(f.name + " (" + f.type + ") " +
                ➥f.size + " bytes");
                pnode.appendChild(tnode);
                ev.target.appendChild(pnode);
            }
            ev.preventDefault();
        }

        window.onload = function() {
            var drophere = document.getElementById("drop1");
            drophere.ondragover = allowDrop;
            drophere.ondrop = drop;
        }
    </script>
</head>
<body>
    <div id="drop1" ></div>
</body>
</html>
```

After creating this file in your editor and loading the resulting page into the browser, you should be able to drag files into the drop area from your local system, and see filename, MIME type, and size listed, as shown in Figure 15.4.

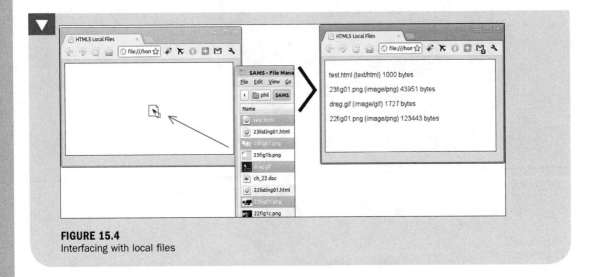

FIGURE 15.4
Interfacing with local files

Summary

HTML5 offers a whole array of facilities to HTML, enabling the markup language to be used as a much better basis for web applications and allowing JavaScript to exploit some more modern APIs.

In this lesson you had a whistle-stop tour of these capabilities, including some hands-on coding experience using some of these more recent APIs and coding techniques.

Q&A

Q. What is the best way for me to learn HTML5?

A. Learn HTML5 by using it. Jump right in and start building pages using HTML5 features. Use the semantic tags; try video and audio playback; play with drag and drop, and the file API; and build animations using `<canvas>`. When you have questions, many Internet-based tutorials, blogs, and code examples are available.

Q. Are there already real live sites using HTML5?

A. Sure, lots of them. Take a look at http://html5gallery.com/ for some examples.

Workshop

Quiz questions and exercises to test your understanding and to stretch your skills.

Quiz

1. Which of the following is NOT a valid HTML5 semantic element?

   a. `<header>`

   b. `<sidebar>`

   c. `<nav>`

2. Which of the following is NOT a valid method for `<audio>` and `<video>` elements?

   a. `play()`

   b. `pause()`

   c. `stop()`

3. Which of the following is NOT a standard drag-and-drop event?

   a. `drag`

   b. `dragover`

   c. `dragout`

4. When using local storage, a web page can access any data

   a. That it has itself stored

   b. That was stored by any page in the current browser session

   c. That was stored by any page listed in the browser history

5. A `<canvas>` element

   a. Can be any size and shape

   b. Can be any size, but is always rectangular

   c. Is always the same size as the browser window

TIP

Register Your Book

Just a reminder for those of you reading these words in the print or e-book edition of this book: If you go to www.informit.com/register and register this book (using ISBN 978-0-672-33809-0), you can receive free access to an online Web Edition that not only contains the complete text of this book but also features an interactive version of this quiz.

Answers

1. b. `<sidebar>` is not a valid HTML5 element.

2. c. There is no `stop()` method.

3. c. There is no `dragout` event; use `dragleave`.

4. a. That it has itself stored

5. b. Can be any size, but is always rectangular

Exercises

Review some of the examples from previous lessons and try to rewrite them using some of the HTML5 interfaces.

The introduction of HTML5 is pretty recent at the time of writing. Check out the current state of browser support for the various aspects of HTML5 at http://caniuse.com/.

LESSON 16
Manipulating CSS in JavaScript

What You'll Learn in This Lesson:

▸ Separating style from content
▸ Using the DOM `style` property
▸ Retrieving styles
▸ Setting styles
▸ Accessing classes using `className`
▸ Using the DOM `styleSheet` object
▸ Enabling, disabling, and switching stylesheets in JavaScript
▸ Changing the mouse cursor

In the early days of the World Wide Web, pages were all about their text content. Early browsers had rudimentary support for graphic effects, and some didn't even support images. Styling a web page was largely a matter of using the few style-related attributes and tags allowed by the early incarnations of HTML.

Things improved markedly with the introduction of browser support for Cascading Style Sheets (CSS), which allowed the styling of a page to be treated independently from its HTML markup.

In earlier lessons you learned how to edit the structure of your page using JavaScript's DOM methods. However, JavaScript can also be used to access and amend CSS styles for the current page. In this lesson you learn how.

A Ten-Minute CSS Primer

If you've decided to learn JavaScript, there's a pretty good chance that you're already familiar with CSS styling. Just in case it's managed to pass you by, let's review the basics.

Separating Style from Content

Before CSS came along, most styling in HTML pages was carried out using HTML tags and/or their attributes. To change the font color of a piece of text, for example, you had to use something like this:

```
<p><font color="red">This text is in red!</font></p>
```

This approach was pretty awful for a number of reasons:

▶ Every single piece of text in the page that you wanted to be colored red had to be marked up with these extra tags.

▶ The created style could not be carried over to other pages; they too had to be marked up individually with additional HTML.

▶ To later change pages' styles, you had to edit each and every page and sift through the HTML, changing every style-related tag and attribute individually.

▶ With all this extra markup, the HTML became very hard to read and maintain.

CSS attempts to separate the styling of an HTML element from the markup function of that element. This is done by defining individual *style declarations* and then applying these to HTML elements or collections of elements.

You can use CSS to style the visual properties of a page element, such as color, font, and size, as well as format-related properties such as positioning, margins, padding, and alignment.

Separating style from content in this way brings with it a lot of benefits:

▶ Style declarations can be applied to more than one element or even (when using external stylesheets) more than one page.

▶ Changes to style declarations affect all associated HTML elements, making updating your site's style more accurate, quick, and efficient.

▶ Sharing styles encourages more consistent styling through your site.

▶ HTML markup is clearer to read and maintain.

Using CSS Style Declarations

The syntax of CSS style declarations is not unlike that of JavaScript functions. Suppose you want to declare a style for all paragraph elements in a page, causing the font color inside the paragraphs to be colored red:

```
p {
    color: red
}
```

You can apply more than one style rule to your chosen element or collection of elements, separating them with semicolons:

```
p {
    color: red;
    text-decoration: italic;
}
```

Since you have used the selector p, the preceding style declarations affect every paragraph element on the page. To select just one specific page element, you can use its ID. When you do so, the selector you use for your CSS style declaration is not the name of the HTML element, but the ID value prefixed by a hash character. For instance, the HTML element

```
<p id="para1">Here is some text.</p>
```

could be styled by the following style declaration:

```
#para1 {
    font-weight: bold;
    font-size: 12pt;
    color: black;
}
```

To style multiple page elements using the same style declaration, you can simply separate the selectors with commas. The following style declaration affects all <div> elements on the page, plus whatever element has the id value para1:

```
div, #para1 {
    color: yellow;
    background-color: black;
}
```

Alternatively, you can select all elements sharing a particular class attribute, by prefixing the class name with a dot to form your selector:

```
<p class="info">Welcome to my website.</p>
<span class="info">Please log in or register using the form below.</span>
```

You can style these elements with one declaration:

```
.info {
    font-family: arial, verdana, sans-serif;
    color: green;
}
```

Deciding Where to Place Style Declarations

Somewhat similarly to JavaScript statements, CSS style declarations can either appear within the page or be saved in an external file and referenced from within the HTML page.

If you want to reference an external stylesheet, normal practice is to add a line to the page `<head>` like this:

```
<link rel="stylesheet" type="text/css" href="style.css" />
```

Alternatively, you can place style declarations directly in the `<head>` of your page between `<style>` and `</style>` tags:

```
<style>
    p {
        color: black;
        font-family: tahoma;
    }
    h1 {
        color: blue;
        font-size: 22pt;
    }
</style>
```

Finally, it's possible to add style declarations directly into an HTML element by using the `style` attribute:

```
<p style="color:red; font-size:12px;">Please see our terms of service.</p>
```

TIP

External Stylesheets

Styles defined in external stylesheets have the advantage that they can easily be applied to multiple pages, whereas styles defined within the page can't.

The DOM `style` Property

You saw in previous lessons how the HTML page is represented by the browser as a DOM tree. The DOM *nodes*—individual "leaves and branches" making up the DOM tree—are objects, each having its own properties and methods.

You've seen various methods that allow you to select individual DOM nodes, or collections of nodes, such as `document.getElementById()`.

Each DOM node has a property called `style`, which is itself an object containing information about the CSS styles pertaining to its parent node. Let's see an example:

```
<div id="id1" style="width:200px;">Welcome back to my site.</div>
<script>
    var myNode = document.getElementById("id1");
    alert(myNode.style.width);
</script>
```

In this case the alert would display the message "200px."

NOTE

Using Square Brackets Notation

In addition to the syntax

`myNode.style.width`

you can also use the equivalent

`myNode.style["width"]`

This is sometimes necessary, such as when passing a property name as a variable:

`var myProperty = "width";`

`myNode.style[myProperty] = "200px";`

Unfortunately, while this method works fine with *inline* styles, if you apply a style to a page element via a `<style>` element in the head of your page or in an external stylesheet, the DOM `style` object won't be able to access it.

NOTE

Accessing Style Properties

In Lesson 17, "More Advanced Control of CSS," you read about another way to access style properties in JavaScript that avoids the limitation of only working for inline styles.

The DOM `style` object, though, is not read-only; you can set the values of style properties using the `style` object, and properties you've set this way *will* be returned by the DOM `style` object.

NOTE

Dealing with Hyphens in Property Names

CSS contains many properties with names that contain hyphens, such as `background-color`, `font-size`, `text-align`, and so on. Since the hyphen is not allowed in JavaScript property and method names, you need to amend the way these properties are written. To access such a property in JavaScript, remove the hyphen from the property name and capitalize the character that follows, so `font-size` becomes `fontSize`, `text-align` becomes `textAlign`, and so on.

▼ TRY IT YOURSELF

Setting Style Properties

Let's write a function to toggle the background color and font color of a page element between two values, using the DOM `style` object:

```
function toggle() {
    var myElement = document.getElementById("id1");
    if(myElement.style.backgroundColor == 'red') {
        myElement.style.backgroundColor = 'yellow';
        myElement.style.color = 'black';
    } else {
        myElement.style.backgroundColor = 'red';
        myElement.style.color = 'white';
    }
}
```

The function `toggle()` first finds out the current `background-color` CSS property of a page element and then compares that color to `red`.

If the `background-color` property currently has the value of `red`, it sets the style properties of the element to show the text in black on a yellow background; otherwise, it sets the style values to show white text on a red background.

You use this function to toggle the colors of a `<span>` element in an HTML document.

The complete listing is shown in Listing 16.1.

LISTING 16.1   Styling Using the DOM `style` Object

```
<!DOCTYPE html>
<html>
<head>
    <title>Setting the style of page elements</title>
    <style>
        span {
            font-size: 16pt;
            font-family: arial, helvetica, sans-serif;
            padding: 20px;
        }
    </style>
    <script>
        function toggle() {
            var myElement = document.getElementById("id1");
            if(myElement.style.backgroundColor == 'red') {
                myElement.style.backgroundColor = 'yellow';
                myElement.style.color = 'black';
            } else {
                myElement.style.backgroundColor = 'red';
                myElement.style.color = 'white';
            }
```

```
        }
        window.onload = function() {
            document.getElementById("btn1").onclick = toggle;
        }
    </script>
</head>
<body>
    <span id="id1">Welcome back to my site.</span>
    <input type="button" id="btn1" value="Toggle" />
</body>
</html>
```

Create the HTML file in your editor and try it out.

You should see that when the page originally loads, the text is in the default black and has no background color. That happens because these style properties are initially not set in the `<style>` instructions in the page head, as an inline style, or via the DOM.

Executing when the button is clicked, the `toggle()` function checks the current background color of the `<span>` element. On finding that its value is not currently red, `toggle()` sets the background color to red and the text color to white.

The next time the button is clicked, the test condition

```
if(myElement.style.backgroundColor == 'red')
```

returns a value of `true`, causing the colors to be set instead to black on a yellow background.

Figure 16.1 shows the program in action.

FIGURE 16.1
Setting style properties in JavaScript

How to Access Classes Using `className`

Earlier in this lesson we discussed separating style from content and the benefits that this can bring.

Using JavaScript to edit the properties of the `style` object, as in the previous exercise, works well, but it does carry with it the danger of reducing this separation of style and content. If your JavaScript code routinely changes elements' style declarations, the responsibility for styling your pages is no longer lodged firmly in CSS. If you later decide to change the styles your JavaScript applies, you'll have to go back and edit all your JavaScript functions.

Thankfully, we have a mechanism by which JavaScript can restyle pages without overwriting individual style declarations. By using the `className` property of the element, you can switch the value of the `class` attribute and with it the associated style declarations for the element. Take a look at Listing 16.2.

LISTING 16.2   Changing Classes Using `className`

```
<!DOCTYPE html>
<html>
<head>
    <title>Switching classes with JavaScript</title>
    <style>
        .classA {
            width: 180px;
            border: 3px solid black;
            background-color: white;
            color: red;
            font: normal 24px arial, helvetica, sans-serif;
            padding: 20px;
        }
    .classB {
            width: 180px;
            border: 3px dotted white;
            background-color: black;
            color: yellow;
            font: italic bold 24px "Times New Roman", serif;
            padding: 20px;
        }
    </style>
    <script>
        function toggleClass() {
            var myElement = document.getElementById("id1");
            if(myElement.className == "classA") {
                myElement.className = "classB";
            } else {
                myElement.className = "classA";
            }
        }
```

```
        window.onload = function() {
            document.getElementById("btn1").onclick = toggleClass;
        }
    </script>
</head>
<body>
    <div id="id1" class="classA"> An element with a touch of class.</div>
    <input type="button" id="btn1" value="Toggle" />
</body>
</html>
```

The `<style>` element in the page `<head>` lists style declarations for two classes, `classA` and `classB`. The JavaScript function `toggleClass()` uses similar logic to the earlier function `toggle()` shown in Listing 16.1, except that `toggleClass()` does not work with the element's `style` object. Instead, `toggleClass()` gets the class name associated with the `<div>` element and switches its value between `classA` and `classB`.

Figure 16.2 shows the script in action.

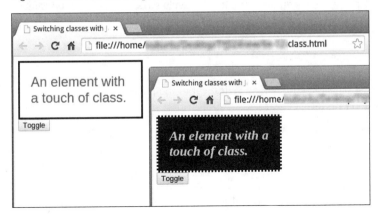

FIGURE 16.2
Switching classes in JavaScript

NOTE

Using the `class` Attribute

As an alternative to using `className`, you could try setting the `class` attribute for an element to the value `classA` by using

```
element.setAttribute("class", "classA");
```

Unfortunately, various versions of Internet Explorer have trouble when trying to set the `class` attribute, but work fine with `className`. The statement

```
element.className = "classA";
```

seems to work in all browsers.

The DOM `styleSheets` Object

The `styleSheets` property of the `document` object contains an array of all the stylesheets on the page, whether they are contained in external files and linked into the page head, or declared between `<style>` and `</style>` tags in the page head. The items in the `styleSheets` array are indexed numerically, starting at zero for the stylesheet appearing first.

TIP

Counting Stylesheets

You can access the total number of stylesheets on your page by using

```
document.styleSheets.length
```

Enabling, Disabling, and Switching Stylesheets

Each stylesheet in the array has a property called `disabled`, containing a value of Boolean `true` or `false`. This is a read/write property, so you are able to effectively switch individual stylesheets on and off in JavaScript:

```
document.styleSheets[0].disabled = true;
document.styleSheets[1].disabled = false;
```

The preceding code snippet "switches on" the second stylesheet in the page (index 1) while "switching off" the first stylesheet (index 0).

Listing 16.3 has a working example. The script on this page first declares the variable `whichSheet`, initializing its value at zero:

```
var whichSheet = 0;
```

This variable keeps track of which of the two stylesheets is currently active. The second line of code initially disables the second of the two stylesheets on the page:

```
document.styleSheets[1].disabled = true;
```

The function `sheet()`, which is attached to the `onClick` event handler of the button on the page when the page loads, carries out three tasks when the button is clicked:

▶ Disables the stylesheet whose index is stored in variable `whichSheet`:

```
document.styleSheets[whichSheet].disabled = true;
```

▶ Toggles the variable `whichSheet` between one and zero:

```
whichSheet = (whichSheet == 1) ? 0 : 1;
```

▶ Enables the stylesheet corresponding to the new value of `whichSheet`:

```
document.styleSheets[whichSheet].disabled = false;
```

The combined effect of these activities is to toggle between the two active stylesheets for the page. The script is shown in action in Listing 16.3 and Figure 16.3.

LISTING 16.3 Toggling Between Stylesheets Using the styleSheets Property

```
<!DOCTYPE html>
<html>
<head>
    <title>Switching Stylesheets with JavaScript</title>
    <style>
        body {
            background-color: white;
            color: red;
            font: normal 24px arial, helvetica, sans-serif;
            padding: 20px;
        }
    </style>
    <style>
        body {
            background-color: black;
            color: yellow;
            font: italic bold 24px "Times New Roman", serif;
            padding: 20px;
        }
    </style>
    <script>
        var whichSheet = 0;
        document.styleSheets[1].disabled = true;
        function sheet() {
            document.styleSheets[whichSheet].disabled = true;
            whichSheet = (whichSheet == 1) ? 0 : 1;
            document.styleSheets[whichSheet].disabled = false;
        }
        window.onload = function() {
            document.getElementById("btn1").onclick = sheet;
        }
    </script>
</head>
<body>
    Switch my stylesheet with the button below!<br />
    <input type="button" id="btn1" value="Toggle" />
</body>
</html>
```

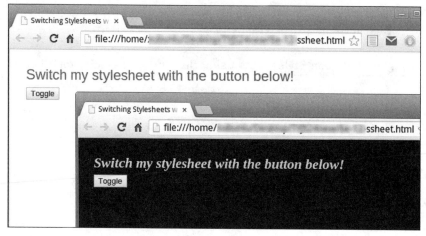

FIGURE 16.3
Switching stylesheets with the `styleSheets` property

▼ TRY IT YOURSELF

Selecting a Particular Stylesheet

Having your stylesheets indexed by number doesn't make it easy to select the stylesheet you need. It would be easier if you had a function to allow you to title your stylesheets and select them by their title attribute.

You need your function to respond in a useful manner if you ask for a stylesheet that doesn't exist; you want it to maintain the previous stylesheet and send the user a message.

To do so, first declare a couple of variables and initialize their values:

```
var change = false;
var oldSheet = 0;
```

The Boolean variable `change` keeps track of whether you've found a stylesheet with the requested title; once you do so, you change its value to `true`, indicating that you intend to change stylesheets.

The integer `oldSheet`, originally set to zero, will eventually be assigned the number of the currently active sheet; in case you don't find a new stylesheet matching the requested title, you set this back to active before returning from the function.

Now you need to cycle through the `styleSheets` array:

```
for (var i = 0; i < document.styleSheets.length; i++) {
  ...
}
```

For each stylesheet:

▶ If you find that this is the currently active stylesheet, store its index in the variable oldSheet:

```
if(document.styleSheets[i].disabled == false) { oldSheet = i;}
```

▶ As you cycle through, make sure all sheets are disabled:

```
document.styleSheets[i].disabled = true;
```

▶ If the current sheet has the title of the requested sheet, enable it by setting its disabled value to false, and immediately set your variable change to true:

```
if(document.styleSheets[i].title == mySheet) {
  document.styleSheets[i].disabled = false;
  change = true;
}
```

When you've cycled through all sheets, you can determine from the state of the variables change and oldSheet whether you are in a position to change the stylesheet. If not, reset the prior stylesheet to be enabled again:

```
if(!change) document.styleSheets[oldSheet].disabled = false;
```

Finally, the function returns the value of variable change, returning true if the change has been made or false if not.

The code is shown in Listing 16.4. Save this code in an HTML file and load it into your browser.

LISTING 16.4   Selecting Stylesheets by Title

```
<!DOCTYPE html>
<html>
<head>
    <title>Switching stylesheets with JavaScript</title>
    <style title="sheet1">
        body {
            background-color: white;
            color: red;
        }
    </style>
    <style title="sheet2">
        body {
            background-color: black;
            color: yellow;
        }
    </style>
    <style title="sheet3">
        body {
            background-color: pink;
```

```
                color: green;
            }
    </style>
    <script>
        function ssEnable(mySheet) {
            var change = false;
            var oldSheet = 0;
            for (var i = 0; i < document.styleSheets.length; i++) {
                if(document.styleSheets[i].disabled == false) {
                    oldSheet = i;
                }
                document.styleSheets[i].disabled = true;
                if(document.styleSheets[i].title == mySheet) {
                    document.styleSheets[i].disabled = false;
                    change = true;
                }
            }
            if(!change) document.styleSheets[oldSheet].disabled = false;
            return change;
        }
        function sheet() {
            var sheetName = prompt("Stylesheet Name?");
            if(!ssEnable(sheetName)) alert("Not found - original stylesheet retained.");
        }
        window.onload = function() {
            document.getElementById("btn1").onclick = sheet;
        }
    </script>
</head>
<body>
    Switch my stylesheet with the button below!<br />
    <input type="button" id="btn1" value="Change Sheet" />
</body>
</html>
```

The small function `sheet()` is added to the button's `onClick` event handler when the page loads. Each time the button is clicked, `sheet()` prompts the user for the name of a stylesheet:

```
var sheetName = prompt("Stylesheet Name?");
```

Then it calls the `ssEnable()` function, passing the requested name as an argument.

If the function returns `false`, indicating that no change of stylesheet has taken place, you alert the user with a message:

```
if(!ssEnable(sheetName)) alert("Not found - original stylesheet retained.");
```

The script is shown operating in Figure 16.4.

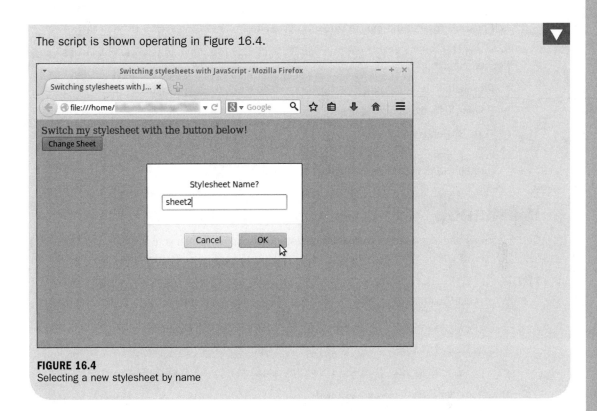

FIGURE 16.4
Selecting a new stylesheet by name

Summary

In this lesson you learned a number of ways in which JavaScript can be put to work on the CSS styles of your page. You learned how to use the `style` property of page elements, how to work with CSS classes, and how to manipulate entire stylesheets.

Q&A

Q. Is it possible for JavaScript to work with individual CSS style rules?

A. Yes, it is, but at the time of writing this does not work perfectly cross-browser. Most modern browsers support the `cssRules` array, while Internet Explorer (before version 9) calls the equivalent array `Rules`. There is also some difference among browsers in how the notion of a "rule" is interpreted. It's to be hoped that future browser versions will finally resolve the remaining differences.

Q. Is it possible to alter the mouse cursor in JavaScript?

A. Yes, it is. The `style` object has a property called `cursor` that can take various values. Popular cursors include the following:

- ▶ **Crosshair:** Pointer renders as a pair of crossed lines like a gun sight.
- ▶ **Pointer:** Usually a pointing finger.
- ▶ **Text:** Text entry caret.
- ▶ **Wait:** The program is busy. Most browsers show an animated cursor, such as a rotating arc, a flashing hourglass, or similar.

Workshop

Quiz questions and exercises to test your understanding and to stretch your skills.

Quiz

1. What would you use to set the `font-family` property for element `myElement` to Verdana?

   a. `myElement.style.font-family = "verdana";`

   b. `myElement.style.fontFamily = "verdana";`

   c. `myElement.style.font-family("verdana");`

2. The property `className` can be used

   a. To access the value of the `class` attribute of an element

   b. To access the value of the `name` attribute of an element

   c. To add the attribute `classname` to an element

3. How can you enable the stylesheet with index `n` in the `styleSheets` array?

   a. `document.styleSheets[n].active = true;`

   b. `document.styleSheets[n].enabled = true;`

   c. `document.styleSheets[n].disabled = false;`

4. The `styleSheets` property is a property of which DOM object?

   a. `document`

   b. `document.head`

   c. `document.body`

5. What can you use to return the total number of stylesheets used on your page?

   a. `document.styleSheets.count`

   b. `document.styleSheets.size`

   c. `document.styleSheets.length`

Answers

1. b. `myElement.style.fontFamily = "verdana";`

2. a. To access the value of the `class` attribute of an element

3. c. `document.styleSheets[n].disabled = false;`

4. a. `document`

5. c. `document.styleSheets.length`

Exercises

Edit the program in Listing 16.1 to change other style properties such as font face and decoration, element borders, padding, and margins.

Change the program in Listing 16.4 so that some of the stylesheets are externally linked, rather than situated between `<style>` and `</style>` tags in the page `<head>`. Does everything work the same?

More Advanced Control of CSS

What You'll Learn in This Lesson:

▶ Some of the capabilities CSS3 brings to CSS

▶ How to use vendor-specific prefixes and extensions

▶ How to set CSS3 properties across browsers

▶ How to set CSS3 properties efficiently in JavaScript

Using CSS3, you can easily achieve plenty of cool effects without having to use lots of JavaScript code and/or external graphics applications such as Photoshop. You can create rounded borders, add shadows to boxes, use an image as a border, and more. CSS3 contains several background properties that give you more control over background elements, including multiple background images, while CSS3 gradients let you display smooth transitions between two or more specified colors. Text features include text shadows and word wrap, as well as easy use of web fonts. And CSS3 lets you easily build really cool transitions, transformations, and animations.

In this lesson you get a taste of what CSS3 can do for your web pages and see how to effectively control CSS3's capabilities using JavaScript.

Vendor-Specific Properties and Prefixes

CSS vendor prefixes are a way for the browser companies to add support for new or experimental CSS features before they become part of the formal CSS3 specification, or to implement features of a specification that hasn't yet been finalized. In due course, these prefixes usually become unnecessary because the features become fully supported via their standard CSS3 nomenclature. To make sure that your pages render as you want them to in the maximum number of browsers, though, it pays to use prefixes.

The CSS3 browser prefixes you're likely to need appear in Table 17.1.

TABLE 17.1   Vendor Prefixes for CSS3

Browser/System	Prefix
Android	-webkit-
Chrome	-webkit-
Firefox	-moz-
Internet Explorer, Microsoft Edge	-ms-
iOS	-webkit-
Opera	-o-
Safari	-webkit-

In most cases, where a prefix is necessary, you take the CSS3 property as listed in the CSS3 specification and add the relevant prefix from Table 17.1 for the browser in use. For example, later in this lesson you read about CSS3 transitions. There you see that, if you want to add a CSS3 transition to your page, you use the transition property with the prefixes added first:

```
-webkit-transition: background 0.5s ease;
-moz-transition: background 0.5s ease;
-o-transition: background 0.5s ease;
transition: background 0.5s ease;
```

The user's browser will respond to whichever version of the transition feature it understands, ignoring the rest.

Thankfully, browser manufacturers are working hard at fully implementing all the CSS3 features, and for most modern browsers, the number of properties requiring a prefix is falling quickly.

TIP

Browser Features

There's a really useful roundup of which feature/browser combinations require a prefix at http://shouldiprefix.com/.

For a frequently updated list of which features are supported by a particular browser and version, visit www.w3schools.com/cssref/css3_browsersupport.asp.

CAUTION

Vendor-prefixed Properties Are Not Always Perfect

The prefixed version of a property might not always be exactly the same as the property as described in the CSS3 specification.

Even though vendor-specific extensions usually avoid conflicts (as each vendor has a unique prefix), please remember that such extensions may also be subject to change by the vendor, as they do not form part of the CSS3 specifications, even though they try to behave like the forthcoming CSS3 properties.

Remember, too, that the vendor-specific extensions will almost certainly fail CSS validation.

CSS3 Borders

CSS3 lets you do some really cool things with borders that were only previously possible with lots of ugly, hard-to-maintain code hacks.

In this section you look at two examples: box shadows and rounded corners.

Creating Box Shadows

The `box-shadow` property enables you to add drop shadows to your page's box elements. As Table 17.2 shows, you can separately specify values for color, size, blur, and offset.

TABLE 17.2 Parameters for the `box-shadow` **Property**

Shadow Parameter	Action
`h-shadow` (required)	The position of the horizontal shadow. Negative values are allowed.
`v-shadow` (required)	The position of the vertical shadow. Negative values are allowed.
`blur` (optional)	The blur distance.
`spread` (optional)	The size of shadow.
`color` (optional)	The color of the shadow. The default is black.

Here's an example using a 10px-wide shadow heading down and to the right, blurred across its full width, and colored mid-gray:

```
#div1 {
    background-color: #8080ff;
    width: 400px;
    height: 250px;
    box-shadow: 10px 10px 10px #808080;
    -webkit-box-shadow: 10px 10px 10px #808080;
    -moz-box-shadow: 10px 10px 10px #808080;
}
```

In Figure 17.1 you can see an example of this style applied to a `<div>` element in a web page.

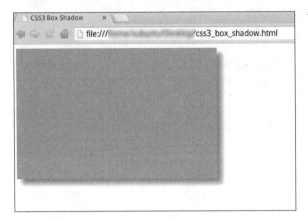

FIGURE 17.1
A CSS3 box shadow

Rounding Corners with the `border-radius` Property

The `border-radius` property enables you to add rounded corners to your page elements without the need for specially created corner images, and is perhaps one of the most popular features of CSS3.

The `border-radius` property has widespread browser support, though Mozilla Firefox required the `-moz-` prefix for a little longer than some of its rivals; therefore, if you need to support Firefox back several versions, you should consider including the prefixed version too:

```
#div1 {
    -moz-border-radius: 25px;
    border-radius: 25px;
}
```

In Figure 17.2 you can see an example of a `<div>` element styled with rounded corners.

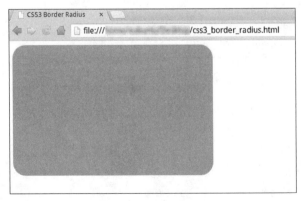

FIGURE 17.2
A CSS3 border radius

Rounded corners can be specified independently using the individual properties `border-bottom-left-radius`, `border-top-left-radius`, `border-bottom-right-radius`, and `border-top-right-radius`, or for all four corners in one statement by using the `border-radius` property, as done here.

CSS3 Backgrounds

CSS3 contains several new background properties that allow more control of the background element.

In this section you learn about the `background-size` and `background-origin` properties, as well as how to use multiple background images.

The `background-size` Property

The `background-size` property adds a new feature to CSS that allows you to set the size of your background images using lengths, percentages, or either of two keywords, `contain` or `cover`.

Specifying the background size using lengths and percentages behaves as you might expect. For each background image, two lengths or percentages can be supplied, relating to the width and height, respectively. (When you use percentages, these relate to the space available for the background, not to the width and height of the background image.)

The `auto` keyword can be used in place of either the width or the height value. If you specify only one value for `background-size`, this will be assumed to be the width. The height will then default to `auto`.

The keyword `cover` tells the browser to make the image cover the entire container, even if it has to stretch or trim the image.

Using the keyword `contain` causes the browser to always show the whole image, even if that introduces a little blank space to the sides or to the bottom of it.

Let's look at an example with the image size set as a px value:

```
#div1 {
    background-size: 400px;
    background-image: url(lake.png);
    width: 400px;
    height: 250px;
    border-radius: 25px;
}
```

Here the background width is set equal to the size of the `<div>` element (the corners are also rounded for good measure). The result is shown in Figure 17.3.

FIGURE 17.3
Setting background size in CSS3

The `background-origin` Property

The `background-origin` property is used to set how the position of a background in a box is calculated.

It takes one of three values: `padding-box`, `border-box`, or `content-box`.

When you supply a value of `padding-box`, the position is relative to the upper-left corner of the padding edge. With `border-box`, it's relative to the upper-left corner of the border, and `content-box` means the background is positioned relative to the upper-left corner of the content.

Multiple Background Images

CSS3 allows you to use multiple background images for box elements, simply by employing a comma-separated list. The order of the list is important, with the first value supplied representing the layer closest to the user, and subsequent entries in the list being rendered as layers successively further behind it. Here's an example:

```
#div1 {
    width: 600px;
    height: 350px;
    background-image: url(boat.png), url(lake.png);
    background-position: center bottom, left top;
    background-repeat: no-repeat;
}
```

Here, boat.png is a drawing of a yacht upon a transparent background, while lake.png is a photograph. In Figure 17.4 you can see the result when applied to a `<div>` element within a web page.

FIGURE 17.4
Using multiple images in CSS3 backgrounds

All the common browsers offer this feature.

CSS3 Gradients

CSS3 gradients allow you to generate smooth transitions between two or more specified colors, where previously you had to employ images to achieve these effects. With CSS3 gradients you can reduce the download time, cache memory, and bandwidth usage that these images would have cost. CSS3 gradients perform better when zoomed, too.

CSS3 offers two types of gradients: *linear gradients*, directed down/up/left/right/diagonally, and *radial gradients*, directed outward from a defined center.

Linear Gradients

To create a linear gradient in CSS3, you must define at least two colors to serve as the end points of the gradient. You can also define a starting point and a direction (that is, top to bottom, left to right, or an angle) for the gradient effect.

```
#div1 {
    width: 600px;
    height: 350px;
    background: -webkit-linear-gradient(red, #6699cc);
```

```
    background: -o-linear-gradient(red, #6699cc);
    background: -moz-linear-gradient(red, #6699cc);
    background: linear-gradient(red, #6699cc);
}
```

This example mixes the ways the colors are defined, using both color names (here red) and #rrggbb notation. It doesn't specify a direction for the gradient, so the browser will use the default top-to-bottom, as shown in Figure 17.5.

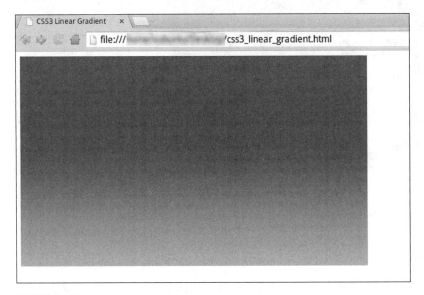

FIGURE 17.5
A CSS3 linear gradient

You can also enter a direction for the gradient; for instance, suppose you want the gradient to be directed left-to-right instead of top-to-bottom, like so:

```
background: linear-gradient(to right, red, #6699cc);
```

The following line defines a diagonal gradient:

```
background: linear-gradient(to bottom right, red, #6699cc);
```

If you want total control over the direction of the gradient, define an angle:

```
background: linear-gradient(135deg, red, #6699cc);
```

Radial Gradients

A radial gradient is defined by its center and (like its linear counterpart) must have at least two colors defined to act as end points for the gradient effect:

```
background: radial-gradient(red, #6699cc);
```

A radial gradient specified this way displays as shown in Figure 17.6.

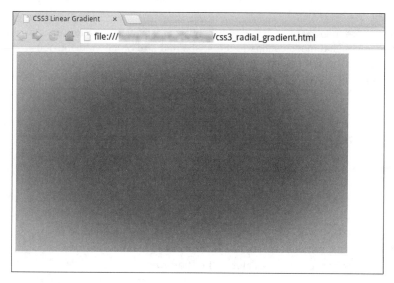

FIGURE 17.6
A CSS3 radial gradient

You can also set a location parameter for the center of the radial gradient, using the `at` keyword:

```
background: radial-gradient(at top left, red, #6699cc);
```

The result is shown in Figure 17.7.

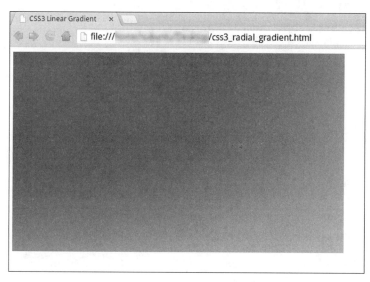

FIGURE 17.7
Moving the center of the radial gradient

TIP

CSS3 Gradients Can Do Much More

CSS3 gradients can do much more than we have space to describe here, including the use of more than two colors, transparency, and modifications to the shape and size of the gradient. You can even add multiple gradients to the same element. Full details are in the W3C documentation at www.w3.org/TR/css3-images/.

CSS3 Text Effects

CSS3 also contains some features to help you manipulate text.

Text Shadow

In CSS3, the `text-shadow` property applies shadow to text in a way almost identical to the `box-shadow` property for block elements. You specify the horizontal and vertical shadow distances and optionally the blur distance and the color of the shadow:

```
h3 {
    text-shadow: 10px 10px 3px #333;
    font-size: 26px;
}
```

You can see an example displayed in Figure 17.8.

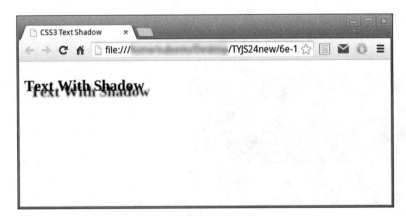

FIGURE 17.8
CSS3 text shadow

Word Wrap

If a word is too long to fit within the block element containing it, it overflows beyond its container. In CSS3, you can use the `word-wrap` property to force the text to wrap, even if has to wrap in the middle of a word:

```
p {
    word-wrap: break-word;
}
```

CSS3 Transitions, Transformations, and Animations

Traditionally, programmers have used custom JavaScript code to create movement in page elements, which can be tricky to implement in a cross-browser way. It would be better if there were easier ways to add simple effects to elements on the page.

These capabilities have been introduced in CSS3, in the form of transitions, transformations, and animations. They already have support to varying degrees in most browsers.

In the following example, we add a transition effect (in those browsers that support it) to change the background color on link hover. As the background color changes, a transition effect will smooth out the transformation.

Here's the code for the sample link:

```
<a href="somepage.html" class="trans" id="link1">Show Me</a>
```

Following are the CSS declarations showing the original and hover background colors, and the declarations used to carry out the transition effect in the various browsers. Note the range of different prefixes required for older browser versions, as discussed earlier in this lesson. The last declaration, without a prefix, is the only one required for up-to-date versions of most modern browsers.

```
a.trans {
    background: #669999;
    -webkit-transition: background 0.5s ease;
    -moz-transition: background 0.5s ease;
    -o-transition: background 0.5s ease;
    transition: background 0.5s ease;
}
a.trans:hover {
    background: #999966;
}
```

NOTE

A Useful Online Reference

You can find comprehensive information about CSS3 transitions, transformations, and animations at http://css3.bradshawenterprises.com/all/.

How to Reference CSS3 Properties in JavaScript

The combination of CSS3 and JavaScript promises some great effects with slick performance, high reliability, and minimum code complexity. In this section you look at some ways to get and set CSS3 properties successfully from within your JavaScript code.

How to Convert CSS Property Names to JavaScript

As you learned in Lesson 16, "Manipulating CSS in JavaScript," to make the names of CSS properties compatible with JavaScript naming conventions, CSS property names need a small conversion from the format they have in stylesheets.

Instead of using lowercase names and hyphens as they do in CSS, the JavaScript versions have the hyphens removed and the following characters capitalized. Hence, `border-radius` becomes `borderRadius`. Property names having no hyphens, such as `width`, are unchanged.

You saw in Lesson 16 how to access element style properties using this naming convention along with the DOM `style` property:

```
var bRad = document.getElementById("div1").style.borderRadius;
```

As you saw in that lesson, while this capability can be useful, it is limited to elements with inline styles; for elements with CSS declarations grouped in `<style>` elements in the page head or in external files, it won't work. Luckily, there's a better way, which we discuss next.

The DOM `getComputedStyle()` Method

Nowadays nearly all browsers support the DOM `getComputedStyle()` method, which accesses the final (that is, computed) style of an element. By final style, we mean the style in which the browser finally displays the element after applying (in their appropriate order) all the styling rules relevant to that element, whether they are inline, external, or inherited from container elements.

NOTE

How Multiple CSS Rules Are Applied

The final style for a page element can be specified in multiple places, such as in multiple stylesheets, which can interact in complex ways. Deciding the order in which multiple style rules are applied is too complex to cover here. You can find a detailed article on the subject at https://developer.mozilla.org/en-US/docs/Learn/CSS/Introduction_to_CSS/Cascade_and_inheritance.

The `getComputedStyle()` method returns an object having various methods, including `getPropertyValue(property)`, which returns the current value for the given CSS property name:

```
var myDiv = document.getElementById("div1");
var bRad = getComputedStyle(myDiv).getPropertyValue("borderRadius");
```

TRY IT YOURSELF ▼

Controlling Lighting Effects

Let's create a small application to use `box-shadow` and `radial-gradient`, both controlled by JavaScript, to control lighting effects in a simple HTML page. To do so, look at the code shown in Listing 17.1.

LISTING 17.1   Controlling CSS3 Effects

```
<!DOCTYPE html>
<html>
<head>
    <title>Controlling CSS3 Effects</title>
    <style>
        #div1 {
            width: 600px;
            height: 350px;
            background-color: #6699cc;
        }
        #div2 {
            background-color: #aaaaff;
            width: 80px;
            height: 80px;
            padding: 20px;
            position: relative;
            left: 240px;
            top: 105px;
        }
    </style>
```

```
<script>
    window.onload = function() {
        document.getElementById("btn1").onclick = function() {
            document.getElementById("div1").style.background = "radial-
            ➡gradient(at top left, white, #6699cc)";
            document.getElementById("div2").style.boxShadow = "10px 10px 10px
            ➡#808080";
        }
        document.getElementById("btn2").onclick = function() {
            document.getElementById("div1").style.background = "radial-
            ➡gradient(at top right, white, #6699cc)";
            document.getElementById("div2").style.boxShadow = "-10px 10px 10px
            ➡#808080";
        }
        document.getElementById("btn3").onclick = function() {
            document.getElementById("div1").style.background = "radial-
            ➡ gradient(at bottom, white, #6699cc)";
            document.getElementById("div2").style.boxShadow = "0px -10px 10px
            ➡#808080";
        }
    }
</script>
</head>
<body>
    <div id="div1">
        <div id="div2">
            LIGHTS:<br/>
            <input type="button" id="btn1" value="Top Left"><br/>
            <input type="button" id="btn2" value="Top Right"><br/>
            <input type="button" id="btn3" value="Bottom">
        </div>
    </div>
</body>
</html>
```

First, look at the `<body>` section of the page. This simple section contains just two nested `<div>` elements, the inner one containing three buttons, labeled Top Left, Top Right, and Bottom, respectively.

Returning to the `<head>` section of the page, you can see that the `window.onload` event causes the attachment of an `onclick` event handler to each of these buttons. In each case, the event handler changes the gradient of the outer `<div>` element's background and the direction of the `box-shadow` style of the inner `<div>` element. The combined effect is to simulate a light source emanating from one of three directions.

You can see the page in action in Figure 17.9.

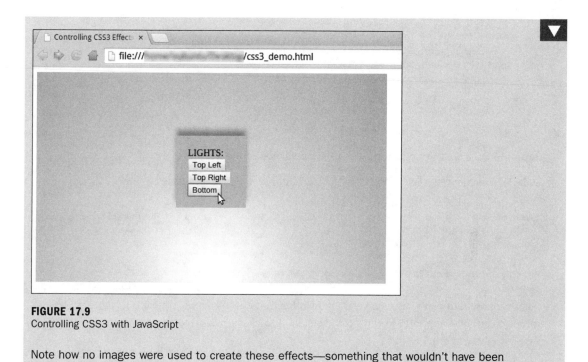

FIGURE 17.9
Controlling CSS3 with JavaScript

Note how no images were used to create these effects—something that wouldn't have been possible prior to CSS3.

How to Set CSS3 Properties with Vendor Prefixes

So you've seen how to get a CSS property, but how can you *set* a CSS3 property using JavaScript when different browsers support different variations of the property (that is, having different prefixes)?

When a browser supports a particular CSS property, it returns a string value when you request the property from a page element. (This is an empty string if the property has not yet been set.) If your browser doesn't support the property, the value undefined is returned instead. So you can easily carry out a test before setting a CSS3 property to determine which variant of the property is supported.

Let's write code that accepts an array of potential CSS3 properties and returns the one supported by the browser:

```
function getCss3Property(properties){
    // loop through all possible property names
```

```
for (var i=0; i<properties.length; i++) {
    // if the property exists for this element
    if (properties[i] in document.documentElement.style) {
        // return the associated string
        return properties[i];
    }
}
}
```

With this code, you can return the appropriate version of the feature.

Now let's see how that might work for the transition used earlier in this lesson:

```
//get the correct CSS3 transition property
var myTrans = getCss3Property(['transition', 'MozTransition', 'WebkitTransition',
'msTransition', 'OTransition'])

//set CSS transition for "link1"
document.getElementById("link1").style[myTrans] = "background 0.5s ease" ;
```

Let's suppose that you're using a version of Firefox that doesn't support the CSS3 transition property but does support Mozilla's own version, MozTransition (corresponding to -moz-transition).

When called, the getCss3Property() function begins to loop through the list of transition properties corresponding to the various vendor types. Having returned a value of undefined for the property transition (because the browser does not support it), it will, on the following trip through the loop, exit the function, returning a string value of MozTransition. You now know which version of the property to set in the following line of code.

Summary

In this lesson you learned about some of the capabilities that CSS3 brings to web design. You saw how different browser manufacturers implement new or experimental CSS3 features via custom prefixes and saw how you can access and set these custom features using JavaScript.

Q&A

Q. What browsers currently support CSS3 transitions, transforms, and animations?

A. 3D transforms are supported natively in up-to-date versions of all the popular browsers, though earlier versions may need vendor-specific prefixes. See www.w3schools.com/css/css3_3dtransforms.asp for detailed information. Most of these effects degrade sensibly, so a user having a browser without support will still be okay but will see the page elements without animation. 2D transforms are available in all popular current browsers.

Q. **Why do several different browser vendors use the** `-webkit-` **prefix?**

A. WebKit is a layout engine used for rendering web pages in web browsers. The webkit engine is the basis of a number of popular browsers, including Safari, Chrome/Chromium, and various other browsers for both desktop and mobile platforms.

Workshop

Quiz questions and exercises to test your understanding and to stretch your skills.

Quiz

1. Which of the following will correctly specify a linear gradient from lower left to upper right?

   a. `linear-gradient(upper right, #112244 , #6699cc);`

   b. `linear-gradient(top right, #112244 , #6699cc);`

   c. `linear-gradient(to top right, #112244 , #6699cc);`

2. How would you reference the `text-shadow` property in JavaScript?

   a. `textShadow`

   b. `text-Shadow`

   c. `text-shadow`

3. Which of the following would correctly render multiple background images with image cactus.png visible in front of image desert.jpg?

   a. `background-image: cactus.png, desert.jpg`

   b. `background-image: url(cactus.png), url(desert.jpg);`

   c. `background-image: url(desert.jpg), url(cactus.png);`

4. Word wrapping in CSS3 can be achieved using what property?

   a. `word-wrap`

   b. `wrap`

   c. `word-wrapping`

5. The `getComputedStyle()` method calculates how an element will be displayed based on

   a. Just inline styles

   b. Just inline and external styles

   c. Inline styles, external styles, and styles inherited from container elements

TIP

Register Your Book

Just a reminder for those of you reading these words in the print or e-book edition of this book: If you go to www.informit.com/register and register this book (using ISBN 978-0-672-33809-0), you can receive free access to an online Web Edition that not only contains the complete text of this book but also features an interactive version of this quiz.

Answers

1. c. `linear-gradient(to top right, #112244 , #6699cc);`

2. a. `textShadow`

3. b. `background-image: url(cactus.png), url(desert.jpg);`

4. a. `word-wrap`

5. c. Inline styles, external styles, and styles inherited from container elements

Exercises

Using the individual properties `border-bottom-left-radius`, `border-top-left-radius`, `border-bottom-right-radius`, and `border-top-right-radius`, use JavaScript to style a `<div>` element to be appear elliptical in shape. (Hint: Set the radius sizes such that all of the element's border is within the radius of exactly one corner.)

In this lesson's "Try It Yourself" section, the box shadow direction was set manually, while you were writing the code, to be appropriate to the simulated lighting direction. Can you write a function in JavaScript to set the shadow properties based on the detected value of the background gradient?

Reading and Writing Cookies

What You'll Learn in This Lesson:

▶ What cookies are

▶ All about cookie attributes

▶ How to set and retrieve cookies

▶ About cookie expiration dates

▶ How to save multiple data items in a single cookie

▶ How to delete cookies

▶ How to escape and unescape data

▶ Limitations of cookies

Something that the JavaScript techniques that you have seen so far can't do is transfer information from one page to another. Cookies provide a convenient way to give your web pages the means to store and retrieve small pieces of information on a user's own computer, allowing your website to save details such as a user's preferences or dates of her prior visits to your site.

In this lesson you learn how to create, save, retrieve, and delete cookies using JavaScript.

What Are Cookies?

The HTTP protocol that you use to load web pages into your browser is a so-called *stateless* protocol. This means that once the server has delivered the requested page to your browser, it considers the transaction complete and retains no memory of it. This makes it difficult to maintain certain sorts of continuity during a browsing session (or between one session and the next) such as keeping track of which information the visitor has already read or downloaded, or of his login status to a private area of the site.

Cookies are a way to get around this problem; you could, for example, use cookies to remember a user's last visit, save a list of that user's preferences, or keep track of shopping cart items while he continues to shop. Correctly used, cookies can help improve the experience perceived by the user while using your site.

The cookies themselves are small strings of information that can be stored on a user's computer by the web pages she visits, to be later read by any other web pages from within the correct domain and path. Cookies are set to expire after a specified length of time.

CAUTION

Cookies

Be aware that many users do not allow websites to leave cookies on their computers, so be sure not to make your websites depend on them.

The usual reason is that some websites use cookies as part of advertising systems, using them to track users' online activities with a view to selecting appropriate advertisements. It may be advisable to show an explanation of why you are going to use the cookie and what you'll use it for.

Limitations of Cookies

Your browser may have a limit to how many cookies it can store—normally a few hundred cookies or more. Usually, 20 cookies per domain name are permitted. A total of 4KB of cookie information can be stored for an individual domain.

In addition to the potential problems created by these size limitations, cookies can also vanish from a hard disk for various reasons, such as the cookie's expiry date being reached or the user clearing cookie information or switching browsers. Cookies should therefore never be used to store critical data, and your code should always be written to cope with situations where an expected cookie cannot be retrieved.

Using the `document.cookie` Property

Cookies in JavaScript are stored and retrieved by using the `cookie` property of the `document` object.

Each cookie is essentially a text string consisting of a name and a value pair, like this:

```
username=sam
```

When a web page is loaded into your browser, the browser marshals all the cookies available to that page into a single string-like property, which is available as `document.cookie`. Within `document.cookie`, the individual cookies are separated by semicolons:

```
username=sam;location=USA;status=fullmember;
```

TIP

A Cookie Isn't a Real String

I refer to `document.cookie` as a *string-like* property, because it isn't really a string; it just behaves like one when you're trying to extract cookie information, as you see during this lesson.

How to Escape and Unescape Data

Cookie values may not include certain characters. Those disallowed include semicolons, commas, and whitespace characters such as space and tab. Before storing data to a cookie, you need to encode the data in such a way that it will be stored correctly.

You can use the JavaScript `escape()` function to encode a value before storing it, and the corresponding `unescape()` function to later recover the original cookie value.

The `escape()` function converts any non-ASCII character in the string to its equivalent two- or four-digit hexadecimal format, so a blank space is converted into `%20` and the ampersand character (&) to `%26`.

For example, the following code snippet writes out the original string saved in variable `str` followed by its value after applying the `escape()` function:

```
var str = 'Here is a (short) piece of text.';
document.write(str + '<br />' + escape(str));
```

The output to the screen would be

```
Here is a (short) piece of text.
Here%20is%20a%20%28short%29%20piece%20of%20text.
```

Notice that the spaces have been replaced by `%20`, the opening parenthesis by `%28`, and the closing parenthesis by `%29`.

All special characters, with the exception of *, @, -, _, +, ., and /, are encoded.

Reviewing Cookie Ingredients

The cookie information in `document.cookie` may look like a simple string of name and value pairs, each in the form of

```
name=value;
```

but really each cookie has certain other pieces of information associated with it, as outlined in the following sections.

NOTE

Read the Cookie Specification

The definitive specification for cookies was published in 2011 as RFC6265. You can read it at http://tools.ietf.org/html/rfc6265.

cookieName and cookieValue

The name and value visible in each `name=value` pair in the cookie string are `cookieName` and `cookieValue`, respectively.

domain

The `domain` attribute tells the browser to which domain the cookie belongs. This attribute is optional, and when not specified, its value defaults to the domain of the page setting the cookie.

The purpose of the `domain` attribute is to control cookie operation across subdomains. If the domain is set to www.example.com, then pages on a subdomain such as code.example.com cannot read the cookie. If, however, `domain` is set to example.com, then pages in code.example.com will be able to access it.

You cannot set the `domain` attribute to any domain outside the one containing your page.

path

The `path` attribute lets you specify a directory where the cookie is available. If you want the cookie to be set only for pages in directory `documents`, set the path to `/documents`. The `path` attribute is optional, the usual default path being /, in which case the cookie is valid for the whole domain.

secure

The optional and rarely used `secure` flag indicates that the browser should use SSL security when sending the cookie to the server.

expires

Each cookie has an `expires` date after which the cookie is automatically deleted. The `expires` date should be in UTC time (Greenwich Mean Time, or GMT). If no value is set for `expires`, the cookie will last only as long as the current browser session and will be automatically deleted when the browser is closed.

Writing a Cookie

To write a new cookie, you simply assign a value to `document.cookie` containing the attributes required:

```
document.cookie = "username=sam;expires=15/06/2018 00:00:00";
```

To avoid having to set the date format manually, you could do the same thing using JavaScript's `Date` object:

```
var cookieDate = new Date ( 2018, 05, 15 );
document.cookie = "username=sam;expires=" + cookieDate.toUTCString();
```

This code produces a result identical to the previous example.

TIP

Cookie Dates Use Coordinated Universal Time

Note the use of

```
cookieDate.toUTCString();
```

instead of

```
cookieDate.toString();
```

because cookie dates always need to be set in UTC time.

In practice, you should use `escape()` to ensure that no disallowed characters find their way into the cookie values:

```
var cookieDate = new Date ( 2018, 05, 15 );
var user = "Sam Jones";
document.cookie = "username=" + escape(user) + ";expires=" + cookieDate.toUTCString();
```

Writing a Function to Write a Cookie

It's fairly straightforward to write a function to write your cookie for you, leaving all the escaping and the wrangling of optional attributes to the function. The code for such a function appears in Listing 18.1.

LISTING 18.1   Function to Write a Cookie

```
function createCookie(name, value, days, path, domain, secure) {
    if (days) {
        var date = new Date();
        date.setTime(date.getTime() + (days*24*60*60*1000));
        var expires = date.toGMTString();
    }
    else var expires = "";
    cookieString = name + "=" + escape (value);
    if (expires) cookieString += "; expires=" + expires;
    if (path) cookieString += "; path=" + escape (path);
    if (domain) cookieString += "; domain=" + escape (domain);
    if (secure) cookieString += "; secure";
    document.cookie = cookieString;
}
```

The operation of the function is straightforward. The `name` and `value` arguments are assembled into a `name=value` string, after escaping the `value` part to avoid errors with any disallowed characters.

Instead of specifying a date string to the function, you are asked to pass the number of days required before expiry. The function then handles the conversion into a suitable date string.

The remaining attributes are all optional and are appended to the string only if they exist as arguments.

CAUTION

You May Need a Web Server

Your browser security may prevent you from trying out the examples in this lesson if you try simply loading the files from your local machine into your browser. To see the examples working, you may need to upload the files to a web server on the Internet or elsewhere on your local network.

▼ TRY IT YOURSELF

Writing Cookies

Let's use this function to set the values of some cookies. The code for the simple page is shown in Listing 18.2. Create a new file named testcookie.html and enter the code as listed. Feel free to use different values for the name and value pairs that you store in your cookies.

LISTING 18.2 Writing Cookies

```
<!DOCTYPE html>
<html>
    <head>
    <title>Using Cookies</title>
    <script>
        function createCookie(name, value, days, path, domain, secure) {
            if (days) {
                var date = new Date();
                date.setTime(date.getTime() + (days*24*60*60*1000));
                var expires = date.toGMTString();
            }
            else var expires = "";
            cookieString = name + "=" + escape (value);
            if (expires) cookieString += "; expires=" + expires;
            if (path) cookieString += "; path=" + escape (path);
            if (domain) cookieString += "; domain=" + escape (domain);
            if (secure) cookieString += "; secure";
            document.cookie = cookieString;
        }
        createCookie("username","Sam Jones", 5);
        createCookie("location","USA", 5);
```

```
        createCookie("status","fullmember", 5);
    </script>
</head>
<body>
    Check the cookies for this domain using your browser tools.
</body>
</html>
```

Upload this HTML file to an Internet host or a web server on your local area network, if you have one. The loaded page displays nothing but a single line of text:

```
Check the cookies for this domain using your browser tools.
```

In the Chromium browser, you can open Developer Tools using Shift+Ctrl+I. If you are using a different browser, check the documentation for how to view cookie information.

My result is shown in Figure 18.1.

TIP

New Values Are Appended

Note that each time the function is called, it sets a new value for `document.cookie`, yet this value does not overwrite the previous one; instead, it appends your new cookie to the cookie values already present. As you learned previously, `document.cookie` sometimes *appears* to act like a string, but it isn't one really.

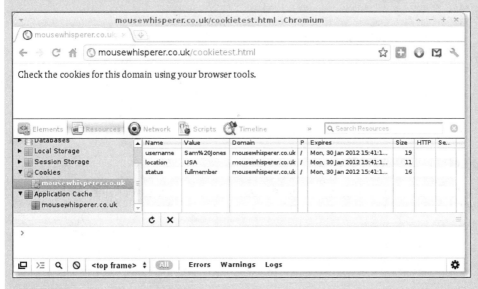

FIGURE 18.1
Displaying your cookies

Reading a Cookie

The function to read the value of a cookie relies heavily on JavaScript's `split()` string method that you learned about in Lesson 7, "Working with Character Strings." You may recall that `split()` takes a string and splits it into an array of items, using a specified character to determine where the string should be divided:

```
myString = "John#Paul#George#Ringo";
var myArray = myString.split('#');
```

The preceding statement would divide string `myString` into a series of separate parts, cutting the string at each occurrence of the hash (#) character: `myArray[0]` would contain `"John"`, `myArray[1]` would contain `"Paul"`, and so forth.

Since in `document.cookie` the individual cookies are divided by the semicolon character, this character is initially used to break up the string returned by `document.cookie`:

```
var crumbs = document.cookie.split(';');
```

You want to search for a cookie of a specific name, so the resulting array `crumbs` is next searched for any items having the appropriate `name=` part.

The `indexOf()` and `substring()` methods are combined to return the value part of the cookie, which is then returned by the function after using `unescape()` to remove any encoding:

```
function getCookie(name) {
    var nameEquals = name + "=";
    var crumbs = document.cookie.split(';');
    for (var i = 0; i < crumbs.length; i++) {
        var crumb = crumbs[i];
        if (crumb.indexOf(nameEquals) == 0) {
            return unescape(crumb.substring(nameEquals.length, crumb.length));
        }
    }
    return null;
}
```

Deleting Cookies

To delete a cookie, you just need to set it with an expiry date before the current day. The browser infers that the cookie has already expired and deletes it.

```
function deleteCookie(name) {
    createCookie(name,"",-1);
}
```

CAUTION

Check Cookies Have Been Deleted

Some versions of some browsers maintain the cookie until you restart your browser even if you
have deleted it in the script. If your program depends on the deletion definitely having happened, do
another `getCookie` test on the deleted cookie to make sure it has really gone.

TRY IT YOURSELF ▼

Using Cookies

Let's put together all you've learned so far about cookies by building some pages to test cookie
operation.

First, collect the functions `createCookie()`, `getCookie()`, and `deleteCookie()` into a single
JavaScript file and save it as cookie.js, using the code in Listing 18.3.

LISTING 18.3   cookies.js

```
function createCookie(name, value, days, path, domain, secure) {
    if (days) {
        var date = new Date();
        date.setTime( date.getTime() + (days*24*60*60*1000));
        var expires = date.toGMTString();
    }
    else var expires = "";
    cookieString = name + "=" + escape (value);
    if (expires) cookieString += "; expires=" + expires;
    if (path) cookieString += "; path=" + escape (path);
    if (domain) cookieString += "; domain=" + escape (domain);
    if (secure) cookieString += "; secure";
    document.cookie = cookieString;
}

function getCookie(name) {
    var nameEquals = name + "=";
    var crumbs = document.cookie.split(';');
    for (var i = 0; i < crumbs.length; i++) {
        var crumb = crumbs[i].trim();
        if (crumb.indexOf(nameEquals) == 0) {
            return unescape(crumb.substring(nameEquals.length, crumb.length));
        }
    }
}
```

```
        return null;
}

function deleteCookie(name) {
    createCookie(name,"",-1);
}
```

This file will be included in the `<head>` of your test pages so that the three functions are available for use by your code.

The code for the first test page, cookietest.html, is listed in Listing 18.4, and that for a second test page, cookietest2.html, in Listing 18.5. Create both of these pages in your text editor.

LISTING 18.4   cookietest.html

```html
<!DOCTYPE html>
<html>
<head>
    <title>Cookie Testing</title>
    <script src="cookies.js"></script>
    <script>
        window.onload = function() {
            var cookievalue = prompt("Cookie Value:");
            createCookie("myCookieData", cookievalue);
        }
    </script>
</head>
<body>
    <a href="cookietest2.html">Go to Cookie Test Page 2</a>
</body>
</html>
```

LISTING 18.5   cookietest2.html

```html
<!DOCTYPE html>
<html>
<head>
    <title>Cookie Testing</title>
    <script src="cookies.js"></script>
    <script>
        window.onload = function() {
            document.getElementById("output").innerHTML = "Your cookie value: " +
            ➥getCookie("myCookieData");
        }
```

```
        </script>
</head>
<body>
    <a href="cookietest.html">Back to Cookie Test Page 1</a><br/>
    <div id="output"></div>
</body>
</html>
```

The only visible page content in cookietest.html is a link to the second page, cookietest2.html. However, the `window.onload` event is captured by the code on the page and used to execute a function that launches a `prompt()` dialog as soon as the page has finished loading. The dialog asks you for a value to be saved to your cookie, and then calls `createCookie()` to set a cookie of name `myCookieData` with the value that you just entered.

The page cookietest.html is shown working in Figure 18.2.

FIGURE 18.2
Entering a value for your cookie

After setting your cookie, use the link to navigate to cookietest2.html.

When this page loads, the `window.onload` event handler executes a function that retrieves the stored cookie value using `getCookie()` and writes it to the page, as shown in Figure 18.3.

FIGURE 18.3
Retrieving the value of your cookie

To try it out for yourself, you need to upload the files cookietest.html, cookietest2.html, and cookies.js to a web server on the Internet (or one on your local network, if you have one) because browser security will probably prevent you from setting cookies when using the `file://` protocol to view a file on your own computer.

Setting Multiple Values in a Single Cookie

Each cookie contains one `name=value` pair, so if you need to store several separate pieces of data such as a user's name, age, and membership number, you need three different cookies.

However, with a little ingenuity, you can make your cookie store all three values by concatenating the required values into a single string, which becomes the value stored by your cookie.

This way, instead of having three separate cookies for name, age, and membership number, you could have just one, perhaps named `user`, containing all three pieces of data. To separate the details later, you place in your value string a special character called a *delimiter* to separate the different pieces of data:

```
var userdata = "Sandy|26|A23679";
createCookie("user", userdata);
```

Here the | (pipe) character acts as the delimiter. When you later retrieve the cookie value, you can split it into its separate variable values by using the | delimiter:

```
var myUser = getCookie("user");
var myUserArray = myUser.split('|');
```

```
var name = myUserArray[0];
var age = myUserArray[1];
var memNo = myUserArray[2];
```

Cookies that store multiple values use up fewer of the 20 cookies per domain allowed by some browsers, but remember that your use of cookies is still subject to the 4KB overall limit for cookie information.

NOTE

Serialization of Data

This is a further example of serialization, which you learned about in Lesson 14, "Meet JSON."

Summary

In this lesson you learned about cookies, and how to set, retrieve, and delete them using JavaScript. You also learned how to concatenate multiple values into a single cookie.

Q&A

Q. When concatenating multiple values into a single cookie, can you use any character as a delimiter?

A. You can't use any character that might appear in your escaped data (except as the delimiter character), nor can you use equal (=) or the semicolon (;) because they are used to assemble and concatenate the `name=value` pairs in `document.cookie`. Additionally, cookies may not include whitespace or commas, so naturally they cannot be used as delimiters either.

Q. Are cookies safe?

A. Questions are often raised over the security of cookies, but such fears are largely unfounded. Cookies *can* help website owners and advertisers track your browsing habits, and they can (and do) use such information to select advertisements and promotions to show on web pages that you visit. Website owners and advertisers can't, however, find out personal information about you or access other items on your hard disk simply through the use of cookies.

Workshop

Quiz questions and exercises to test your understanding and to stretch your skills.

Quiz

1. Cookies are small pieces of text information stored

   a. On a user's hard disk

   b. On the server

   c. At the user's Internet service provider

2. What can you use to encode a string to store it safely in a cookie?

   a. `escape()`

   b. `unescape()`

   c. `split()`

3. What is a character used to separate multiple values in a single cookie known as?

   a. An escape sequence

   b. A delimiter

   c. A semicolon

4. How much cookie information can be stored for a single domain?

   a. 400 bytes

   b. 4 kilobytes

   c. 40 kilobytes

5. Which of these object properties is used to store and retrieve cookie information?

   a. `document.cookie`

   b. `window.cookie`

   c. `navigator.cookie`

TIP

Register Your Book

Just a reminder for those of you reading these words in the print or e-book edition of this book: If you go to www.informit.com/register and register this book (using ISBN 978-0-672-33809-0), you can receive free access to an online Web Edition that not only contains the complete text of this book but also features an interactive version of this quiz.

Answers

1. a. Cookies are stored on a user's hard disk.

2. a. You can use `escape()` to safely encode string values for storage in a cookie.

3. b. Multiple values are separated by a character called a delimiter.

4. b. 4 kilobytes

5. a. `document.cookie`

Exercises

Find out how to view cookie information in your favorite browser. Use the browser tools to examine the cookie set by the code in Listing 18.4.

Rewrite the code for cookietest.html and cookietest2.html to write multiple values to the same cookie and separate them on retrieval, displaying the values on separate lines. Use the hash character (#) as your delimiter.

Add a button to cookietest2.html to delete the cookie set in cookietest.html and check that it works as requested. (Hint: Use the button to call `deleteCookie()`.)

Matching Patterns Using Regular Expressions

What You'll Learn in This Lesson:

▶ What is meant by the term *regular expression*

▶ What regular expressions can do

▶ How to work with regular expression literals and special characters

▶ How to use the `RegExp` object

▶ How to use regular expression methods

▶ Ways of using regular expressions to process strings

In Lesson 7, "Working with Character Strings," you learned how to manipulate strings in various ways using JavaScript's string methods. Sometimes, though, you need a way to apply a more rigorous or detailed pattern match against a piece of text. That's where regular expressions come into play.

TIP

Regular Expression and Regex Mean the Same Thing

The shorter term **regex** is often used instead of **regular expression**, especially in speech or other informal communications. I use both terms in the course of this lesson, but they mean the same thing.

A regular expression is a special character string used to describe a search pattern. Such a pattern can be used in your programs to find, replace, or otherwise manage character strings appearing in blocks of text.

There are countless situations where regular expressions can help you. Some common examples include

▶ Verifying the format of user-inputted data such as email addresses, telephone numbers, or zip/postal codes

▶ Finding and updating a URL appearing multiple times in an article

▶ Manipulating particular tags and attributes in HTML source code

In this lesson you learn how to construct regular expressions and try some practical examples of using them in your scripts.

The syntax of regular expressions can seem a little overwhelming at first, but we take it step by step. Let's get to it.

NOTE

Many Languages Support Regular Expressions

Regular expressions are not used uniquely by JavaScript. Many other computer languages support them, though the details of the implementation vary slightly from language to language.

Creating a Regular Expression

JavaScript has two ways to make a regular expression. You can do so via a string literal or via JavaScript's `RegExp` object.

Using Regular Expression String Literals

Regular expressions are sequences of characters that JavaScript interprets as search patterns to apply to the text being examined.

Here's an example of such a pattern, created as a so-called *regular expression string literal*:

```
var myRegExp = /FooBar/;
```

This expression is similar to the declaration of a string, as you first saw in Lesson 7, but notice that here the expression is contained between forward slashes, rather than quotes.

This pattern is one of the simplest regular expressions you could create, and it is used simply to match the string `FooBar` exactly. Before going any further, let's see how you might use it in a snippet of JavaScript code (assuming that the text to be examined is contained in a `<div>` element having an ID of `"txt"`):

```
var myRegExp = /FooBar/; //regular expression matching the exact pattern FooBar
if (document.getElementById("txt").value.search(myRegExp) == -1) {
        //if no match found
        alert("The string 'FooBar' was not found");
    } else {
        // if match found
        alert("The string 'FooBar' occurs in the text");
    }
```

So far, so good. But what if you want to match regardless of case, so that you find not only `FooBar` but `foobar`, `FOOBAR`, or `fooBar`? In that case (no pun intended), you can add the character `i` after the end of the string literal:

```
var myRegExp = /FooBar/i;
```

The regex will now search for the pattern and match it regardless of case.

The character `i` in this example is known as a *modifier*. Table 19.1 lists the available modifiers:

TABLE 19.1   **Regular Expression Modifiers**

Modifier	Description
i	Perform case-insensitive matching
g	Perform a global match (find all occurring matches rather than terminating at the first)
m	Perform multiline matching

TIP

Flags

Another commonly used name for modifiers is **flags**.

Here is an example using the `g` modifier to find all matches of a given string. The matches are returned as an array. In this example the regex search is wrapped up in a little function:

```
var str = "Stupid is as stupid does";
function mySearch(input) {
    var pattern = /stupid/gi;
    return input.match(pattern);
}
var output = mySearch(str);
```

Notice that the string literal now has two modifiers—`i` (match regardless of case) and `g` (match globally, that is, return all matches). In this case, the function would return the array

```
["Stupid", "stupid"]
```

which would be stored in the variable `output`.

To allow the regex to search for *ranges* of characters, you can use brackets within the string literal. For example, to find instances of *hubble* or *bubble* within a piece of text, you could use

```
var pattern = /[hb]ubble/gi;
```

Table 19.2 lists examples showing how you can use brackets to find ranges of characters.

TABLE 19.2   Using Brackets to Find a Range of Characters

Expression	Finds
[abcd]	Any character specified between the brackets
[^abcd]	Any character NOT specified between the brackets
[0-9]	Any numeral specified between the brackets
[^0-9]	Any numeral NOT specified between the brackets
(a|b)	Any of the specified alternatives

Note that you can enter ranges in addition to specific characters, so, for instance,

```
[0-9]
```

is equivalent to

```
[0123456789]
```

In the same way, the expression

```
[a-z]
```

matches any lowercase letter of the alphabet.

Definitions can be grouped together within the square brackets, so that

```
[a-zA-Z]
```

would match any upper- or lowercase letter.

CAUTION

Mind Your Language!

The expression [a-z] actually matches all lowercase letters in the **English** alphabet. If you are using another language that employs further characters—ones with accents, for example—you need to add them into your expression.

Note the last line in Table 19.2. Another way of selecting either *hubble* or *bubble* would be to use the following string literal:

```
var pattern = /(hubble|bubble)/gi;
```

Regular expressions also have a shorthand for dealing with special characters known as *metacharacters*. Table 19.3 lists metacharacters and their meanings.

TABLE 19.3   Regular Expression Metacharacters

Metacharacter	Finds
.	A single character, except a new line or line terminator
\w	A word character
\W	A nonword character
\d	A digit
\D	A nondigit character
\s	A whitespace character
\S	A nonwhitespace character
\b	A match at the beginning or end of a word
\B	A match not at the beginning or end of a word
\0	A null character
\n	A new line character
\f	A form-feed character
\r	A carriage return character
\t	A tab character
\v	A vertical tab character
\xxx	The character specified by an octal number xxx
\xdd	The character specified by a hexadecimal number dd
\uxxxx	The Unicode character specified by a hexadecimal number xxxx

Once again there is some duplication here with examples we've already seen; for example, the metacharacter \d meaning "a digit" is exactly equivalent to the expression [0-9].

NOTE

Word Characters

Table 19.3 makes reference to "word" characters. This set of characters consists of the alphabet in both upper- and lowercase, decimal digits, and the underscore character. It is therefore equivalent to the expression [a-zA-Z0-9_]

Take a look at this regex string literal:

```
var pattern = /\W/;
```

This pattern would seek out any characters in the target text that are NOT word characters.

For example, it would find the character % within this string:

```
"75% of people questioned"
```

Regular expression literals can also contain so-called *quantifiers*. These shorthand expressions define the number of occurrences of a pattern and/or the location in the target text where the pattern is found. Table 19.4 lists some examples.

TABLE 19.4   Regular Expression Quantifiers

Quantifier	Matches
$n+$	Any string containing at least one n
$n*$	Any string containing zero or more occurrences of n
$n?$	Any string containing zero or one occurrence of n
$n\{X\}$	Any string containing a sequence of X n's
$n\{X, Y\}$	Any string containing a sequence of X to Y n's
$n\{X, \}$	Any string containing a sequence of at least X n's
$n\$$	Any string with n at the end
$\wedge n$	Any string with n at the beginning
$?=n$	Any string that is followed by a string n
$?!n$	Any string that is not followed by a string n

Let's use metacharacters and quantifiers to find whitespace at the start of a string using a regex:

```
var pattern = /^[\s]+/;
```

Here the caret character ^ is used as a quantifier to indicate that you are looking for something only at the beginning of the target string. The expression [\s] indicates that you're looking for whitespace characters. Finally, the + character indicates that you don't care how many whitespace characters are found at this position (so long as there's at least one); you want to match to them all. (Later in the lesson you see how you can not only find such whitespace but also remove it, if that's what you need to do.)

TIP

Use an Online Tester

A quick and easy way to test your prototype regular expression is through one of the many online testing tools, such as the example at www.regextester.com/.

Regular string literals offer the best performance when you are using regular expressions that don't change while a script is running. Sometimes, though, your script or its users will want to define new patterns while the script is running. In that case it's usually easier to use the RegExp object instead.

Using the JavaScript RegExp Object

JavaScript's RegExp object is instantiated just like any other object, as you first saw in Lesson 11, "Introducing Object-Oriented Programming":

```
var myPattern = new RegExp("Foobar");
```

In this case the regular expression string is passed to the object constructor as a parameter. Note that you no longer need to enclose the pattern between forward slashes.

Using test() and exec()

The RegExp object's test() and exec() methods can be used to perform searches using your newly created object.

Here's how the test() method might be used to perform a regex search:

```
var myString = "The boy stood on the burning deck";
var myPattern = new RegExp("boy");
var result = myPattern.test(myString);
```

Since there is an occurrence of *boy* in myString, the value returned to the variable result will be true.

The test() method always returns a result of Boolean true or false, depending on whether or not the test was successful.

The exec() method tests for a match in a string, returning an array of information about the matched text if successful; otherwise, it returns null.

```
var myString = "The boy stood on the burning deck";
var myPattern = new RegExp("boy");
var result = myPattern.exec(myString);
```

Since there is an occurrence of *boy* in myString, the variable result will contain an array:

```
["boy", index: 4, input: "The boy stood on the burning deck"]
```

TIP

Use exec() on String Literals

You can also use exec() without explicitly creating a RegExp object:

```
var result = /boy/.exec("The boy stood on the burning deck");
console.log(result[0]);
```

This logs a message containing "boy".

Using String Methods with Regular Expressions

Back in Lesson 7 you learned about many of the methods associated with JavaScript's `string` object.

Some of these string methods can use regular expressions directly to perform their tasks. Table 19.5 lists these methods.

TABLE 19.5 String Methods Using Regular Expressions

Quantifier	Description
match	Searches the string for occurrences matching the regular expression. Returns an array containing information about matches found, or `null` if there are none.
search	Tests for a match in the string and returns the index of the match, or −1 if there are none.
replace	Searches for a match in the string and replaces the match with a specified alternative string.
split	Breaks a string into an array of substrings based on the regular expression.

Using your browser's JavaScript console, you can try some of these for yourself.

▼ TRY IT YOURSELF

Regular Expressions Using String Methods

Let's look at a few examples.

In the first, let's use the `match()` method to select only the numeric data from a string, returning the result as an array:

```
var myString="John has 7 apples and Diane has 5"
var outString = myString.match(/\d+/g) // outString will contain the array [7,5]
```

Open your browser's JavaScript console. I use the Chrome browser, so for me the key combination is Ctrl+Shift+I.

At the console prompt, enter the following line and press Enter:

```
var myString="John has 7 apples and Diane has 5"
```

If all goes well, the console will return `undefined` (because the statement does not return a value).

Now enter the statement

```
myString.match(/\d+/g)
```

and the console should respond with the result of the regex match, as mine has in Figure 19.1.

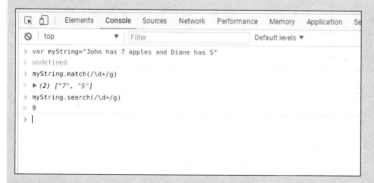

FIGURE 19.1
A regex match performed in the JavaScript console

If you use the `search()` method in place of `match()`, the method returns the index (that is, the location in the string) of the first match found:

```
var myString="John has 7 apples and Diane has 5"
var outString = myString.search(/\d+/g) // outString will contain the value '9'
```

Once again, you can test this in the console. The test string has already been saved in the variable `myString`, so you only need to enter the expression

```
myString.search(/\d+/g)
```

The console should respond with the answer 9, as in Figure 19.2.

FIGURE 19.2
A regex search performed in the JavaScript console

Now let's try the `split()` method. In this case you want to not only split the string at every occurrence of a semicolon but also remove any whitespace from around the numbers:

```
var myString="1  ;2; 3;4;  5"
var outString = myString.split(/\s*;\s*/) // outString contains
["1","2","3","4","5"]
```

This time you enter a new string to work with, so at the console prompt, enter the following and press Enter:

```
var myString="1  ;2; 3;4;  5"
```

The console should once again respond with `undefined`.

Finally, enter the expression

```
myString.split(/\s*;\s*/)
```

Now the console should respond with the correct result, as shown in Figure 19.3.

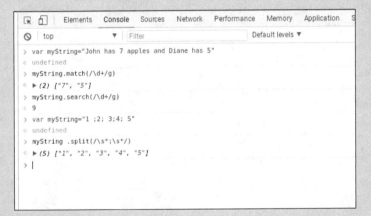

FIGURE 19.3
A regex string split performed in the JavaScript console

The simplest syntax for using the `replace()` method on a string `myString` is

```
var newstring = myString.replace(regexp, replacement_string);
```

Note that when this statement executes, it leaves the original string `myString` unchanged and returns a new string containing replacement substrings for any matches found.

Let's turn one more time to the console and enter the following:

```
var myString = "Stupid is as stupid does";
```

Now you can use the `replace()` method to replace some of the string:

```
myString.replace(/stupid/ig, "cupid");
```

The console output is shown in Figure 19.4. On the last line you can see the original string `myString` displayed once more, demonstrating how it remains unchanged by the `replace()` operation.

```
  Elements   Console   Sources   Network   Performance   Memory   Application
  top              ▼   Filter                Default levels ▼
> var myString = "Stupid is as stupid does";
< undefined
> myString.replace(/stupid/ig, "cupid");
< "cupid is as cupid does"
> myString
< "Stupid is as stupid does"
> |
```

FIGURE 19.4
A regex string replace performed in the JavaScript console

Experiment using different test strings with various string methods and regex patterns of your own.

To remove unwanted substrings, you can simply use `replace()` with an empty string as the replacement string. For example, earlier in the lesson you used the following pattern to find whitespace at the beginning of a string:

```
var pattern = /^[\s]+/;
```

The following code snippet will not only find but also remove any such whitespace in the string `myString`:

```
myString = myString.replace(pattern, "");
```

To remove whitespace from both the beginning and end of the string just requires a small change to the regex pattern:

```
var pattern = /^\s+|\s+$/g;
```

Using `replace()` with a Function as a Parameter

A cool capability of the `replace()` method is to accept a function instead of a string as the second parameter. After the match has been performed, the function will be called once for each match found, and the function's return value will then be used as the replacement string.

For example, suppose you want to edit a passage of text so it refers to temperatures in degrees Fahrenheit rather than its current references to degrees Celsius. To convert between the two, you can write a simple function to operate on each match:

```
function CtoF(match) {
    return ((match * 9) /5 ) + 32;
}
```

Now let's use this function as a parameter in a `replace()` operation.

```
var myString = "for temperatures between 5 and 65 degrees";
myString = myString.replace(/\d+/g, CtoF);
```

Each match found by the regex will be passed to the function `CtoF` as parameter `match`.

The variable `myString` will afterward contain the following value:

```
"for temperatures between 41 and 149 degrees"
```

Summary

In this lesson you learned the basics of using regular expressions to manipulate strings.

Generating regular expressions can be complicated and takes a lot of practice to master, but the investment is well worthwhile because their use can hugely simplify a whole host of programming tasks.

Q&A

Q. Where can I find online resources about regular expressions?

A. There are many resources online. Try MDN (https://developer.mozilla.org/en-US/docs/Web/JavaScript/Guide/Regular_Expressions) and W3 Schools (www.w3schools.com/jsref/jsref_obj_regexp.asp) as a starting point.

Q. Who invented regular expressions?

A. Regular expressions originated in the 1950s, when mathematician Stephen Cole Kleene described regular languages using his concept called *regular sets*. Regexes were subsequently used for text processing on Unix systems, and were later adopted by a wide range of computer applications and languages. So the concept predates JavaScript itself.

Workshop

Quiz questions and exercises to test your understanding and to stretch your skills.

Quiz

1. Which of these examples tests whether the first character of a string is uppercase or not?

   a. `regexp = /^[A-Z]/;`

   b. `var regexp = /[^A-Z]/;`

   c. `var regexp = /[A-Z][a-z]/;`

2. Which of the following string snippets matches `regexp /ab+c?/`?

   a. `ac`

   b. `abbb`

   c. `cab`

3. Which of the following matches strings composed entirely of letters and exactly seven characters long?

   a. `regexp = /^[a-zA-Z]{7,}$/;`

   b. `regexp = /^[a-zA-Z]{7}$/;`

   c. `regexp = /^[a-zA-Z]{6,8}$/;`

4. Which of the following could the regex `192\.168\.1\.\d{1,3}` be used for?

   a. Match any IP address

   b. Match any IP address beginning with 192 or 168

   c. Match any IP address within the range 192.168.1.0 to 192.168.1.255

5. Look at the following code snippet:

   ```
   var regexp = /^\d{2}$/;
   var myString = "29";
   alert(regex.test(myString));
   ```

   What will the alert display?

   a. `true`

   b. `1`

   c. `29`

TIP

Register Your Book

Just a reminder for those of you reading these words in the print or e-book edition of this book: If you go to www.informit.com/register and register this book (using ISBN 978-0-672-33809-0), you can receive free access to an online Web Edition that not only contains the complete text of this book but also features an interactive version of this quiz.

Answers

1. a. `regexp = /^[A-Z]/;`

2. b. `abbb`

3. b. `regexp = /^[a-zA-Z]{7}$/;`

4. c. Match any IP address within the range 192.168.1.0 to 192.168.1.255

5. a. `true`

Exercises

Write a JavaScript function using a regular expression to return the number of words in a supplied string. (Hint: Remember to strip away whitespace from the beginning and end of the string first.)

Write code to find all instances of *JavaScript* within a piece of text, irrespective of case, and replace them all with the word *JAVASCRIPT* in uppercase.

Understanding and Using Closures

If you're anything like me, then you find some concepts really tricky to understand, no matter how you approach them. You can furrow your brow, drink unwise amounts of caffeine, and read every reference the Internet can offer you, and a grasp of the matter still eludes you. Then, one day, the penny drops and you wonder how you ever *didn't* get it. For many people the concept of closures is a little bit like that.

In this lesson I try to break down closures into easy bite-size chunks. If it's still confusing, just hang in there until the penny drops.

Revisiting Scope

Lesson 3, "Introducing Functions," and Lesson 4, "More Fun with Functions," introduced the concept of a variable's *scope* and in particular how it relates to those variables declared within functions. Let's look at this snippet of code:

```
function sayHi(){
    let msg = 'Hello world!';
    console.log(msg);
}
```

Executing the function is straightforward:

```
sayHi()
```

Assuming nothing has gone wrong, `'Hello world!'` is logged to the JavaScript console. But what happens when you try to access the variable `msg` directly? If you were to try to execute

```
console.log(msg);
```

anywhere outside the function—for instance, by typing the command into the JavaScript console—JavaScript would be quick to point out your error:

```
Uncaught ReferenceError: msg is not defined
```

You'll recall from Lessons 3 and 4 that variables defined within a function in this way are only accessible within that function. This describes the so-called *scope* of the variable. When you made the call to `sayHi()`, the variable `msg` was created; when `sayHi()` completed execution, it was destroyed again.

Suppose you had written the original code like this:

```
var msg = 'Hello world!';
function sayHi(){
    console.log(msg);
}
```

In this case, the variable is declared outside the function `sayHi()` and is in *global* scope. The call to `console.log(msg)` would in this case have worked just fine, wherever you had made the call.

Returning a Function from a Function

In the preceding code, the function `sayHi()` doesn't return anything. But what if you were to ask it to return another function? Now look at this code:

```
function sayHi() {
    return function logMessage() {
        let msg = 'Hello world!';
        console.log(msg);
    }
}
```

To call `sayHi()` and then store the function it returns to a variable, you can simply write

```
var hello = sayHi();
```

When `sayHi()` is executed, the function `logMessage()` is stored in the variable `hello`. If you now execute

```
console.log(msg);
```

you'll once again simply receive a terse error, as shown in Figure 20.1.

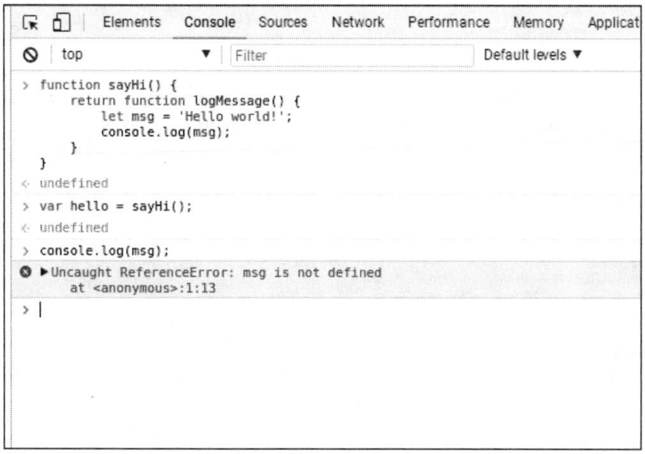

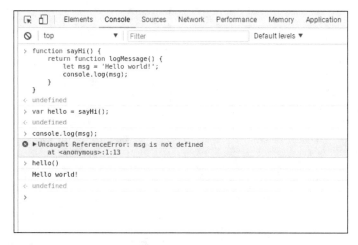

FIGURE 20.1
The variable `msg` is no longer accessible, which is what you might reasonably have expected

The variable `hello` now contains the returned function `logMessage()`. So what if you try to execute this function?

```
hello()
```

The result is shown in Figure 20.2.

FIGURE 20.2
The `hello()` function executes successfully

Success! The variable `msg` was declared inside the function, so it's still accessible, and everything is working as you would expect.

TIP

Traveling First Class

In JavaScript, functions are so-called first-class values. In other words, functions are to be passed as arguments, returned from function calls, and so forth, just like types such as strings and integers.

Achieving Closure

Now let's rewrite the code a little:

```
function sayHi() {
    let msg = 'Hello world!';
    return function logMessage() {
        console.log(msg);
    }
}
var hello = sayHi();
```

Once again the code has returned the function `logMessage()` and stored it in variable `hello`. But this time the variable `msg` was declared outside the function declaration for `logMessage()`. Rather, it was declared within the scope of the *parent* function of `logMessage()`. What will happen if you try to execute the function stored in variable `hello`? It would be reasonable to assume that the variable `msg` disappeared when `sayHi()` completed execution and that it's therefore no longer accessible by `logMessage()`. The outcome of running the command

```
hello();
```

is shown in Figure 20.3.

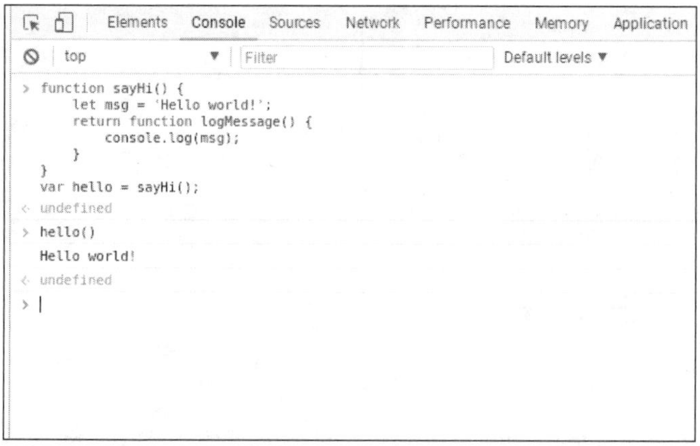

FIGURE 20.3
Running the revised `hello()` function

Whoa! What happened here? You seem to have access to the variable `msg` again!

What happened? When the function `logMessage()` was created and stored in the variable `hello`, that returned function retained access to any variables in the scope of its parent, even when the scope of the parent has closed. This is called a *closure*.

TIP

A Handy Definition for a Closure

A closure is a function that has access to the parent scope, even after that scope has closed.

Passing Parameters

Let's look at another example, this time making the closure just a little more useful. It's trivially easy to amend the string stored in variable `msg` by passing an argument to the parent function `sayHi()`, as in the following snippet:

```
function sayHi(visitor) {
    let msg = visitor + ' says: hello world!';
    return function logMessage() {
        console.log(msg);
    }
}
```

You can now pass in information, with the predictable results displayed in Figure 20.4.

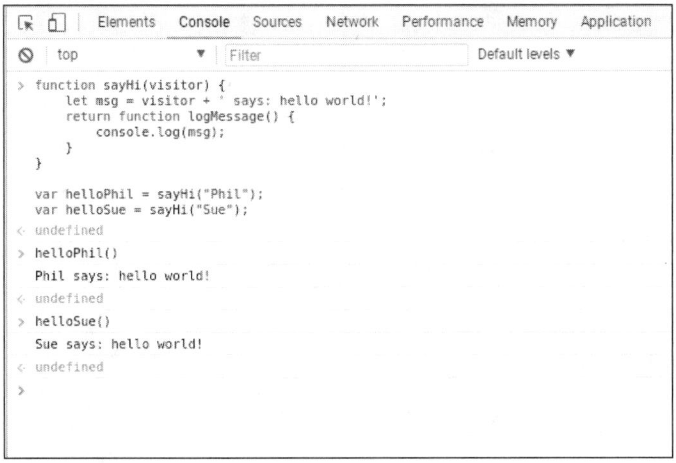

FIGURE 20.4
Passing parameters to `hello()`

Editing a Closed-over Variable

All well and good. But what if you want the returned function—the closure—to not only access the variable declared in the parent scope but also change it? Here's an example that does that by rewriting the returned function to also accept an argument:

```
function sayHi(visitor) {
    let msg = visitor + ' says: ';
    return function logMessage(extra) { // the returned function now accepts an argument
        msg = msg + extra;
        console.log(msg);
    }
}
```

You store the returned functions in the same variables as previously:

```
var helloPhil = sayHi("Phil");
var helloSue = sayHi("Sue");
```

Now the returned function can be passed a parameter that will be used to amend the value of the closed-over variable `msg`. You can see the result in Figure 20.5.

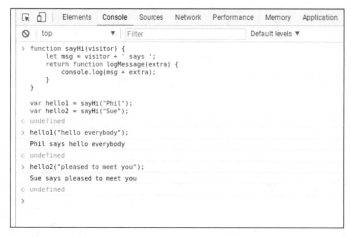

FIGURE 20.5
Passing parameters to edit a closure

Let's recap briefly what has happened here:

- ▶ The function `sayHi(visitor)` has been executed twice with different values of the parameter `visitor`.

- ▶ In each case, a returned function `logMessage()` has formed a closure over a variable `msg`, which was declared in its parent scope. Each of the two returned functions has been saved to a different variable.

▶ The two functions contained in these variables are *closures*. They each close over "their own" variable `msg` and modify the value of that variable when called with a parameter. Note that in each case the parent scope in which `msg` was declared has long since closed. The only access to the values stored in the two versions of `msg` is via the closures `helloPhil` and `helloSue`.

Let's look at another example.

TRY IT YOURSELF ▼

Building a Click Counter Using a Closure

Let's look at the code in Listing 20.1.

LISTING 20.1 A Program to Demonstrate Closures

```
<!DOCTYPE html>
<html>
<head>
    <title>Closure Tester</title>
    <script>
    function setup() {
        let counter = 0;
        console.log("Click count: " + counter);
        return function () {
            counter += 1;
            console.log("Click count: " + counter);
        }
    }

    var add = setup();

    window.onload = function() {
        document.getElementById("b1").onclick = add();
    }
    </script>
</head>
<body>
    <button id="b1" type="button">GO</button>
</body>
</html>
```

This ultra-simple HTML page contains only one button, which has an `id` attribute with value `b1`. When the page has finished loading, an `onclick` handler `add()` is applied to the button.

Take a look at the code, in particular the function `setup()`. This function is run only once, by the line

```
var add = setup();
```

The `setup()` function declares a variable `counter`, sets its value to zero, and then returns a function that is saved in variable `add`.

The key issue to understand is that the resulting function `add()` still has access to the variable `counter` that was created within the (no longer existing) parent scope of the anonymous function returned by `setup()`.

The variable `counter` is now protected by the scope of the `add()` function and can only be changed using this function.

The closure has essentially allowed the function `add()` to have its own private variable.

Save the code from Listing 20.1 into an HTML file and load it into your browser. While watching the JavaScript console, click the button a few times. You should get a result something like the one shown in Figure 20.6.

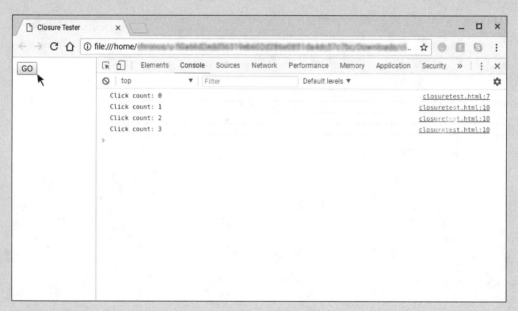

FIGURE 20.6
Counting clicks with a closure

The first logged message was created when `setup()` ran, declaring the variable `counter` and setting its value to 0.

Each subsequent message was logged by the returned function stored in variable `add`. Note how it is able to change the value of `counter`, even though that variable was created in the returned function's parent scope.

NOTE

Using Closures for Data Privacy

In JavaScript, closures are most commonly used to ensure data privacy. When you use closures this way, the enclosed variables are not accessible from an outside scope except through the intended functions.

NOTE

Closures Work Out of the Box

Functions in JavaScript exhibit closure action automatically. You don't need to do anything to enable the effect.

Closures Versus Objects

In Lesson 11, "Introducing Object-Oriented Programming," you learned how objects allow you to associate some data (the properties of the object) with one or more methods that operate on that data.

As you've already seen, closures also allow you to associate some data with a function that operates on that data. You can often use a closure where you might have decided to use an object instead. Let's use a closure from earlier in this lesson as an example:

```
// Using a closure
function sayHi(visitor) {
    let msg = visitor + ' says: hello world!';
    return function logMessage() {
        console.log(msg);
    }
}
var helloPhil = sayHi("Phil");
helloPhil() // Phil says: hello world!
```

You could have achieved similar functionality by using an object, using what you learned in Lesson 11:

```
// Using an object
function SayHi(visitor) {
    this.visitor = visitor;
    this.msg = visitor + ' says: hello world!';
}
SayHi.prototype.logMessage = function () {
    console.log(this.msg);
};
var helloPhil = new SayHi("Phil");
helloPhil.logMessage(); // Phil says: hello world!
```

In both cases the private data can only be accessed via the associated function, but in one case that data is stored in a closure; in the other it's stored as an object property.

Which approach you use depends on the situation.

Objects offer more *flexibility*. You can change the functionality or stored data of an object via statements anywhere in your source code. For example, elsewhere in your code, you may find the following:

```
SayHi.prototype.clearMessage = function () {
    this.msg = '';
};
helloPhil.clearMessage();
```

This flexibility can be a two-edged sword, however; other parts of your code can access and modify the properties of your object, maybe introducing bugs that are hard to trace.

With a closure, the only way to modify the behavior is to define the new functionality within the parent function that creates the closure. The details of the closed-over data can only be accessed via the returned function.

Summary

In this lesson, you learned about creating and using closures. The use of closures is a powerful JavaScript technique that essentially allows functions to have private variables.

After a review of function scope, you saw examples of how closures could be created and used and saw how closures compare to objects.

Finally, you employed a closure to create a counter to record user clicks of a button on a web page.

Closures can be a tricky subject for many programmers, especially those new to JavaScript, but mastery of the technique can help you write more concise and reliable code.

Q&A

Q. Are closures unique to JavaScript?

A. Not at all. The concept has been around for many years and is used in a wide variety of computer languages.

Q. At what point is a closure created?

A. A closure is created each time an outer (parent) function is called. The inner function does not need to be called for a closure to be created.

Q. Does the inner function make a copy of the enclosed variable?

A. No. Functions are assigned by reference. If the closed-over variable changes before the returned function is called, the updated (that is, latest) value will be used by the closure.

Q. Can multiple closures share the same parent scope?

A. Yes. If you define multiple functions in the same parent scope, that scope (and its associated variables) is shared among all the created closures. Here's an example:

```
function outer() {
    let count = 0;

    function increment() {
        count++;
        console.log(count);
    }

    function decrement() {
        count--;
        console.log(count);
    }

    function clear() {
        count = 0;
        console.log(count);
    }

    return {increment, decrement, clear}
}
let {increment, decrement, clear} = outer();
increment(); // logs 1
increment(); // logs 2
increment(); // logs 3
decrement(); // logs 2
clear(); // logs 0
increment(); // logs 1
```

Workshop

Quiz questions and exercises to test your understanding and to stretch your skills.

Quiz

1. Which of these statements is not a description of a closure?

   a. A closure is an inner function that has access to the variables defined in the environment of its outer function.

   b. A closure is a function that has acccss to the parent scope, even after the scope has closed.

   c. A closure is an outer function that has access to the variables defined in the environment of its inner function.

2. Consider the following code. What will be logged to the console by each of the calls to `f1()` and then `f2()` if they are called in the order shown?

   ```
   let x = "apple";
   var f1 = function() {
     console.log(x);
     x = "pear";
   }
   x = "banana";
   var f2 = function() {
     console.log(x);
   }
   f1();
   f2();
   ```

   a. `f1()` logs "banana", `f2()` logs "pear"

   b. `f1()` logs "pear", `f2()` logs "apple"

   c. `f1()` logs "pear", `f2()` logs "banana"

3. Take a look at the following code:

   ```
   var x = 4;
   function myFunc() {
       var x = 3;
       return function(y) {
           console.log(x*y);
       }
   }
   var f1 = myFunc();
   f1(5);
   ```

What is logged to the console?

a. 20

b. 15

c. `NaN`

4. What do closures store?

a. References to the outer function's variables

b. Copies of the outer function's variables

c. Both of the above

5. Which of these statements is incorrect? JavaScript closures and JavaScript objects

a. Are different terms meaning the same thing

b. Can both be used to make data private, that is, only accessible via predefined functions

c. Are both popular ways of associating some data with functions that operate on that data

---

TIP

Register Your Book

Just a reminder for those of you reading these words in the print or e-book edition of this book: If you go to www.informit.com/register and register this book (using ISBN 978-0-672-33809-0), you can receive free access to an online Web Edition that not only contains the complete text of this book but also features an interactive version of this quiz.

Answers

1. c. A closure is an outer function that has access to the variables defined in the environment of its inner function.

2. a. `f1()` logs `"banana"`, `f2()` logs `"pear"`

3. b. 15

4. a. References to the outer function's variables

5. a. Are different terms meaning the same thing

Exercise

One of your colleagues has written the following code routine, but it isn't working the way she expected. Can you explain why? How would you fix the code so that it gives the output your colleague was expecting?

```
var output = [];

for (var i = 0; i < 5; i++) {
  output[i] = function () {
    console.log(i);
  }
}

output[0](); // logs 5, not the expected 0
output[1](); // logs 5, not the expected 1
output[2](); // logs 5, not the expected 2
output[3](); // logs 5, not the expected 3
output[4](); // logs 5, not the expected 4
```

Organizing Code with Modules

What You'll Learn in This Lesson:

- ▶ What we mean by the term *modules*
- ▶ Some reasons for using modules
- ▶ How to write, declare, and use modules
- ▶ How to import and export module values

In the lessons so far, you have usually used only one source file to store your JavaScript code. While this approach is fine for the examples used here, and for small applications in general, it has its limitations for larger projects where a monstrous codebase can make your code hard to debug and maintain. In such cases it would be better if your code could be divided in some logical way among several source files.

By default, anything you declare in one file of JavaScript source code is not available outside that file, which is a problem if you want to use a number of functionally separated source files. It would be great to have a means to make variables, functions, and objects that have been declared in one file available in others. That way, larger projects could be written in a modular fashion.

Surprisingly, until recently JavaScript did not have such a facility built into the language, though users and developers have invented workarounds with projects like CommonJS and Asynchronous Module Definition (AMD). In its latest versions, however, JavaScript now has native support for modules.

In this lesson you learn how to use modules to structure your code for larger projects into manageable chunks.

NOTE

Third-Party Solutions for Modules

Users and developers created their own solutions with projects like CommonJS and Asynchronous Module Definition (AMD). The new native JavaScript modules have some similarities to these solutions, but with more functionality and more concise syntax.

When I refer to JavaScript modules in this lesson, I always refer to the native JavaScript implementation of modules, not to any third-party project such as CommonJS or AMD.

Why Use Modules?

Among the many reasons for writing modular code, three in particular stand out. Let's look at each in turn.

Modules Make Code Easier to Maintain

When you're unfamiliar with some code, finding what you're looking for can be frustrating. It's so much easier when logically related components are grouped together in appropriately named modules.

Further development of modular code is easier too. Well-written modules have few, if any, dependencies on external code. Therefore, further development of the code contained inside an individual module, or additions to the module's functionality, can be done more easily, quickly, and efficiently than if the code were coupled to other parts of a complex application. Also, those new developments become immediately available to any project that uses the same module.

Modules Help You Reuse Code

There are few things more frustrating than having to reinvent the wheel by rewriting code that you used in another project. Copying the code from previous projects is far from foolproof too, especially where that code had complicated dependencies within its original application. Reusing a module can save you a lot of these headaches.

Modules Make for Tidier Globals

One of the common problems of large and complex JavaScript codebases is the tendency of the global scope to become cluttered with variables. Any part of your code in which some variable is declared with the `var` keyword and outside a function places that variable in the global scope.

Having multiple developers work on a large project can make matters even worse. Imagine the situation where two developers have used the same name for a global variable; when both of their scripts are run on a web page, the declaration that executes second will overwrite the one that ran first!

This is another situation where modules can be helpful. Variables declared in the top level of a module are not part of the shared global scope; instead, they exist within the highest-level scope of just that module.

Module Basics

In the JavaScript native implementation of modules, each module is stored in its own JavaScript file—one file per module. Any and all variables, functions, or objects declared inside a module remain inaccessible to code outside the module unless they are specifically exported from the module and imported into another script. We look at export and import routines shortly.

CAUTION

The CORS Gotcha!

You can try out pretty much all the examples you've seen in previous lessons simply by loading the HTML and JavaScript code into your browser from a local source, such as your computer's hard disk. However, unlike regular scripts, modules are fetched with CORS, which stands for Cross-Origin Resource Sharing. This security feature may prevent you from running the examples in this lesson by simply loading them into your browser from your own PC. You may instead need to upload the HTML and JavaScript files to a web server.

How to Include a JavaScript Module

Modules are included in your web page in a similar way to other scripts, except for the presence of a `type` parameter with value of `"module"` in the `<script>` element:

```
<head>
    <script type="module" src="./myModule.js"></script>
</head>
```

CAUTION

Use Relative Paths

At the time of writing, JavaScript requires a relative path to your module. Trying to access a module in the same folder as the main script by using the following call will probably fail:

```
import { convertCtoF, convertFtoC } from 'tempConvert.js';
```

Instead, replace `'tempConvert.js'` with `'./tempConvert.js'` as in the preceding example. You can also use, for example, `../` or `../../` or full URLs such as `'http://www.example.com/tempConvert.js'`.

The `nomodule` Keyword

Although at the time of writing, modules are a recent addition to JavaScript, the latest versions of most browsers already offer support. However, there is a means to allow older browsers to access alternative code if they don't support modules.

Any browsers that understand `type='module'` should ignore all scripts having the `nomodule` attribute:

```
<script type="module" src="./myModule.js"></script>
<script nomodule src="fallback-option.js"></script>
```

This lets you offer modular code to browsers that understand it, while providing an alternative code to other browsers.

Exporting

All variables, functions, and objects declared inside a module remain inaccessible to code outside the module unless they are specifically exported.

To export items from a module, you simply use the keyword `export`. Here's one example, in this case exporting a single function:

```
function func1(x) {
    alert(x);
}
export func1;
```

That's all there is to it. The function `func1()` is now available to be imported elsewhere in the codebase.

Let's look at another simple but slightly more complete example.

A Simple Sample Module

Now let's create a basic module that exports two functions:

```
convertCtoF(c) : // Converts Celsius temperature c to Fahrenheit.
convertFtoC(f) : // Converts Fahrenheit temperature f to Celsius.
```

Here you also create a file named tempConvert.js to contain this module and export both functions for use elsewhere in the application.

The code for tempConvert.js is shown in Listing 21.1.

LISTING 21.1   A Temperature Conversion Module

```
function convertCtoF(c) {
    return (c*1.8) + 32;
}
function convertFtoC(f) {
    return (f-32)/1.8;
}
export { convertCtoF, convertFtoC }
```

The `export` keyword on the last line exports all functions listed between the curly braces—in this case both of the functions defined within the module.

NOTE

Exporting Lists

As you can see in the preceding example, JavaScript modules let you export lists of items with a single `export` keyword. These items can be variables, functions, objects, or combinations of these types:

```
export { func1, var1, obj1 }
```

This syntax is one of many that can be used with `export`. You see some others elsewhere in the lesson.

Items don't need to have been already declared before you can export them; you can add the keyword `export` before your declaration of a new item with `var`, `let`, `function`, `class`, and so on. Here are some examples of valid export statements:

```
// Export a named variable
export var a = 'something';

// Export a named function
export function func1() { console.log('Hello world!'); };

// Export an existing variable
var a = 'something';
export { a };

// Export a list of existing variables
var a = 'something';
var b = 'another thing';
var c = 'just one more thing';
export { a, b, c };
```

TIP

Bindings

Note that your modules export bindings to variables, not copies of those variables.

How to Rename While Exporting

You can rename items at the same time they are exported, if you wish. Suppose that within your module you have an array `arr` from which you want to export one item as a variable called `distance`:

```
export var distance = arr[1];
```

Alternatively, you might want to export the entire array but change its name in the process:

```
export { arr as routeProperties };
```

Named and Default Exports

The preceding examples use a type of export usually referred to as *named exports*, since each value is named. Where you need to export only one item from a module, you can set the item as the module's default export. Obviously, there can be only one default export in any module. To set the default export, you use the `default` keyword:

```
function mmToInches(d) {
    return d/25.4;
}
export default mmToInches;
```

Importing

Now that you've seen how to export things, I'm sure you'll want to know how to import them into other scripts. As you may already have guessed, you need the `import` keyword.

Here's the simple module `tempConvert.js` made earlier:

```
function convertCtoF(c) {
    return (c*1.8) + 32;
}
function convertFtoC(f) {
    return (f-32)/1.8;
}
export { convertCtoF, convertFtoC }
```

You can import the functions from this module into another program:

```
import { convertCtoF, convertFtoC } from './tempConvert.js';
```

The preceding line imports both of the functions from the `tempConvert` module. If you need only one of the functions, you can easily import just that function in the same way:

```
import { convertCtoF } from './tempConvert';
```

Default Imports

When you want to import an item that another module has exported as its default export, you can name the item during the import process. Returning to the example of a default export from earlier in the lesson:

```
function mmToInches(d) {
    return d/25.4;
}
export default mmToInches;
```

Let's assume that this code is in module `convert.js`. Then in the importing script, you can simply use

```
import toInches from './convert.js';
console.log(toInches(100)); // logs 3.937007874015748
```

How to Rename While Importing

Just as it's possible to rename named items as you export them (as you saw earlier in this lesson), it's also easy to rename things at the moment of import:

```
import { convertCtoF as cF } from './tempConvert.js';
```

How to Import a Module as an Object

If you prefer, you can create an object as you import from another module. You then have access to the imported values and functions as properties of the object you created. The following code snippet imports the two functions from the temperature conversion module as an object called `temps` and then uses one of the imported functions:

```
import * as temps from './tempConvert.js';
var cTemp = temps.convertFtoC(212);
```

CAUTION

No Conditional Imports or Exports Are Allowed

Note that you can't conditionally import or export modules. Expressions like

```
if( myVar == 0 ) {
    import { convertCtoF } from './tempConvert.js';
}
```

will produce a syntax error.

NOTE

Imports Are "Hoisted"

Module imports are internally moved to the beginning of the current scope. That is, it doesn't matter where in your module you mention them. The code

```
var cTemp = convertFtoC(212);

import { convertFtoC } from './tempConvert.js';
```

will work fine. This is called *hoisting*.

▼ TRY IT YOURSELF

Creating a Temperature Conversion Module

For this example, let's use the simple temperature conversion module written earlier in a JavaScript web application.

First, create the module using the code you saw in Listing 21.1. Call the module `tempConvert.js`:

```
function convertCtoF(c) {
    return (c*1.8) + 32;
}
function convertFtoC(f) {
    return (f-32)/1.8;
}
export { convertCtoF, convertFtoC }
```

The ultra-simple HTML page will accept a temperature in degrees Celsius and, at the click of a button, convert it to Fahrenheit and display the result. Here's the bare-bones HTML:

```
<!DOCTYPE html>
<html>
<head>
    <title>Module Example</title>
    <style>div { padding: 5px; }</style>
</head>
<body>
    <input type="text" id="temp" /> degrees C<br/>
    <input type="button" id="btn" value="Convert to Fahrenheit" /><br/>
    <div id="out"></div>
</body>
</html>
```

You now need to add code to build the application. Here are the steps to perform:

1. Load the required module into the application.

2. Make sure the code imports the required function(s) from the module.

3. When the page has loaded, add an onclick handler to the button element. The handler should apply an imported conversion function to the user-supplied input temperature and display the resulting output value in the page.

First, you need a `<script>` element in the page head. Remember that, since you'll be using the `import` command, you need to specify the `script` element as a module:

```
<script type="module">
</script>
```

Next, you need to import the conversion function from the module `tempConvert.js`. In this example, you'll actually import everything that this module exports, creating as you do so an object called `temps`:

```
import * as temps from './tempConvert.js';
```

Remember that (at the time of writing) `tempConvert.js` must be prefixed with a valid local path prefix, in this case `./` because the module will be placed in the same folder as the HTML file.

Now, you're ready to code the `onclick` handler for the button element.

First, you need to get the temperature value that the user entered:

```
var t = document.getElementById("temp").value;
```

You can use the `convertCtoF()` function to carry out the conversion. Remember, though, that this function has now become a method of object `temps`:

```
var o = temps.convertCtoF(t);
```

Finally, you can output the converted value to the page. In this example, you use a `<div>` element with the id value `"out"`:

```
document.getElementById("out").innerHTML = o + " degrees F";
```

The completed code is shown in Listing 21.2. Enter the code into a file called convert.html.

LISTING 21.2   The Temperature Conversion Application

```
<!DOCTYPE html>
<html>
<head>
    <title>Module Example</title>
    <style>div { padding: 5px; }</style>
    <script type="module">
        import * as temps from './tempConvert.js';
        window.onload = function() {
        document.getElementById("btn").onclick = function() {
            var t = document.getElementById("temp").value;
            var o = temps.convertCtoF(t);
            document.getElementById("out").innerHTML = o + " degrees F";
        }
    }
    </script>
</head>
<body>
    <input type="text" id="temp" /> degrees C<br/>
    <input type="button" id="btn" value="Convert to Fahrenheit" /><br/>
    <div id="out"></div>
</body>
</html>
```

Load the two files into the web folder of your web server and navigate to convert.html. If all has gone correctly, you should have a working, if simplistic, application like the one shown in Figure 21.1.

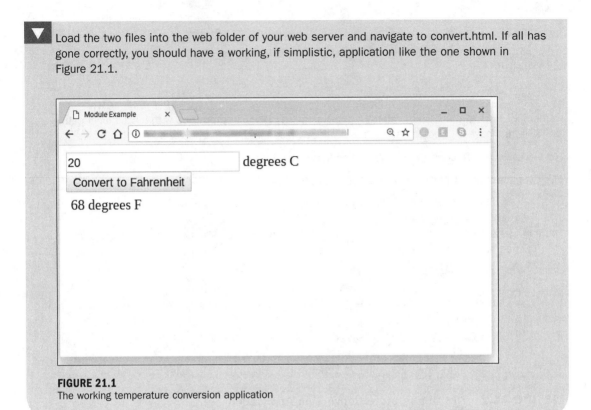

FIGURE 21.1
The working temperature conversion application

Summary

In this lesson you learned about the recently introduced JavaScript implementation of modules and how they can help you to write maintainable, reusable code.

You also saw examples of how flexible and straightforward the syntax is for exporting and importing variables, functions, and other objects between modules.

Writing modular code can greatly improve larger JavaScript applications by making them easier to read and easier to maintain. If written well, modules can be reused in other projects with little or no modification.

The module handling recently introduced to JavaScript allows you to write modular code without having to rely on any third-party solutions.

Q&A

Q. Can I use variables to form expressions in an `import` statement?

A. No. What is imported cannot be computed at runtime, so code like the following will not work:

```
import myVar from './myModule' + module_number + '.js';
```

Q. How can I find out which browsers support JavaScript native modules?

A. At the time of writing, most browsers have at least some support for these features. For older browsers, visit an online resource like https://caniuse.com/#feat=es6-module.

Q. What will happen if I inadvertently import a module more than once?

A. You can import JavaScript modules multiple times, but they'll execute only once.

In the following code, `myModule.js` executes only once:

```
<script type="module" src="./myModule.js"></script>
<script type="module">
    import "./myModule.js";
</script>
```

Workshop

Quiz questions and exercises to test your understanding and to stretch your skills.

Quiz

1. Which of the following module declarations is correct?

   a. `<script module src='./myModule.js'></script>`

   b. `<script type='module' src='./myModule.js'></script>`

   c. `<script module='./myModule.js'></script>`

2. What is the keyword `nomodule` used for?

   a. To indicate a script that should be used by browsers that don't support JavaScript modules

   b. To indicate that no modules are used in the application

   c. To indicate the number of modules used in the applications

3. Which of the following commands correctly exports two functions `func1` and `func2` from a module?

   a. `export { func1(), func2() }`

   b. `export [ func1(), func2() ]`

   c. `export { func1, func2 }`

4. Which of the following will correctly import the variable exported by default from `myModule.js` and name it `var1`?

   a. `import name=var1 from './myModule.js'`

   b. `import as var1 from './myModule.js'`

   c. `import var1 from './myModule.js'`

5. You have imported items from a module using this line of code:

   `import * as utils from './utilModule.js';`

   Which of the following will successfully use the imported function `func1()`?

   a. `var y = func1(x);`

   b. `var y = utils.func1(x);`

   c. `var y = utils{ func1(x) };`

TIP

Register Your Book

Just a reminder for those of you reading these words in the print or e-book edition of this book: If you go to www.informit.com/register and register this book (using ISBN 978-0-672-33809-0), you can receive free access to an online Web Edition that not only contains the complete text of this book but also features an interactive version of this quiz.

Answers

1. b. `<script type='module' src='./myModule.js'></script>`
2. a. To indicate a script that should be used by browsers that don't support JavaScript modules
3. c. `export { func1, func2 }`
4. c. `import var1 from './myModule.js'`
5. b. `var y = utils.func1(x);`

Exercise

Create a module containing routines to convert a person's weight between metric (Kg) and imperial (pounds and ounces) units. The module should export functions to convert in both directions.

Test your module in a simple application similar to the one in Listing 21.2.

LESSON 22
Good Coding Practice

What You'll Learn in This Lesson:

▶ How to avoid overuse of JavaScript

▶ How to write readable and maintainable code

▶ About graceful degradation

▶ About progressive enhancement

▶ How to separate style, content, and code

▶ How to write unobtrusive JavaScript

▶ How to use feature detection

▶ How to avoid inline code such as event handlers

▶ How to handle errors well

JavaScript has gained an unfortunate reputation in certain circles. Since its main goal as a scripting language was to add functionality to web page designs, accessibility for first-time programmers has always been an important aspect of the language. Unfortunately, that has often led to poorly written code being allowed into web pages, leading to frustration for more software-savvy users.

The lessons so far have made reference to aspects of coding that are good and bad. In this lesson we pull all that together to form some general guidelines for good coding practice.

Don't Overuse JavaScript

How much JavaScript do you need? There's often a temptation to include JavaScript code and enhanced interaction where it's not strictly necessary or advisable.

It's important to remember that your users are likely to spend most of their Internet time on sites other than yours. Experienced Internet users become accustomed to popular interface components such as menus, breadcrumb trails, and tabbed browsing. These elements are popular, in general, because they work well, can be made to look good, and don't require the user to read a manual first. Is familiarity with a site's operation likely to increase a user's productivity more than the potential benefits of your all-new whizz-bang design?

Many of the visual effects that once needed to be coded in JavaScript can now be achieved perfectly well using CSS. Where both approaches are possible (image rollovers and some types of menus come immediately to mind), CSS is usually preferable. It's well supported across browsers (despite a few variations) and isn't as commonly turned off by the user. In the rare case that CSS isn't supported, the page is rendered as standard HTML, usually leaving a page that's at least perfectly functional, even if it's not so pretty.

Users in many areas of the world are still using outdated, underpowered, hand-me-down computers and may also have slow and/or unreliable Internet access. The CPU cycles taken up by your unnecessary code may be precious to them.

In some cases you may cost yourself a degree of search engine page rank, since their spiders don't always correctly index content that's been generated by JavaScript, or designs that require it for navigation.

Used carefully and with forethought, JavaScript can be a great tool, but sometimes you can have too much of a good thing.

How to Write Readable and Maintainable Code

There is no way of knowing who will one day need to read and understand your code. Even if that person is you, several years and many projects may have intervened; the code that is so familiar to you at the time of writing can seem mystifying further down the line. If others have to interpret your code, they may not share your coding style, naming conventions, or areas of expertise, and you may not be available to help them out.

Use Comments Sensibly

Well-chosen comments at critical places in your code can make all the difference in such situations. Comments are your notes and pointers for those who come later. The trick is in deciding what comments are likely to be helpful. The subject has often raised debate, and opinions vary widely, so what follows is largely my own opinion.

It's perhaps reasonable to assume that the person who ends up reading your code has an understanding of JavaScript, so a commentary on the way the language itself works is going too far; JavaScript developers may vary widely in their styles and abilities, but the one thing we do all share is the language syntax!

Harder to interpret when reading code are the thought processes and algorithms that lie behind the code's operation. When reading code written by others, I find it helpful to see the following features:

▶ A prologue to any object or function containing more than a few lines of simple code:

```
function calculateGroundAngle(x1, y1, z1, x2, y2, z2) {
  /**
  * Calculates the angle in radians at which
  * a line between two points intersects the
  * ground plane.
  * @author Phil Ballard phil@www.example.com
  */
  if(x1 > 0) {
  .... more statements
```

▶ Inline comments wherever the code would otherwise be confusing or prone to misinterpretation:

```
// need to use our custom sort method for performance reasons
var finalArray = rapidSort(allNodes, byAngle) {
  .... more statements
```

▶ A comment wherever the original author can pass on specialist knowledge that the reader is unlikely to know:

```
// workaround for image onload bug in browser X version Y
if(!loaded(image1)) {
  .... more statements
```

▶ Instructions for commonly used code modifications:

```
// You can change the following dimensions to your preference:
var height = 400px;
var width = 600px;
```

TIP

Code Comments

Various schemes use code comments to help you generate documentation for your software. See, for example, http://code.google.com/p/jsdoc-toolkit/.

Choose Helpful File, Property, and Method Names

The number of comments required in your source code can be greatly reduced by making the code as self-commenting as possible. You can go some way toward this by choosing meaningful human-readable names for methods and properties.

JavaScript has rules about the characters allowed in the names of methods (or functions) and properties (or variables), but there's still plenty of scope to be creative and concise.

A popular convention is to put the names of constants into all uppercase:

```
MONTHS_PER_YEAR = 12;
```

For regular function, method, and variable names, so-called CamelCase is a popular option; names constructed from multiple words are concatenated with each word except the first initialized. The first letter can be upper- or lowercase:

```
var memberSurname = "Smith";
var lastGroupProcessed = 16;
```

It's recommended that constructor functions for instantiating objects have the first character capitalized:

```
function Car(make, model, color) {
  .... statements
}
```

The capitalization provides a reminder that the new keyword needs to be used:

```
var herbie = new Car('VW', 'Beetle', 'white');
```

Reuse Code Where You Can

Generally, the more you can modularize your code, the better. Let's look at this function:

```
function getElementArea() {
    var high = document.getElementById("id1").style.height;
    var wide = document.getElementById("id1").style.width;
    return high * wide;
}
```

The function here attempts to return the area of screen covered by a particular HTML element. Unfortunately, it can only ever work with an element having id = "id1", which is really not very helpful at all.

Collecting your code into modules such as functions and objects that you can use and reuse throughout your code is a process known as *abstraction*. You can give the function *a higher level of abstraction* to make its use more general by passing as an argument the ID of the element to which the operation should be applied:

```
function getElementArea(elementId) {
    var elem = document.getElementById(elementId);
    var high = elem.style.height;
```

```
        var wide = elem.style.width;
        return parseInt(high) * parseInt(wide);
}
```

You could now call your function into action for any element having an ID:

```
var area1 = getElementArea("id1");
var area2 = getElementArea("id2");
```

Don't Assume

What happens in the previous function when you pass a value for `elementId` that doesn't correspond to any element on the page? The function causes an error, and code execution halts.

The error is to assume that an allowable value for `elementId` will be passed. Let's edit the function `getElementArea()` to carry out a check that the page element does indeed exist and also that it has a numeric area:

```
function getElementArea(elementId) {
    if(document.getElementById(elementId)) {
        var elem = document.getElementById(elementId);
        var high = elem.style.height;
        var wide = elem.style.width;
        var area = parseInt(high) * parseInt(wide);
        if(!isNaN(area)) {
            return area;
        } else {
            return false;
        }
    } else {
        return false;
    }
}
```

That's an improvement. Now the function will return `false` if it cannot return a numeric area, either because the relevant page element couldn't be found, or because the ID corresponded to a page element without accessible `width` and `height` properties.

Graceful Degradation

Among the earliest web browsers were some that didn't even support the inclusion of images in HTML. When the `<img>` element was introduced, a way was needed to allow those text-only browsers to present something helpful to the user whenever such a nonsupported tag was encountered.

In the case of the <img> tag, that facility was provided by the alt (alternative text) attribute. Web designers could assign a string of text to alt, and text-only browsers would display this text to the user instead of showing the image. At the whim of the page designer, the alt text might be simply a title for the image, a description of what the picture would have displayed, or a suggestion for an alternative source of the information that would have been carried in the graphic.

This was an early example of *graceful degradation*, the process by which a user whose browser lacks the required technical features to make full use of a web page's design—or has those features disabled—can still benefit as fully as possible from the site's content.

Let's take JavaScript itself as another example. Virtually every browser supports JavaScript, and few users turn it off. So do you really need to worry about visitors who don't have JavaScript enabled? The answer is probably yes. One type of frequent visitor to your site will no doubt be the spider program from one of the search engines, busy indexing the pages of the Web. The spider will attempt to follow all the navigation links on your pages to build a full index of your site's content; if such navigation requires the services of JavaScript, you may find some parts of your site not being indexed. Your search ranking will probably suffer as a result.

Another important example lies in the realm of accessibility. No matter how capable a browser program is, there are some users who suffer with other limitations, such as perhaps the inability to use a mouse, or the necessity to use screen-reading software. If your site does not cater to these users, they're unlikely to return.

Progressive Enhancement

When we talk about graceful degradation, it's easy to imagine a fully functional web page with all the bells and whistles providing charitable assistance to users whose browsers have lesser capabilities.

Supporters of *progressive enhancement* tend to look at the problem from the opposite direction. They favor the building of a stable, accessible, and fully functional website, the content of which can be accessed by just about any imaginable user and browser, to which they can later add extra layers of additional usability for those who can take advantage of them.

This ensures that the site will work for even the most basic browser setup, with more advanced browsers simply gaining some additional enhancements.

Separate Style, Content, and Code

The key resource of a web page employing progressive enhancement techniques is the content. HTML provides markup facilities to allow you to describe your content semantically; the markup tags themselves identify page elements as being headings, tables, paragraphs, and so on. We might refer to this as the *semantic layer*.

What this semantic layer should ideally *not* contain is any information about how the page should appear. You can add this additional information afterward, using CSS techniques to form the *presentation layer*. By linking external CSS stylesheets into the document, you avoid any appearance-related information from appearing in the HTML markup itself. Even a browser having no understanding of CSS, however, can still access and display all of the page's information, even though it might not look so pretty.

When you now come to add JavaScript into the mix, you do so as yet another notional layer—you might think of it as the *behavior layer*. Users without JavaScript still have access to the page content via the semantic markup; if their browser understands CSS, they'll also benefit from the enhanced appearance of the presentation layer. If the JavaScript of the behavior layer is applied correctly, it will offer more functionality to those who can use it, without prejudicing the abilities of the preceding layers.

To achieve that, you need to write JavaScript that is *unobtrusive*.

Unobtrusive JavaScript

There is no formal definition of unobtrusive JavaScript, but the concepts upon which it's built all involve maintaining the separation between the behavior layer and the content and presentation layers.

Leave That HTML Alone

The first and perhaps most important consideration is the removal of JavaScript code from the page markup. Early applications of JavaScript clutter the HTML with inline event handlers such as the `onClick` event handler in this example:

```
<input type="button" style="border: 1px solid blue;color: white"
onclick="doSomething()" />
```

Inline style attributes, such as the one in the preceding example, can make the situation even worse.

Thankfully, you can effectively remove the style information to the style layer, for example, by adding a `class` attribute to the HTML tag referring to an associated style declaration in an external CSS file:

```
<input type="button" class="blueButtons" onclick="doSomething()" />
```

And in the associated CSS definitions:

```
.blueButtons {
 border: 1px solid blue;
 color: white;
}
```

Alternative Methods

You could, of course, define your style rule for the button via any one of a number of different selectors, including the `input` element or via an `id` instead of a `class` attribute.

To make your JavaScript unobtrusive, you can employ a similar technique to the one just used for CSS. By adding an `id` attribute to a page element within the HTML markup, you can attach the required `onClick` event listener from within your external JavaScript code, keeping it out of the HTML markup altogether. Here's the revised HTML element:

```
<input type="button" class="blueButtons" id="btn1" />
```

The `onClick` event handler is attached from within your JavaScript code:

```
function doSomething() {
  .... statements ....
}
document.getElementById("btn1").onclick = doSomething;
```

DOM Availability

Remember that you can't use DOM methods until the DOM is available, so any such code must be attached via a method such as `window.onload` to guarantee DOM availability. There are plenty of examples throughout these lessons.

Use JavaScript Only as an Enhancement

In the spirit of progressive enhancement, you want your page to work even if JavaScript is turned off. Any improvements in the usability of the page that JavaScript may add should be seen as a bonus for those users whose browser setup permits them.

Let's imagine you want to write some form validation code—a popular use for JavaScript. Here's a little HTML search form:

```
<form action="process.php">
    <input id="searchTerm" name="term" type="text" /><br />
    <input type="button" id="btn1" value="Search" />
</form>
```

You want to write a routine to prevent the form from being submitted if the search field is blank. You might write this function `checkform()`, which will be attached to the `onClick` handler of the search button:

```
function checkform() {
    if(document.forms[0].term.value == "") {
```

```
            alert("Please enter a search term.");
            return false;
        } else {
            document.forms[0].submit();
        }
    }
}
window.onload = function() {
    document.getElementById("btn1").onclick = checkform;
}
```

That should work just fine. But what happens when JavaScript is switched off? The button now does nothing at all, and the form can't be submitted by the user. Your users would surely prefer that the form could be used, albeit without the *enhancement* of input checking.

Let's change the form slightly to use an input button of `type="submit"` rather than `type="button"`, and edit the `checkform()` function:

```
<form action="process.php">
    <input id="searchTerm" name="term" type="text" /><br />
    <input type="submit" id="btn1" value="Search" />
</form>
```

Here's the modified `checkform()` function:

```
function checkform() {
    if(document.forms[0].term.value == "") {
        alert("Please enter a search term.");
        return false;
    } else {
        return true;
    }
}
window.onload = function() {
    document.getElementById("btn1").onclick = checkform;
}
```

If JavaScript is active, returning a value of `false` to the submit button will prevent the default operation of the button, preventing form submission. Without JavaScript, however, the form will still submit when the button is clicked.

Feature Detection

Where possible, try to directly detect the presence or absence of browser features, and have your code use those features only where available.

As an example, let's look at the `clipboardData` object, which is only supported in Internet Explorer. Before using this object in your code, it's a good idea to perform a couple of tests:

▶ Does JavaScript recognize the object's existence?

▶ If so, does the object support the method you want to use?

The following `setClipboard()` function attempts to write a particular piece of text directly to the clipboard using the `clipboardData` object:

```
function setClipboard(myText){
    if((typeof clipboardData != 'undefined') && (clipboardData.setData)){
        clipboardData.setData("text", myText);
    } else {
        document.getElementById("copytext").innerHTML = myText;
        alert("Please copy the text from the 'Copy Text' field to your clipboard");
    }
}
```

First, it tests for the object's existence using `typeof`:

```
if((typeof clipboardData != 'undefined') ....
```

NOTE

Return Values for `typeof`

The `typeof` operator returns one of the following, depending on the type of the operand:

`"undefined"`, `"object"`, `"function"`, `"boolean"`, `"string"`, or `"number"`

Additionally, the function insists that the `setData()` method must be available:

```
... && (clipboardData.setData)){
```

If either test fails, the user is offered an alternative, if less elegant, method of getting the text to the clipboard; it is written to a page element and the user is invited to copy it:

```
document.getElementById("copytext").innerHTML = myText;
alert("Please copy the text from the 'copytext' field to your clipboard");
```

At no point does the code try to explicitly detect that the user's browser is Internet Explorer (or any other browser); should some other browser one day implement this functionality, the code should detect it correctly.

How to Handle Errors Well

When your JavaScript program encounters an error of some sort, a warning or error will be created inside the JavaScript interpreter. Whether and how this is displayed to the user depends on the browser in use and the user's settings; the user may see some form of error message, or the failed program may simply remain silent but inactive.

Neither situation is good for the user; he is likely to have no idea what has gone wrong or what to do about it.

As you try to write your code to handle a wide range of browsers and circumstances, it's possible to foresee some areas in which errors might be generated. Examples include

▶ The uncertainty over whether a browser fully supports a certain object and whether that support is standards compliant

▶ Whether an independent procedure has yet completed its execution, such as an external file being loaded

Use `try` and `catch`

A useful way to try to intercept potential errors and deal with them cleanly is to use the `try` and `catch` statements.

The `try` statement allows you to attempt to run a piece of code. If the code runs without errors, all is well; however, should an error occur, you can use the `catch` statement to intervene before an error message is sent to the user, and determine what the program should then do about the error.

```
try {
    doSomething();
}
catch(err) {
    doSomethingElse();
}
```

Note the syntax:

```
catch(identifier)
```

Here `identifier` is an object created when an error is caught. It contains information about the error; for instance, if you wanted to alert the user to the nature of a JavaScript runtime error, you could use a code construct like

```
catch(err) {
    alert(err.description);
}
```

to open a dialog containing details of the error.

▼ TRY IT YOURSELF

Converting Code into Unobtrusive Code

From time to time you may find yourself in the position of having to modernize code to make it less obtrusive. Let's do that with some code written way back in Lesson 5, "Using DOM Objects and Built-in Objects," presented once again here in Listing 22.1.

LISTING 22.1   An Obtrusive Script

```
<!DOCTYPE html>
<html>
    <head>
        <title>Current Date and Time</title>
        <style>
            p {font: 14px normal arial, verdana, helvetica;}
        </style>
        <script>
            function telltime() {
                var out = "";
                var now = new Date();
                out += "<br />Date: " + now.getDate();
                out += "<br />Month: " + now.getMonth();
                out += "<br />Year: " + now.getFullYear();
                out += "<br />Hours: " + now.getHours();
                out += "<br />Minutes: " + now.getMinutes();
                out += "<br />Seconds: " + now.getSeconds();
                document.getElementById("div1").innerHTML = out;
            }
        </script>
    </head>
    <body>
        The current date and time are:<br/>
        <div id="div1"></div>
        <script>
            telltime();
        </script>
        <input type="button" onclick="location.reload()" value="Refresh" />
    </body>
</html>
```

As it stands, this script has a number of areas of potential improvement:

▶ The JavaScript statements are placed between `<script>` and `</script>` tags on the page; they would be better in a separate file.

▶ The button has an inline event handler.

▶ A user without JavaScript would simply see a page with a nonfunctioning button.

First, let's move all the JavaScript to a separate file and remove the inline event handler. You can also give the button an `id` value, so that you can identify it in JavaScript to add the required event handler via our code.

Next, you need to address the issue of users without JavaScript enabled. You use the `<noscript>` page element so that users without JavaScript enabled will see, instead of the button, a short message with a link to an alternative source of time information:

```
<noscript>
    Your browser does not support JavaScript<br />
    Please consult your computer's operating system for local date and
time information or click <a href="clock.php" target="_blank">HERE</a>
to read the server time.
</noscript>
```

TIP

Using the `noscript` Element

The `<noscript>` element provides additional page content for users with disabled scripts or with a browser that can't support client-side scripting. Any of the elements that you can put in the `<body>` element of an HTML page can go inside the `<noscript>` element and will automatically be displayed if scripts cannot be run in the user's browser.

The HTML file after modification is shown in Listing 22.2.

LISTING 22.2   The Modified HTML Page

```
<!DOCTYPE html>
<html>
<head>
    <title>Current Date and Time</title>
    <style>
        p {font: 14px normal arial, verdana, helvetica;}
    </style>
    <script src="datetime.js"></script>
</head>
<body>
    The current date and time are:<br/>
    <div id="div1"></div>
    <input id="btn1" type="button" value="Refresh" />
    <noscript>
    <p>Your browser does not support JavaScript.</p>
    <p>Please consult your computer's operating system for local date and time
information or click <a href="clock.php" target="_blank">HERE</a> to read the
server time.</p>
    </noscript>
</body>
</html>
```

Within the JavaScript source file telltime.js, you use `window.onload` to add the event listener for the button. Finally, you call `telltime()` to generate the date and time information to display on the page. This JavaScript code is shown in Listing 22.3.

LISTING 22.3 datetime.js

```
function telltime() {
    var out = "";
    var now = new Date();
    out += "<br />Date: " + now.getDate();
    out += "<br />Month: " + now.getMonth();
    out += "<br />Year: " + now.getFullYear();
    out += "<br />Hours: " + now.getHours();
    out += "<br />Minutes: " + now.getMinutes();
    out += "<br />Seconds: " + now.getSeconds();
    document.getElementById("div1").innerHTML = out;
}

window.onload = function() {
    document.getElementById("btn1").onclick= function() {location.reload();}
    telltime();
}
```

With JavaScript enabled, the script works just as it did in Lesson 5. However, with JavaScript disabled, the user now sees the page shown in Figure 22.1.

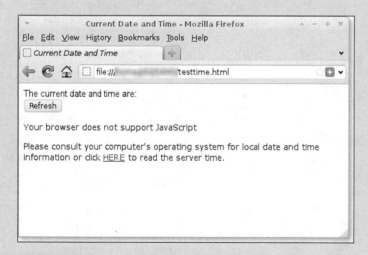

FIGURE 22.1
Extra information for users without JavaScript

Summary

This lesson rounded up and presented various examples of good practice in writing JavaScript. Used together, they should help you deliver your code projects more quickly, with higher quality and much easier maintenance.

Q&A

Q. Why would a user turn off JavaScript?

A. Remember that the browser might have been set up by the service provider or employer with JavaScript turned off by default, in an effort to improve security. This is particularly likely in an environment such as a school or an Internet cafe.

Additionally, some corporate firewalls, ad-blocking, and personal antivirus software prevent JavaScript from running, and some mobile devices have web browsers without complete JavaScript support.

Q. Are there any other options besides `<noscript>` **for dealing with users who don't have JavaScript enabled?**

A. An alternative that avoids `<noscript>` is to send users who *do* have JavaScript support to an alternative page containing JavaScript-powered enhancements:

```
<script>window.location="enhancedPage.html";</script>
```

If JavaScript is available and activated, the script redirects the user to the enhanced page. If the browser doesn't have JavaScript support, the script won't be executed, and the user is left viewing the more basic version.

Workshop

Quiz questions and exercises to test your understanding and to stretch your skills.

Quiz

1. What is the modularization of code into reusable blocks for more general use called?

   a. Abstraction

   b. Inheritance

   c. Unobtrusive JavaScript

2. The CSS for your page should be confined as much as possible to the

  a. Semantic layer

  b. Presentation layer

  c. Behavior layer

3. Unobtrusive JavaScript code should, wherever possible, be placed

  a. In an external file

  b. Between `<script>` and `</script>` tags in the page `<head>`

  c. Inline

4. By convention, the names of constants are put into

  a. Lowercase

  b. Uppercase

  c. CamelCase

5. When `catch()` is used to handle an error, the object passed as an argument to `catch()`

  a. Contains information about the error

  b. Contains the line number of the error

  c. Neither of the above

TIP
_____

Register Your Book

Just a reminder for those of you reading these words in the print or e-book edition of this book: If you go to www.informit.com/register and register this book (using ISBN 978-0-672-33809-0), you can receive free access to an online Web Edition that not only contains the complete text of this book but also features an interactive version of this quiz.
_____

Answers

  1. a. Abstraction

  2. b. Where possible, all CSS goes in the presentation layer.

  3. a. Use external JavaScript files where it's feasible to do so.

  4. b. Uppercase

  5. a. Contains information about the error

Exercises

Pick some Try It Yourself sections from earlier lessons and see what you can do to make the code more unobtrusive, without adversely affecting the script's operation.

Can you work out how to further modify the code in Listing 22.2 and Listing 22.3 to ensure that users without JavaScript enabled see just the content of the `<noscript>` tag, without the additional text and button being present? (Hint: Write these items to the page with innerHTML or via DOM methods.)

Debugging Your Code

What You'll Learn in This Lesson:

▶ Recognizing the types of errors common in JavaScript code

▶ Carrying out simple debugging with `alert()`

▶ Using the browser console and `console.log()`

▶ Grouping messages in the console

▶ Using breakpoints

As you delve into more advanced scripting, now and then you'll create JavaScript programs that contain errors.

JavaScript errors can be caused by a variety of minor blunders, such as mismatched opening and closing parentheses, mistyped variable names or keywords, calls made to nonexistent methods, and so on.

This lesson aims to offer some straightforward tips and suggestions for diagnosing errors and correcting your code, making your programming hours more pleasurable and productive.

An Introduction to Debugging

The process of locating and correcting bugs is known as *debugging*, and it can be one of the most tricky and frustrating parts of the development process.

Recognizing Types of Errors

The errors that can crop up in your code usually conform to one of three types:

▶ **Syntax errors:** These errors can include typographical and spelling errors, missing or mismatched quote marks, missing or mismatched parentheses/braces, and case-sensitivity errors.

▶ **Runtime errors:** These errors occur when the JavaScript interpreter tries to do something it can't make sense of. Examples include trying to treat a string as if it were a numerical value and trying to divide a number by zero.

▶ **Faulty program logic:** These mistakes don't always generate error messages—the code may be perfectly valid—but your script doesn't do what you want it to. These are usually problems associated with algorithms or logical flow within the script.

Choosing a Programmer's Editor

Whatever platform you work on, and whatever your browser of choice, it makes sense to have a good code editor. While it's certainly possible to write code in simple programs like the Windows Notepad text editor, a dedicated editor makes life a lot easier.

Many such programs are available, often free of charge under open source and similar licenses. Here is a small selection of no-cost editors, but you should look around for one that suits your platform, your working style, and your wallet:

▶ Notepad++ (Windows)

▶ JEdit (should work on any platform that has Java installed)

▶ PSPad (Windows)

▶ Geany (Windows, Linux)

▶ Atom (macOS, Windows, Linux)

Editors offer a range of features and capabilities, but at a minimum I suggest looking for an editor with the following:

▶ **Line numbering:** This capability is especially useful if you store your JavaScript in external files (and is yet another reason you should do so, wherever feasible). That way, the line numbers of any error messages generated by your browser's debugger will usually match those in the source file open in the editor.

▶ **Syntax highlighting:** When you become familiar with your editor's scheme of syntax highlighting, you can on many occasions spot coding errors simply because the code in the editor "looks wrong." It's surprising how quickly you get used to the colors of keywords, variables, string literals, objects, and so on in your favorite editing program. Many editors let you alter the syntax highlighting color scheme to your own taste.

▶ **Parentheses matching:** As an error-seeking missile, parentheses matching is invaluable. Good editors will show matching pairs of open/close occurrences and for all types of brackets, braces, and parentheses. When your code has several levels of nested parentheses, it's easy to lose count.

▶ **Code completion or tooltip-style syntax help:** Some editors offer pop-up tooltip-style help for command functions and expressions. This feature can save you from having to take your eyes from the editor window to look up an external reference.

Simple Debugging with `alert()`

Sometimes you want a really simple and quick way to read a variable's value or to track the order in which your code executes.

Perhaps the easiest way of all is to insert JavaScript `alert()` statements at appropriate points in the code. Let's suppose you want to know whether an apparently unresponsive function is actually being called, and if so, with what parameters:

```
function myFunc(a, b) {
    alert("myFunc() called.\na: " + a + "\nb: " + b);
    // .. rest of function code here ...
}
```

When the function is called at runtime, the `alert()` method executes, producing a dialog like the one in Figure 23.1.

This page says

myFunc() called.
a: 12.5
b: south

OK

FIGURE 23.1
Using a JavaScript `alert()`

Remember to put a little more information in the displayed message than just a variable value or one-word comment; in the heat of battle, you'll likely forget to what variable or property the value in the `alert()` refers.

More Advanced Debugging

Placing `alert()` calls in your code is perhaps okay for a quick-and-dirty debug of a short piece of code. The technique does, however, have some serious drawbacks:

▶ You have to click OK on each dialog to allow processing to continue. Repeating this step can be demoralizing, especially when you're dealing with long loops!

▶ The messages received are not stored anywhere, and they disappear when the dialog is cleared; you can't go back later and review what was reported.

▶ You need to go back into the editor and erase all the `alert()` calls before your code can "go live."

In the following sections, we look at some more advanced debugging techniques.

Using the Console

Thankfully, most modern browsers provide a JavaScript Console that you can use to better effect for logging debugging messages. You used your own browser's console in some of the previous lessons.

The console normally forms part of a browser's bundled set of developer tools. How to open the developer tools varies from browser to browser:

- ▶ In Internet Explorer: F12

- ▶ In Chrome, Opera, or Firefox: Ctrl+Shift+I

- ▶ In Microsoft Edge: F12 or Ctrl+Shift+I

The examples in this section assume that you're using one of the preceding debuggers. If not, you may have to consult your debugger's documentation to see how to carry out some of the tasks described here. How your browser presents such errors to you differs from browser to browser.

▼ TRY IT YOURSELF

Using Your Browser's Debugging Tools

Let's look at the code in Listing 23.1.

LISTING 23.1   A Program with Errors

```
<!DOCTYPE html>
<html>
<head>
    <title>Strings and Arrays</title>
</head>
<body>
    <script>
        function sayHi() {
            alert("Hello!);
        }
    </script>
    <input type="button" value="good" onclick="sayHi()" />
    <input type="button" value="bad" onclick="sayhi()" />
</body>
</html>
```

This code listing has two different types of errors. First, in the call to the `alert()` method, the argument is missing its closing quotation mark.

Second, the `onclick` handler of the second button calls the function `sayhi()`. Remember that function names are case sensitive, so in fact there is no function defined with the name `sayhi()`.

Loading the page into Google Chrome, you can see the expected two buttons, one labeled "good" and the other "bad." Neither seems to do anything. You can open Chrome's JavaScript Console like I did by pressing Ctrl+Shft+J (or by opening the developer tools using Ctrl+Shft+I and then selecting the console), and the result is shown in Figure 23.2.

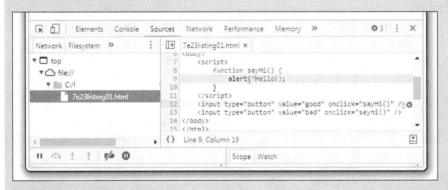

FIGURE 23.2
The Chrome JavaScript Console

That's a helpful start. Chrome indicates that it found an ***invalid or unexpected token*** and provides a link to the offending line number. Clicking on that link takes you to a code listing with this line highlighted, as shown in Figure 23.3.

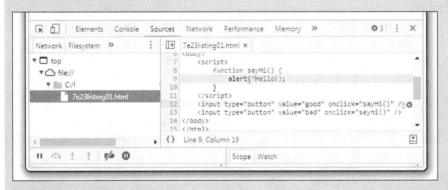

FIGURE 23.3
Showing the line containing the error

With the error corrected and the file saved again, you can try again by reloading the test page.

That looks better. This time the page comes up again, and the console stays blank. Clicking on the button labeled "good" opens the expected `alert()` dialog—so far, so good.

But clicking on the button labeled "bad" doesn't seem to do anything, so you can refer again to the JavaScript Console, as shown in Figure 23.4.

FIGURE 23.4
The second error

Chrome again identifies the problem: "sayhi is not defined." Now you're well on the way to having the code fully debugged and working correctly.

Every browser has its own way of dealing with errors. Figure 23.5 shows how the Firefox browser reports the initial error, which it correctly describes as an ***unterminated string literal***.

FIGURE 23.5
The initial error in Firefox's console

TIP

Practice with Your Favorite Browser

It's worth getting to know the debugging tools in your favorite browser. You might even think about switching browsers if you particularly prefer the tools on offer in another. If you plan to regularly write JavaScript code, it makes sense to do so in a development environment in which you feel comfortable, where you'll be more productive and less frustrated.

TIP

Read About Developer Tools for Your Browser

We have only scratched the surface here of the capabilities of the debugger in Google Chrome. To learn more, there is a good tutorial at https://developers.google.com/web/tools/chrome-devtools/javascript/ to get you started.

If Firefox is your browser of choice for development work, you can read about the developer tools at https://developer.mozilla.org/en-US/docs/Tools/Tools_Toolbox.

If you're using Microsoft Edge, you can find good information on debugging with the Developer Tools at https://docs.microsoft.com/en-us/microsoft-edge/devtools-guide.

Opera contains the Dragonfly debugging tool, which you can read about at www.opera.com/dragonfly/.

The console provides a number of methods you can use in your code in place of the cumbersome and limited `alert()` call, perhaps the most well-known being `console.log()`:

```
function myFunc(a, b) {
    console.log("myFunc() called.\na: " + a + "\nb: " + b);
    // ... rest of function code here ...
}
```

Rather than interrupt program operation, `console.log()` operates invisibly to the user unless she happens to be looking at the console. Figure 23.6 shows the result of running the preceding code with the console open in Google Chrome.

FIGURE 23.6
A message logged in the console

In addition to `console.log()`, you can also take advantage of `console.warn()`, `console.info()`, and `console.error()`. These all record messages at the console in slightly different styles, allowing you to build up a picture of how your script is running.

Figure 23.7 shows how Chrome console displays each one; the display will be slightly different in other browsers.

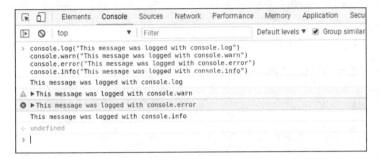

FIGURE 23.7
Different types of console messages

Grouping Messages

Sorting console debugging messages into groups makes them even more readable. You can name the individual message groups any way you like:

```
function myFunc(a, b) {
    console.group("myFunc execution");
    console.log("Executing myFunc()");
    if(isNaN(a) || isNaN(b)) {
        console.warn("One or more arguments non-numeric");
    }
    console.groupEnd();
    myOtherFunc(a+b);
}

function myOtherFunc(c) {
    console.group("myOtherFunc execution");
    console.log("Executing myOtherFunc()");
    if(isNaN(c)) {
        console.info("Argument is not numeric");
    }
    console.groupEnd();
    // ... rest of function code here ...
}
```

This code snippet defines two `console.group()` sections, which are named to associate with the functions in which they execute. Each group ends with a `console.groupEnd()` statement. When the code runs, any console messages display in groups, as shown in Figure 23.8.

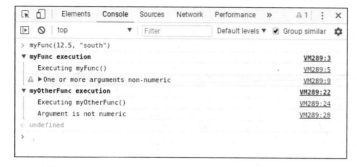

FIGURE 23.8
Grouped messages

Using Breakpoints to Halt Code Execution

As your scripts grow in complexity, you're likely to find that even console logging isn't enough to let you debug effectively.

To perform more detailed debugging, you can set so-called breakpoints in the code at places of interest. When code execution arrives at a breakpoint, it pauses; while time remains frozen, you can examine how your code is operating, check variable values, read logged messages, and so on.

To set a breakpoint in most popular debuggers, you need to go to the Scripts or Sources panel, where you'll see your code listed. Click on a line number (or just to the left of it) to set a breakpoint at that line. In Figure 23.9, a breakpoint has been set on line 8 of the code. The execution has stopped at this point, and you can see the current values of the individual variables in the right panel. You can remove breakpoints by clicking again on the breakpoint icon in the left margin.

FIGURE 23.9
Execution stopped at a breakpoint

▼ TRY IT YOURSELF

A Banner-Cycling Script

Let's put to use some of what you learned in this lesson by writing a script to cycle images on the page. You've surely seen this sort of program before, either as an image slideshow or perhaps as rotating advertisement banners.

To rotate the banner images, you are going to use JavaScript's `setInterval()` function. You may recall from Lesson 10, "Controlling Program Flow," that this function allows you to run a JavaScript function repeatedly, with a preset delay between successive executions.

The `setInterval()` function takes two arguments. The first is the name of the function you want to run, and the second is the delay (in milliseconds) between successive executions of the function. As an example, the line

```
setInterval(myFunc, 5000);
```

would execute the `myFunc()` function every five seconds.

Here you use `setInterval()` to rotate the banner image at a regular interval.

To start, create a new file named banner.html and enter the code from Listing 23.2.

LISTING 23.2 A Banner Rotator

```
<!DOCTYPE html>
<html>
<head>
    <title>Banner Cycler</title>
    <script>
        var banners = ["banner1.jpg", "banner2.jpg", "banner3.jpg"];
        var counter = 0;
        function run() {
            setInterval(cycle, 2000);
        }
        function cycle() {
            counter++;
            if(counter == banners.length) counter = 0;
            document.getElementById("banner").src = banners[counter];
        }
    </script>
</head>
<body onload = "run();">
    <img id="banner" alt="banner" src="banner1.jpg" />
</body>
</html>
```

The HTML part of the page could hardly be simpler; the body of the page just contains an image element. This image will form the banner, which will be "rotated" by changing its `src` property.

Now let's look at the code.

The `run()` function contains only one statement, the `setInterval()` function. This function executes another function, `cycle()`, every two seconds (2000 milliseconds).

Every time the `cycle()` function executes, you carry out three operations:

1. Increment a counter:

```
counter++;
```

2. Use a conditional statement to check whether the counter has reached the number of elements in the array of image names; if so, reset the counter to zero:

```
if(counter == banners.length) counter = 0;
```

3. Set the `src` property of the displayed image to the appropriate filename selected from the array of image filenames:

```
document.getElementById("banner").src = banners[counter];
```

The operation of the script is shown in Figure 23.10.

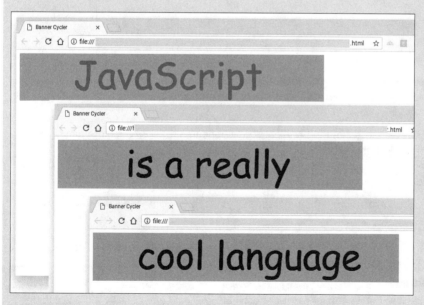

FIGURE 23.10
Our banner cycler

Now let's examine the script operation using browser-based debug tools. To use Chrome like I did, open the Developer Tools console again as done in Figure 23.5—in Chrome, that's Settings > More Tools > Developer Tools or the shortcut Ctrl+Shift+I.

This time select the Sources tab to display the code; you can click on the line number for line 15 to set a breakpoint, as shown in Figure 23.11.

FIGURE 23.11
Setting a breakpoint

While this breakpoint remains set, code execution will halt every time this line of code is reached, before executing the code in the line—in this case, before completing the current execution of the `cycle()` function.

On the right side of the same pane, the breakpoint now appears in the Breakpoints panel. In the same pane, you can click in the Watch Expressions panel and add the names of any variables or expressions whose values you want to examine each time the program pauses. For this example, enter `counter` and `getElementById("Banner").src` to see what values they contain.

Figure 23.12 shows the display when the program next pauses, showing the values of the two chosen expressions.

TIP

Watch Expressions

Instead of simply watching variable names or DOM objects, you could enter one or more *watch expressions*. A watch expression is a valid JavaScript expression that the debugger continuously evaluates, making the value available for you to inspect. Any valid expression can be used, ranging from a simple variable name to a formula containing logical and arithmetic expressions or calls to other functions.

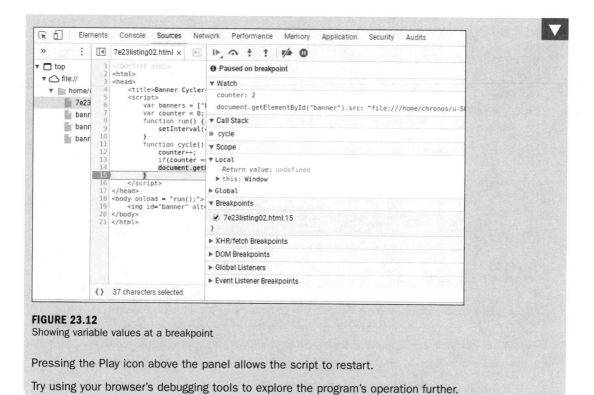

FIGURE 23.12
Showing variable values at a breakpoint

Pressing the Play icon above the panel allows the script to restart.

Try using your browser's debugging tools to explore the program's operation further.

Setting Conditional Breakpoints

Sometimes it helps to break code execution only when a particular situation occurs. You can set a conditional breakpoint by right-clicking the breakpoint icon in the left column and entering a conditional statement.

Your code will execute without interruption until the condition is fulfilled, at which point execution will halt. For instance, in Figure 23.13, the code will halt if the sum of a and b is less than 12. You can edit the expression at any time just by right-clicking once more on the breakpoint icon.

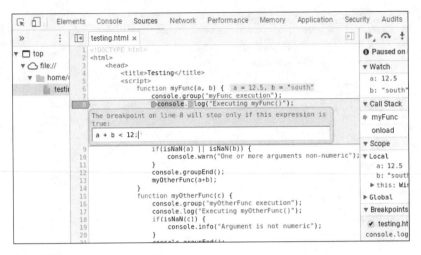

FIGURE 23.13
A conditional breakpoint

When code execution halts at a breakpoint, you can choose to continue code execution or step through your code one statement at a time, by using one of the code execution buttons. These buttons usually look something like video playback controls and appear at the top of one of the panels in the debugger. In most debuggers, the options are

- ▶ **Continue:** Resume execution and pause again only if/when another breakpoint is reached.

- ▶ **Step Over:** Execute the current line, including any functions that are called, then move to the next line.

- ▶ **Step Into:** Move to the next line, as with Step Over, unless the line calls a function; in that case jump to the first line of the function.

- ▶ **Step Out:** Leave the current function and return to the place from which it was called.

Launching the Debugger from Your Code

It's also possible, and often useful, to set breakpoints from within the JavaScript code. You can do this by using the keyword `debugger`:

```
function myFunc(a, b) {
    if(isNaN(a) || isNaN(b)) {
        debugger;
    }
    // ... rest of function code here ...
}
```

In this example, code execution will be halted and the debugger opened only if the conditional expression evaluates to `true`.

The debugging tools allow you to halt code execution in other circumstances too, such as when the DOM has been altered, or when an uncaught exception has been detected, but these are more advanced cases outside the scope of this discussion.

Validating JavaScript

A different and complementary approach to checking your JavaScript code for problems is to use a validation program. It will check that the code conforms to the correct syntax rules of the language. These programs are sometimes bundled with commercial JavaScript editors, or you can simply use Douglas Crockford's JavaScript Lint, which is available free online at www.jslint.com/.

Here you can simply paste your code into the displayed window and click the button.

Don't be too dismayed if the program reports a lot of errors. Just work through them one at a time. JSLint is very thorough and will even report various issues of coding style that wouldn't affect your code's running at all but do help to improve how you program!

Summary

In this lesson you learned a lot about debugging your JavaScript code, including using the browser console, as well as setting breakpoints and stepping through code in the debugger.

Q&A

Q. How should I choose a programmer's editor?

A. It's completely up to personal choice. Many are free or have a free version, so there's nothing to stop you from trying several before deciding.

Q. Where can I find out more about JavaScript debugging?

A. Many tutorials exist online. Start with the one published by W3Schools, at www.w3schools.com/js/js_debugging.asp.

Workshop

Quiz questions and exercises to test your understanding and to stretch your skills.

Quiz

1. Which of these error types are you not likely to find in your JavaScript programs?

    a. Syntax errors

    b. Compilation errors

    c. Runtime errors

2. What does a breakpoint do?

    a. Pauses code execution at a given place

    b. Causes JavaScript to step out of a loop

    c. Produces a JavaScript error

3. What line in your code will launch the debugger?

    a. `debug;`

    b. `debugger;`

    c. `pause;`

4. A watch expression can contain

    a. Just a variable name

    b. Any valid JavaScript expression

    c. Neither of the above

5. When `console.log()` is used to record a message in the console

    a. Program execution ends

    b. Program execution halts temporarily

    c. Program execution continues uninterrupted

TIP

Register Your Book

Just a reminder for those of you reading these words in the print or e-book edition of this book: If you go to www.informit.com/register and register this book (using ISBN 978-0-672-33809-0), you can receive free access to an online Web Edition that not only contains the complete text of this book but also features an interactive version of this quiz.

Answers

1. b. JavaScript is an interpreted, rather than a compiled, language, so you won't encounter compilation errors.

2. a. Pauses code execution at a given place.

3. b. To launch the debugger, type

   ```
   debugger;
   ```

4. b. Any valid JavaScript expression.

5. c. Program execution continues uninterrupted.

Exercise

Using your knowledge of random number generation using the `Math` object, can you rewrite the banner-cycling script in Listing 23.2 to show a random banner at each change, instead of cycling through them in order? Use your browser's built-in debugging tools to help you.

Where to Go Next

What You'll Learn in This Lesson:

▶ How third-party libraries can make coding easier

▶ About some popular JavaScript libraries

▶ How to include and use the jQuery library

▶ How to improve user experience with Ajax

▶ About Node.js and server-side programming

We've been on quite a journey in the lessons so far and covered many of the fundamental techniques used in JavaScript. But the journey doesn't end here—in fact, it's barely begun. In this lesson we consider some ways you can further extend your JavaScript skills by embracing projects that other users and developers have created, notably some of the JavaScript libraries that have become popular in the development community.

Why Use a Library?

You'll often see opinions expressed, mainly on the Internet, by JavaScript developers who strongly advocate writing your own code instead of using one of the many available libraries. Popular objections include

▶ You won't ever really know how the code works because you're simply employing someone else's algorithms and functions.

▶ JavaScript libraries contain a lot of code you'll never use but that your users have to download anyway.

Like many aspects of software development, these are matters of opinion. Personally, I believe that there are some very good reasons for using libraries *sometimes*:

▶ Why invent code that somebody else has already written? Popular JavaScript libraries tend to contain the sorts of abstractions that programmers need often, which means you'll likely need those functions too from time to time. The thousands of downloads and pages of online comments generated by the most-used libraries pretty much guarantee that the code they contain will be more thoroughly tested and debugged than your own home-cooked code would be.

▶ Take inspiration from other coders. There are some *really* clever programmers out there; take their work and use it to improve your own.

▶ Using a well-written library can really take away some of the headaches of writing cross-browser JavaScript. You won't have every browser always at your disposal, but the library writers—and their communities of users—test on every leading browser.

▶ Download size for most libraries is not horrific. For the few occasions when you need the shortest of download times, compressed versions are available for most of the popular libraries that you can use in your "production" websites. There's also the possibility of examining the library code and extracting just the parts you need.

What Sorts of Things Can Libraries Do?

The specifics of what libraries can do differ depending on the library concerned and the needs and intentions of its creator. However, most libraries include certain recurring themes:

▶ **Encapsulation of DOM methods:** As you see later in this lesson when you look at prototype.js, JavaScript libraries can offer appealing shorthand ways to select and manage page elements and groups of elements.

▶ **Animation:** In Lesson 10, "Controlling Program Flow," you learned about the use of timers. Timers can be used to animate page elements, but writing such code can be tricky and the resulting code complicated to maintain. Many of the popular libraries wrap these sorts of operations into convenient functions to slide, fade, shake, squish, fold, snap, and pulsate parts of your page's interface, all in a cross-browser way and with just a few lines of code.

▶ **Drag and drop:** A truly cross-browser drag and drop has always been one of the trickiest effects to code for all browsers. Libraries can make it easy.

▶ **Ajax:** Libraries provide easy methods to update page content without needing to worry about the nitty-gritty of instantiating `XMLHttpRequest` objects and managing callbacks and status codes.

Some Popular Libraries and Frameworks

New libraries are popping up all the time; others have seen continual development over a number of years. This section by no means provides a complete list; it simply attempts to point out some of the more popular current players.

Prototype Framework

The Prototype Framework (www.prototypejs.org) has been around for a few years now and as of this writing is currently in version 1.7.3. Prototype's major strengths lie in its DOM extensions and Ajax handling, though it has many more tricks up its sleeve, including JSON support and methods to help with creating and inheriting classes.

Prototype is distributed as a standalone library but also as part of larger projects, such as Ruby on Rails and the script.aculo.us JavaScript library.

Dojo

Dojo (www.dojotoolkit.org/) is an open source toolkit that adds power to JavaScript to simplify building applications and user interfaces. It has features ranging from extra string and math functions to animation and Ajax, which we discuss later in this lesson. The latest versions support not only all major desktop browsers but also mobile environments, including Apple iOS, Android, and BlackBerry with their "Dojo Mobile" HTML5 mobile JavaScript framework.

At the time of writing, Dojo is at version 1.13 and Dojo 2 is in beta.

React

React (https://reactjs.org/) is a JavaScript library for building user interfaces, and is maintained by Facebook, Instagram, and a community of other developers. React is all about front-end components, often for single-page applications or to add interactivity to existing web apps. The project began at Facebook but is now available under an open source license.

NOTE

More About React.js

If you're keen to read about React, try *Learning React: A Hands-On Guide to Building Web Applications Using React and Redux*, Second Edition, by Kirupa Chinnathambi (www.informit.com/store/learning-react-a-hands-on-guide-to-building-web-applications-9780134843551).

Node.js

Node.js (https://nodejs.org/) is, at the time of writing, rapidly gaining popularity. Unusually for the world of JavaScript, Node.js allows you to write and execute JavaScript on the server, offering similar capabilities to other server-side languages such as PHP and Java but with some distinct advantages. We take a brief look at Node.js later in the lesson.

jQuery

jQuery (http://jquery.com/) is a fast and compact JavaScript library that simplifies various development tasks, including HTML document traversing, event handling, animation, and Ajax calls for rapid development of interactive websites.

A Closer Look at jQuery

Many JavaScript libraries are available, but jQuery is arguably the most popular and also the most extensible. A huge number of developers contribute open source plug-ins for jQuery, and you can find a suitable plug-in for almost any application you might have. The wide range of plug-ins and the simple syntax make jQuery such a great library. In the following sections you learn the basics of jQuery and get a taste of how powerful it is.

Including jQuery in Your Pages

Before you can use jQuery, you need to include it in your pages. There are two main options, detailed in the following sections.

Download jQuery

You can download jQuery from the official website at http://jquery.com/download/, where you find both Compressed and Uncompressed versions of the code. The Compressed version is for your live pages, because it has been compressed to the smallest possible file size to download as quickly as possible.

For development purposes, choose the Uncompressed version. Thanks to the well-formatted, commented source, you can read the jQuery code to see how it works.

You need to include the jQuery library in the `<head>` section of your pages, using a `<script>` tag. The easiest way is to place the downloaded jquery.js file in the same directory as the page where you want to use it and then reference it like this:

```
<script src="jquery-3.3.1.js"></script>
```

Of course, if you place jQuery in another directory, you'll have to change the (relative or absolute) path in the value you give to the `src` attribute to reflect the location of the file.

NOTE

Get the Latest Version of jQuery

The actual jQuery filename depends on the version you download. At the time of writing, 3.3.1 is the current release.

Use a Remote Version

Instead of downloading and hosting jQuery yourself, you can include it from a so-called Content Delivery Network, or CDN. In addition to saving you from having to download the jQuery library, using a CDN version has a further advantage: it's quite likely that when users visit your page and their browser requests jQuery, it'll already be in their browser cache. Additionally, CDNs generally ensure that they serve the file from the server geographically closest to them, further cutting the loading time.

Find out about jQuery's current CDNs at https://code.jquery.com/.

You can modify your `<script>` tag to suit the chosen CDN. For example, this snippet uses Google's CDN:

```
<script src="https://ajax.googleapis.com/ajax/libs/jquery/3.3.1/jquery.min.js">
</script>
```

Unless you have a particular reason for hosting jQuery yourself, this is usually the best way.

TIP

Link to the Latest Version

If you want to make sure your code is always using the latest release of jQuery, simply link to http://code.jquery.com/jquery-latest.min.js.

Using jQuery's `$(document).ready` Handler

At various places throughout earlier lessons, you used the `window.onload` handler. jQuery has its own equivalent:

```
$(document).ready(function() {
    // jQuery code goes here
});
```

Pretty much all the jQuery code you write will be executed from within a statement like this.

Like `window.onload`, it accomplishes two things:

▶ It ensures that the code does not run until the DOM is available—that is, that any elements your code may be trying to access already exist—so your code doesn't return any errors.

▶ It helps make your code unobtrusive, by separating it from the semantic (HTML) and pre-sentation (CSS) layers.

The jQuery version, though, has an advantage over the `window.onload` event; it doesn't block code execution until the entire page has finished loading, as would be the case with `window.onload`. With jQuery's `(document).ready`, the code begins to execute as soon as the DOM tree has been constructed, before all images and other resources have finished loading, speeding up performance a little.

Selecting Page Elements

jQuery lets you select elements in your HTML by enclosing them in the jQuery wrapper $("").

TIP

Quotation Marks in jQuery Functions

You can also use single quotes in the wrapper function: $('').

Here are some examples of sets of page elements wrapped with the $ operator:

```
$("span"); // all HTML span elements
$("#elem"); // the HTML element having id "elem"
$(".classname"); // HTML elements having class "classname"
$("div#elem"); // <div> elements with ID "elem"
$("ul li a.menu"); // anchors with class "menu" that are nested in list items
$("p > span"); // spans that are direct children of paragraphs
$("input[type=password]"); // inputs that have specified type
$("p:first"); // the first paragraph on the page
$("p:even"); // all even numbered paragraphs
```

So much for DOM and CSS selectors. But jQuery also has its own custom selectors, such as the following:

```
$(":header"); // header elements (h1 to h6)
$(":button"); // any button elements (inputs or buttons)
$(":radio"); // radio buttons
$(":checkbox"); // checkboxes
$(":checked"); // selected checkboxes or radio buttons
```

The jQuery statements shown in the preceding examples each return an object containing an array of the DOM elements specified by the expression inside the wrapper function. Note that none of the preceding lines of code specify an action; you are simply getting the required elements from the DOM. In the sections that follow you learn how to work with these selected elements.

Working with HTML Content

One of jQuery's most useful time-saving tricks is to manipulate the content of page elements. The html() and text() methods allow you to get and set the content of any elements you've selected using the previous statements, while attr() lets you get and set the values of individual element attributes. Let's look at some examples.

html()

The html() method gets the HTML of any element or collection of elements. It works pretty much like JavaScript's innerHTML:

```
var htmlContent = $("#elem").html();
/* variable htmlContent now contains all HTML
(including text) inside page element
with id "elem" */
```

Using similar syntax, you can set the HTML content of a specified element or collection of elements:

```
$("#elem").html("<p>Here is some new content.</p>");
/* page element with id "elem"
has had its HTML content replaced*/
```

text()

If you want only the text content of an element or collection of elements without the HTML, you can use text():

```
var textContent = $("#elem").text();
/* variable textContent contains all the
text (but not HTML) content from inside a
page element with id "elem" */
```

Once more you can change the text content of the specified element(s):

```
$("#elem").text("Here is some new content.");
/* page element with id "elem"
has had its text content replaced*/
```

If you want to append content to an element, rather than replacing it, you can use the following:

```
$("#elem").append("<p>Here is some new content.</p>");
/* keeps current content intact, but
adds the new content to the end */
```

And likewise:

```
$("div").append("<p>Here is some new content.</p>");
/* add the same content to all
<div> elements on the page. */
```

attr()

When passed a single argument, the attr() method gets the value for the specified attribute:

```
var title = $("#elem").attr("title");
```

If applied to a set of elements, it returns the value for only the first element in the matched set.

You can also pass a second argument to `attr()` to set an attribute value:

```
$("#elem").attr("title", "This is the new title");
```

Showing and Hiding Elements

Using plain old JavaScript, showing and hiding page elements usually means manipulating the value of the `display` and `visibility` properties of the element's `style` object. While that works okay, it can lead to pretty long lines of code:

```
document.getElementById("elem").style.visibility = 'visible';
```

You can use jQuery's `show()` and `hide()` methods to carry out these tasks with rather less code. The jQuery methods also offer some useful additional functionality, as you see in the following code examples.

show()

A simple way to make an element or set of elements visible is to call the `show()` method:

```
$("div").show(); // makes all <div> elements visible
```

However, you can also add some additional parameters to spice up the transition.

In the following example, the first parameter `"fast"` determines the speed of the transition. As an alternative to `"fast"` or `"slow"`, jQuery is happy to accept a number of milliseconds for this argument as the required duration of the transition. If no value is set, the transition will occur instantly, with no animation.

TIP

How Slow Is Slow?

The value `"slow"` corresponds to 600ms, while `"fast"` is equivalent to 200ms.

The second argument is a function that operates as a callback; that is, it executes once the transition is complete:

```
$("#elem").show("fast", function() {
    // do something once the element is shown
});
```

This example uses an anonymous function, but a named function works just fine too.

hide()

The hide() method is, of course, the exact reverse of show(), allowing you to make page elements invisible with the same optional arguments as you saw for hide():

```
$("#elem").hide("slow", function() {
    // do something once the element is hidden
});
```

toggle()

The toggle() method changes the current state of an element or collection of elements; it makes visible any element in the collection that is currently hidden and hides any currently being shown. The same optional duration and callback function parameters are also available to toggle().

```
$("#elem").toggle(1000, function() {
    // do something once the element is shown/hidden
});
```

TIP

Grouping Elements

Remember that the show(), hide(), and toggle() methods can be applied to collections of elements, so the elements in that collection will appear or disappear all at once.

Command Chaining

A further handy behavior of jQuery is that most jQuery methods return a jQuery object that can then be used in your call to another method. You could combine two of the previous examples, like this:

```
$("#elem").fadeOut().fadeIn();
```

The preceding code will fade out all the chosen elements and then fade them back in. The number of items you can chain is arbitrarily large, allowing for several commands to successively work on the same collection of elements:

```
$("#elem").text("Hello from jQuery").fadeOut().fadeIn();
```

Handling Events

You can attach event handlers to elements or collections of elements a number of ways in jQuery. First, you can add event handlers directly, like this:

```
$("a").click(function() {
    // execute this code when any anchor element is clicked
});
```

Alternatively, you can use a named function, like this:

```
function hello() {
    alert("Hello from jQuery");
}
$("a").click(hello);
```

In these two examples the function will be executed when an anchor is clicked. Some other common events you might use in jQuery include blur, focus, hover, keypress, change, mousemove, resize, scroll, submit, and select.

To help you add multiple event handlers, jQuery wraps the attachEvent and addEventListener JavaScript methods in a cross-browser way:

```
$("a").on('click', hello);
```

The on() method can be used to attach handlers both to elements already present in the original HTML page and to elements that have been dynamically added to the DOM.

The jQuery UI

The jQuery UI provides advanced effects and theme-able widgets that help you build interactive web applications.

What jQuery UI Is All About

The jQuery development team decided to launch an "official" collection of plug-ins for jQuery, bringing together a wide range of popular user interface components and giving them a common interface style. Using these components, you can build highly interactive and attractively styled web applications with a minimum of code.

Using jQuery UI in your programs gives you access to

- ▶ **Interactions:** The jQuery UI library provides support for dragging and dropping, resizing, selecting, and sorting page elements.

- ▶ **Widgets:** These feature-rich controls include accordion, autocomplete, button, date picker, dialog, progress bar, slider, and tabs.

- ▶ **Theme building:** You are able to give your site a coherent look and feel across all the user interface components. A ThemeRoller tool is available at http://jqueryui.com/themeroller/. The ThemeRoller online tool allows you to choose a theme from the gallery of prewritten designs or create a custom theme based on an existing theme as a starting point.

In this lesson we see an example use of one of the more popular plug-ins. Thanks to the consistent user interface of jQuery UI, it will then be easy to explore the many other available plug-ins by using the jQuery documentation.

The jQuery UI Date Picker Widget

Expecting visitors to correctly fill out date fields has always been a tricky business, mainly due to the wide range of possible date formats that may be used.

A date picker is a pop-up calendar widget that allows the user to simply click on the required day, leaving the widget to format the selected date and enter the appropriate data into the correct input field.

Suppose you have a form field to accept a date:

```
<input type="text" id="datepicker">
```

You can implement a date picker widget for that field with a single line of code:

```
$("#datepicker").datepicker();
```

Listing 24.1 has a complete example you can try.

LISTING 24.1   Using a Date Picker Widget

```
<!DOCTYPE html>
<html>
<head>
    <link rel="stylesheet" type="text/css"
href="http://ajax.googleapis.com/ajax/libs/jqueryui/1.10.3/themes/smoothness/
➡jquery-ui.css"/>
    <title>Date Picker</title>
    <script src="http://code.jquery.com/jquery-latest.min.js"></script>
    <script src="http://codeorigin.jquery.com/ui/1.10.3/jquery-ui.min.js"></script>
    <script>
        $(function() {
            $( "#datepicker" ).datepicker();
        });
    </script>
</head>
<body>
    Date: <input type="text" id="datepicker">
</body>
</html>
```

Figure 24.1 shows the date picker in action.

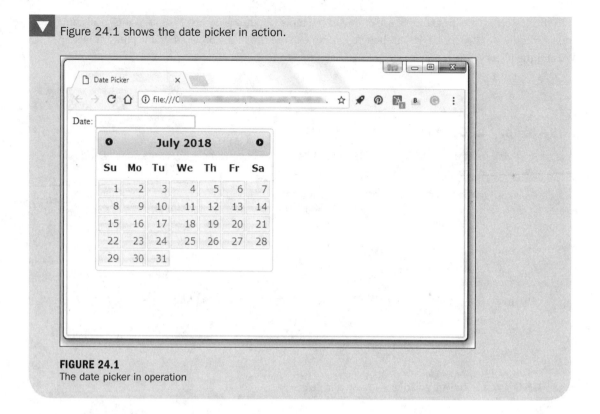

FIGURE 24.1
The date picker in operation

An Introduction to Ajax

So far we've discussed only the traditional page-based model of a website user interface.

When you interact with such a website, individual pages containing text, images, data entry forms, and so forth are presented to you one at a time. Each page must be dealt with individually before navigating to the next.

For instance, you may complete the data entry fields of a form, editing and re-editing your entries as much as you want, knowing that the data will not be sent to the server until the form is finally submitted.

This interaction is summarized in Figure 24.2.

After you submit a form or follow a navigation link, you then must wait while the browser screen refreshes to display the new or revised page that has been delivered by the server.

Unfortunately, interfaces built using this model have quite a few drawbacks. First, there is a significant delay while each new or revised page is loaded. This interrupts what we, as users, perceive as the "flow" of the application.

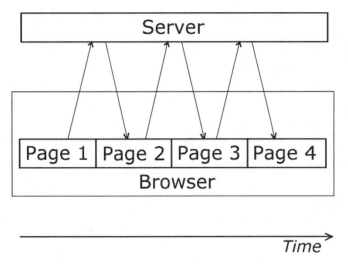

FIGURE 24.2
Traditional client/server interaction

Furthermore, a *whole* page must be loaded on each occasion, even when most of its content is identical to that of the previous page. Items common to many pages on a website, such as header, footer, and navigation sections, can amount to a significant proportion of the data contained in the page.

This unnecessary download of data wastes bandwidth and further exacerbates the delay in loading each new page.

The combined effect of the issues just described is to offer a much inferior user experience compared to that provided by the vast majority of desktop applications. On the desktop, you expect the display contents of your programs to remain visible and the interface elements to continue responding to your commands, while the computing processes occur quietly in the background.

Introducing Ajax

Ajax enables you to add to your web application interfaces some of this functionality more commonly seen in desktop applications. To achieve this, Ajax builds an extra "layer" of processing between the web page and the server.

This layer, often referred to as an Ajax Engine or Ajax Framework, intercepts requests from the user and in the background handles server communications quietly, unobtrusively, and *asynchronously*. This means that server requests and responses no longer need to coincide with particular user actions but may happen at any time convenient to the user and to the correct operation of the application. The browser does not freeze and await the completion by the server of the last request, but instead lets you carry on scrolling, clicking, and typing in the current page.

Ajax also looks after the updating of page elements to reflect the revised information received from the server, which happens dynamically while the page continues to be used.

Figure 24.3 represents how these interactions take place.

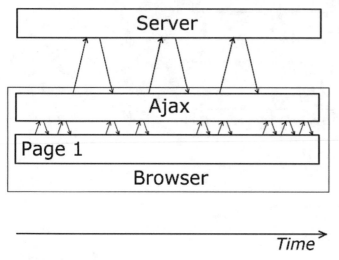

FIGURE 24.3
Ajax client/server interaction

Using the XMLHttpRequest Object

When you click on a hyperlink or submit an HTML form, you send an HTTP request to the server, which responds by serving to you a new or revised page. For your web application to work asynchronously, however, you must have a means to send HTTP requests to the server *without* an associated request to display a new page.

You can do so by means of the XMLHttpRequest object. This JavaScript object is capable of making a connection to the server and issuing an HTTP request without the necessity of an associated page load.

TIP

Calls Must Go to the Same Domain

As a security measure, the XMLHttpRequest object can generally only make calls to URLs within the same domain as the calling page and cannot directly call a remote server.

Creating the Request Object

The following line creates an XMLHttpRequest object called request:

```
var request = new XMLHttpRequest();
```

This line assigns the name request to your new object.

Using Methods and Properties

Now that you have created an instance of your `XMLHttpRequest` object, let's look at some of the object's properties and methods, by referring to Table 24.1.

TABLE 24.1 `XMLHttpRequest` **Objects and Methods**

Properties	Description
onreadystatechange	Determines which event handler will be called when the object's readyState property changes
readyState	Integer reporting the status of the request:
	0 = uninitialized
	1 = loading
	2 = loaded
	3 = interactive
	4 = completed
responseText	Data returned by the server in text string form
responseXML	Data returned by the server expressed as a document object
status	HTTP status code returned by server
statusText	HTTP reason phrase returned by server

Methods	Description
abort()	Stops the current request
getAllResponseHeaders()	Returns all headers as a string
getResponseHeader(x)	Returns the value of header x as a string
Open('method','URL','a')	Specifies the HTTP method (for example, GET or POST), the target URL, and whether the request should be handled asynchronously (if yes, a='true' [default]; if no, a='false')
send(content)	Sends the request, optionally with POST data
setRequestHeader('x','y')	Sets a parameter and value pair x=y and assigns it to the header to be sent with the request

Talking with the Server

In the traditional style of web pages, when you issue a server request via a hyperlink or a form submission, the server accepts that request, carries out any server-side processing required, and subsequently serves to you a new page with content appropriate to the action you've taken.

While this processing takes place, your user interface is effectively frozen. You are made aware when the server has completed its task by the appearance in the browser of the new or revised page.

With asynchronous server requests, however, such communications occur in the background, and the completion of such a request does not necessarily coincide with a screen refresh or a new page being loaded. You must therefore make other arrangements to find out what progress the server has made in dealing with your request.

The `XMLHttpRequest` object possesses a convenient property to report on the progress of the server request. You can examine this property using JavaScript routines to determine the point at which the server has completed its task, and the results are available for you to use.

Your Ajax armory must therefore include a routine to monitor the status of your request and act accordingly. We look at this in more detail later in the lesson.

What Happens at the Server?

So far as the server-side script is concerned, the communication from your `XMLHttpRequest` object is just another HTTP request. Ajax applications care little about what languages or operating environments exist at the server. Provided that the client-side Ajax layer receives a timely and correctly formatted HTTP response from the server, everything will work just fine.

Dealing with the Server Response

Once notified that an asynchronous request has been successfully completed, you may then use the information returned by the server.

Ajax allows for this information to be returned to you in a number of formats, including ASCII text and XML data.

Depending on the nature of the application, you may then translate, display, or otherwise process this information within your current page.

But There's an Easier Way, Right?

Luckily, plenty of JavaScript libraries out there make a good job of packaging these rather complicated procedures into easy-to-use functions and methods.

Let's see how the jQuery library can make writing Ajax scripts a piece of cake.

How to Use jQuery to Implement Ajax

As you probably now realize, Ajax programming from scratch can be a little cumbersome. Fortunately, jQuery solves this issue for you, letting you write Ajax routines in few lines of code.

There are a number of jQuery methods for performing Ajax calls to the server; the more frequently used ones are described here.

load()

When you simply want to grab a document from the server and display it in a page element, `load()` might be all you require. The following code snippet gets the file newContent.html and adds its content to the element with `id="elem"`:

```
$(function() {
    $("#elem").load("newContent.html");
});
```

A neat trick is that you can pass a selector along with the URL and get only the part of the page corresponding to that selector:

```
$(function() {
    $("#elem").load("newContent.html #info");
});
```

This example adds a jQuery selector after the URL, separated by a space. This causes jQuery to pass back only the content of the container specified by the selector; in this case, the element with ID of `info`.

When `load()` gives you too little control, jQuery offers methods to send GET and POST requests too.

get() **and** post()

The two methods are similar, simply invoking different request types. You don't need to select a jQuery object (such as a page element or set of elements); instead, you can call `get()` or `post()` directly using `$.get()` or `$.post()`. In its simplest form, the `get()` or `post()` method takes a single argument, the target URL.

You'll often want to send data to the server using `get()` or `post()`. Such data is sent as a set of parameter and value pairs in an encoded string.

TIP

The jQuery serialize() Method

If you are collecting data from form fields, jQuery offers the handy serialize() method that can assemble the form data for you:

```
var formdata = $('#form1').serialize();
```

In most cases, though, you'll want to do something with the returned data. To do that, you pass a callback function as an argument:

```
$.get("serverScript.php",
    {param1: "value1", param2: "value2"},
```

```
    function(data) {
    alert("Server responded: " + data);
});
```

The syntax for `post()` is essentially the same:

```
$.post("serverScript.php",
    {param1: "value1", param2: "value2"},
    function(data) {
    alert("Server responded: " + data);
});
```

ajax()

For the ultimate flexibility, the `ajax()` method allows you to set virtually every aspect of the Ajax call and how to handle the response. For full details of using `ajax()`, see the documentation at http://api.jquery.com/jQuery.ajax/.

NOTE

Find Out More About jQuery

If you want to explore jQuery further, a great place to start would be a copy of Sams Teach Yourself jQuery and JavaScript in 24 Hours by Brad Dayley. You can find it at www.informit.com/store/jquery-and-javascript-in-24-hours-sams-teach-yourself-9780672337345.

A Brief Look at Node.js

Until recently, JavaScript has commonly been used for client-side programming—that is, for code that executes in the visitor's browser and performs actions of some sort on a web page.

When you build a Node.js application, you can still use JavaScript on the client side to alter your pages. Node.js, however, offers a server-side environment where you can use the JavaScript language, much as you would with more traditional server-side languages such as PHP or Java.

Under the hood, Node.js uses Google's V8 JavaScript engine—the same one that powers its Chrome browser—repurposed to work in the server environment.

So what does JavaScript have that traditional server languages don't?

Using a Nonblocking Code Model

As you've seen in the course of these lessons, JavaScript relies heavily on events. By using event listeners and callback functions, JavaScript can listen for things happening and respond when they do. These events don't have to be user-generated (though on the client side they often are); they might, for instance, involve a task completing or a particular program state being detected.

These capabilities let JavaScript, unlike many other server-side languages, offer a nonblocking code model. In such a model, the server-side program doesn't have to wait for an action to be completed; instead, it can process other instructions while it's waiting.

Let's take a file upload as an example.

In the more traditional blocking model, the program would begin the file upload, hang around until the upload completed, and then perform its next command (display the file on the screen, perhaps).

Using a nonblocking model, however, once the upload is requested, the program can carry on with other activities. It will detect when the file upload has completed and can then return to dealing with it. This is the model used by Node.js.

The result is that Node.js applications never need to hang around waiting for something to happen; instead, they are always busy, making for some fast and responsive applications.

TIP

Find Out More About Node.js

A thorough look at Node.js is outside the scope of these lessons. If you'd like to explore its capabilities, take a look at *Learning Node.js: A Hands-On Guide to Building Web Applications in JavaScript*, Second Edition, by Marc Wandschneider (www.informit.com/store/learning-node.js-a-hands-on-guide-to-building-web-applications-9780134663708).

Summary

In this lesson you learned about a few ways in which you might further extend your knowledge of JavaScript, especially by using third-party libraries and code projects.

You also found out how some of these additions can make your projects easier to code and maintain.

Q&A

Q. Can I use more than one third-party library in the same script?

A. Yes, in theory: If the libraries are well written and designed not to interfere with each other, there should be no problem combining them. In practice, this depends on the libraries you need and how they were written.

Q. Where did jQuery come from?

A. jQuery was written by John Resig and launched in 2006. There are currently several jQuery projects, including jQuery Core and jQuery UI (used in this lesson). These projects are under active development by John and a team of volunteers. You can read about the team and the projects at jquery.org.

Q. How can I make the other elements on my page have the same styles as those generated by jQuery UI?

A. When jQuery UI generates markup, it applies classes to the newly created markup items. These classes correspond to CSS declarations in the jQuery UI CSS Framework. Full details for each widget are given in the jQuery UI documentation.

Q. Do other libraries besides jQuery implement Ajax?

A. Certainly. Many libraries and frameworks help you implement Ajax, some popular ones being Dojo, MooTools, and Prototype.

Workshop

Quiz questions and exercises to test your understanding and to stretch your skills.

Quiz

1. Which of the following is not a JavaScript library?

    a. jQuery

    b. Prototype

    c. Ajax

2. In jQuery, how could you select all page elements having `class = "sidebar"`?

    a. `$(".sidebar")`

    b. `$("class:sidebar")`

    c. `$(#sidebar)`

3. What does the jQuery expression `$("p:first").show()` do?

    a. Displays paragraph elements before displaying any other elements

    b. Makes the first paragraph element on the page visible

    c. Makes the first line of all paragraph elements visible

4. To use the jQuery UI in your pages, each page must contain as a minimum

    a. The jQuery and jQuery UI JavaScript libraries and a link to a jQuery UI theme CSS file

    b. Just the jQuery and jQuery UI libraries

    c. Just the jQuery UI JavaScript library and a link to a jQuery UI theme CSS file

5. Which of these code lines will grab an element with `id=source` from the server file examples.html and insert it into a page element with `id=target`?

a. `$("#target").load("examples.html #source");`

b. `$("#source").load("examples.html #target");`

c. `$(#source).load("examples.html #info");`

TIP

Register Your Book

Just a reminder for those of you reading these words in the print or e-book edition of this book: If you go to www.informit.com/register and register this book (using ISBN 978-0-672-33809-0), you can receive free access to an online Web Edition that not only contains the complete text of this book but also features an interactive version of this quiz.

Answers

1. c. Ajax

2. a. `$(".sidebar")`

3. b. Makes the first paragraph element on the page visible

4. a. The jQuery and jQuery UI JavaScript libraries and a link to a jQuery UI theme CSS file

5. a. `$("#target").load("examples.html #source");`

Exercises

Skip back to Lesson 8, "Storing Data in Arrays," and review Listing 8.1. Rewrite this program using jQuery's element selection and `html()` methods instead of using `document.getElementById()` and the `innerHTML` property. Remove the `<script>` element from the body of the page and run it instead via jQuery's `$(document).ready` feature. Remember that your program will need to include the jQuery source; you can either download this and use a local copy, or use a CDN source as described in the lesson.

Visit the jQuery site at jquery.com and take a look at the documentation and examples, especially for the many jQuery methods that we didn't have space to discuss here.

Data Visualization Using JavaScript

What You'll Learn in This Lesson:

▶ What the D3 JavaScript library can do

▶ How to include D3 in your scripts

▶ About SVG

▶ How to use events in D3

▶ How to bind data to D3 graphics

Most of our discussions about JavaScript have been about its use to make web pages do cool things, and one of the coolest things a web page can do is to present information.

When that information is simple—such as the latest football scores or what time the nearest store closes—it's not too hard to present it clearly in text form. Some information, though, is sufficiently complex to need a different approach.

Data visualization is the presentation of information in a visual format to make it easier to understand. It allows visitors to drill down into data for more detailed insights into not just what the data is but also what it *means*.

In this lesson we check out D3, a JavaScript library designed for presenting data visually.

What Is D3?

D3 is a JavaScript library designed for producing dynamic, interactive data visualizations in web pages using SVG, HTML5, and CSS. It does so by allowing you to bind data to elements of the DOM and then apply transformations to those elements based on the underlying data. (If you don't know what SVG is, don't worry; we get to that in the next section).

For example, you might use D3 to turn numerical lists into HTML tables, graphs, or animated charts.

NOTE

It's a Steep Curve

D3 is not for the fainthearted. The library has a lot of advanced functionality and an interface that can seem daunting at first. In this lesson, we explore some basics to get started. When you feel ready, there's extensive documentation at https://github.com/d3/d3/wiki that you can use to take things further. If you want a quick preview of the amazing things D3 can do, look at the examples in the gallery at https://github.com/d3/d3/wiki/Gallery. You can click on each example to browse the underlying code.

Including D3 in Your Scripts

There are two methods for including the D3 library code in your scripts.

If you want to download a copy of the D3 library and include it in your scripts, you can head over to D3's website at https://d3js.org/ and download a copy. Then it's just a matter of including the library in the head of your page in the usual manner:

```
<script src="d3.v4.min.js"></script>
```

Alternatively, you can link to the latest code directly at D3's site, like this:

```
<script src="https://d3js.org/d3.v4.min.js"></script>
```

This is the way we work for the examples in this lesson.

Introducing SVG

SVG stands for *scalable vector graphics*. You're probably already familiar with graphics stored as bitmaps—a rectangular array of pixel values like those found in most image file types such as .bmp or .jpg. These images are usually optimized to work at a given size and will look pixelated if you try to scale them too much. A vector graphic, however, will scale as much as you need it to without distorting, because vector graphics aren't stored as pixel arrays, but as mathematical definitions.

TIP

Play with SVG Graphics

You can create SVG images with the free online editor at http://editor.method.ac/. When you save an image, the mathematical recipe for your SVG graphics is stored in the XML language, so you can examine the code in any text editor just by opening the .svg file you created.

D3 uses SVG graphics drawn on `<canvas>` elements attached to the DOM of your web page. You don't need to worry about creating any of the XML for the SVG elements, since D3 handles all of that for you by building these elements using its own set of methods.

Getting Started Using D3

D3 works by attaching a canvas to a page element and drawing SVG shapes on that canvas.

For the purposes of this example, let's assume that your HTML page has the following `<div>` element:

```
<div id="out"></div>
```

This is where you'll have D3 attach the `canvas` element on which to draw.

Let's jump straight in with just about the simplest example imaginable: you'll use D3 to draw a rectangle.

Before you can do that, though, we need to talk about the coordinate system, which is shown in Figure 25.1.

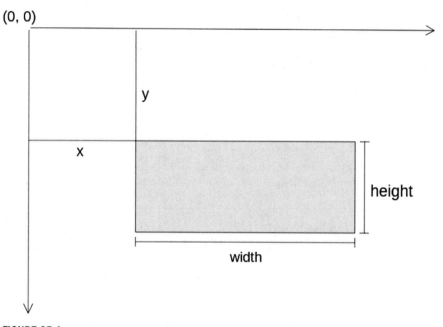

FIGURE 25.1
The coordinate system for the rectangle

D3 uses a two-dimensional system with *x* measuring horizontally from the left and *y* measuring vertically from the top of the canvas. So the origin of the system is in the top-left corner.

You specify your rectangle by telling D3 where to place the top-left corner of the rectangle and by specifying its width and height.

First, though, you need to create the `canvas` element.

Selecting and Appending in D3

Including the D3 library in your page automatically creates an object called d3. You use the properties and methods of the d3 object to do the heavy lifting.

TIP

Loading D3 as a Module

You learned about modules in Lesson 21, "Organizing Code with Modules."

When using D3 in an environment that supports native JavaScript modules, you can import the D3 as you would from a module:

```
import * as d3 from "d3";
```

You can then use the d3 object as detailed elsewhere in this lesson.

First, you need to select the page element where you want the canvas attached:

```
var mySVG = d3.select("#out")
```

You can then chain the append() method to attach the canvas:

```
var mySVG = d3.select("#out").append("svg")
```

TIP

Does This Look Familiar?

The way of defining element selectors and chaining commands in D3 is almost identical to that used in jQuery, which you read about in Lesson 24, "Where to Go Next." Skip back there for a refresher if you feel you need it. We'll wait.

Finally, the canvas needs a couple of attributes—width and height. Here's the complete command:

```
var mySVG = d3.select("#out").append("svg").attr("width", 300).attr("height", 300);
```

NOTE

A Clearer Coding Style

These chained commands can get pretty long in D3. I prefer to write lines like the preceding one in this way:

```
var mySVG = d3.select("#out")
        .append("svg")
        .attr("width", 300)
        .attr("height", 300);
```

The command is exactly the same but avoids so many annoying word wraps or scrolls of the editor pane.

Now for the rectangle: once again you need the `append()` method, but this time with the parameter `"rect"`, which D3 uses for a rectangle. Once again you'll use the `attr()` method, this time to add dimensions and position. You can also add some styling to the rectangle by using D3's `style()` method to add line and fill colors:

```
mySVG.append("rect")
        .style("stroke", "black")
        .style("fill", "#aabbcc")
        .attr("x", 50)
        .attr("y", 100)
        .attr("height", 100)
        .attr("width", 80);
```

The `style()` method can be used to add many styling features to D3 shapes. In the preceding example, `stroke` determines line color, while `fill` defines a color to pour into the shape. Both of these can take any color definition that makes sense in CSS; you can see two different styles in the preceding example. You can also use opacity, with a value between 0 (transparent) and 1 (solid color). It's tough to demonstrate opacity with just one shape, so let's overlay a `circle` element:

```
mySVG.append("circle")
        .style("stroke", "black")
        .style("fill", "#88cc88")
        .style("opacity", "0.5")
        .attr("r", 40)
        .attr("cx", 120)
        .attr("cy", 90)
```

Figure 25.2 shows the two shapes drawn on the canvas.

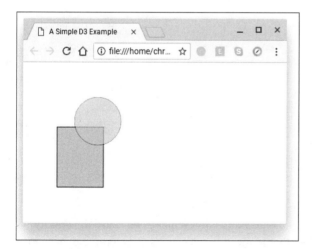

FIGURE 25.2
The rectangle and circle drawn on the canvas

Binding Events to Selections

D3 also supports handling of events. You can bind an event listener to any DOM element using D3's `on()` method.

Chaining the `on()` method to a selection statement adds an event listener to the selected DOM element(s). The first parameter passed to `on()` is an event type, such as `click`, `mouseover`, or `mouseout`. The second parameter is a callback function that will be executed when the given type of event is detected:

```
.on(event, callback);
```

Here's an example using an anonymous function (note, though, that `on()` can use named callback functions too):

```
.on("mouseover", function(){d3.select(this).style("fill", "#88cc88");})
```

This `on()` statement changes the color of the selection on `mouseover`.

NOTE

Using `this`

The use of `this` in the preceding code example provides a handy way to refer to the selection to which `on()` is being applied.

Let's apply some event listeners to the `circle` element from Figure 25.2:

```
mySVG.append("circle")
        .style("stroke", "black")
        .style("fill", "#88cc88")
        .style("opacity", "0.5")
        .attr("r", 40)
        .attr("cx", 120)
        .attr("cy", 90)
        .on("mouseover", function(){
                d3.select(this).style("fill", "#000088");
                d3.select(this).style("opacity", "1");
            })
        .on("mouseout", function(){
                d3.select(this).style("fill", "#88cc88");
                d3.select(this).style("opacity", "0.5")
            });
```

This code snippet uses two `on()` statements—one to change the element's fill color and opacity in response to a `mouseover` event, and the other to revert the element's fill color and opacity to their original values when the mouse pointer leaves.

Figure 25.3 shows the effect in action.

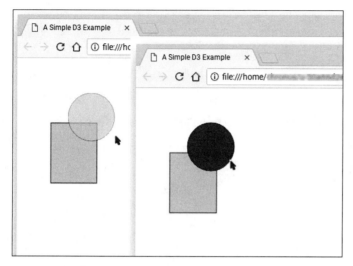

FIGURE 25.3
Changing behavior on `mouseover`

Binding Data to D3 Graphics

So far, so good. You know how to load D3, create and attach a canvas, draw some shapes, and even have elements you've created respond to events.

That's all pretty cool. The whole point of data visualization, though, is to present data. One of the big advantages of using a library such as D3 is its capability to closely bind your presentation to the data being represented, so the value of the data can affect the way it's displayed.

Later in this lesson you use real-world data. For now, though, let's get some random numbers to play with:

```
var myData = [];
for(let i=0; i<10; i++){
    myData[i] = Math.round(Math.random()*100);
}
```

This simple piece of code produces the array `myData` containing 10 integers with values in the range 0 to 100. In the real world these figures might represent temperature measurements, exam scores, or any number of other types of data.

You could fairly easily wrangle a quick horizontal bar chart by looping through the data array and drawing a rectangle for each data item, as in this snippet of code:

```
var barHeight = 30;
for(let n=0; n<myData.length; n++) {
```

```
mySVG.append("rect")
    .style("stroke", "black")
    .style("fill", "#88cc88")
    .attr("y", 100 + (n * barHeight))
    .attr("x", 200)
    .attr("width", myData[n])
    .attr("height", barHeight);
}
```

This example would produce output something like that shown in Figure 25.4.

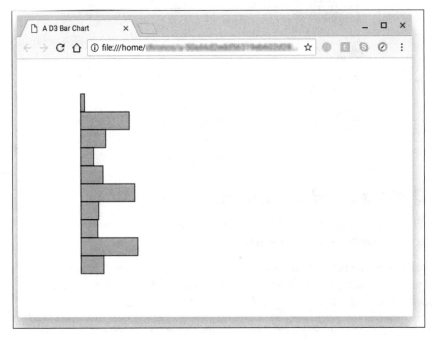

FIGURE 25.4
A simple horizontal bar chart

That works, but it's inflexible. The code is hard to read and to maintain, and overall the result is not very useful.

Instead, let's see how D3 can bind the data to chart elements.

Using `data()` and `enter()`

D3 lets you bind a set of data to the display elements you create, and manipulate the attributes and styles of the display based on the values of the bound data.

Let's look at the following code snippet. How it works might not be obvious at first, but we'll step through it.

```
mySVG.selectAll("rect")
        .data(myData)
        .enter()
        .append("rect")
```

First, this example forms a selection of all the rectangle elements on mySVG canvas:

```
mySVG.selectAll("rect")
```

Next, you attach myData as a data source:

```
.data(myData)
```

Now you want to tell D3 to add a new entry to the selection for each piece of data it encounters:

```
.enter()
```

And finally, you tell it that each addition should be another rectangle:

```
.append("rect")
```

When you're ready to specify attributes for your new items, you can base those attributes on the *index* (that is, the position of the element in the data array) and *value* of the data item itself. In the case of your horizontal bar chart, you want the width of each rectangle to change with the value of the data. Let's look at an example:

```
mySVG.selectAll("rect")
        .data(myData)
        .enter()
        .append("rect")
        .attr("height", 100)
        .attr("width", function(d, i){ return d })
```

Did you notice the callback function in the last line? D3 will use this function (instead of a static value, like the one in the line above it) to set the attribute value.

The callback function takes two parameters—the first being the value of the current item of data (it's called d here, but you can call it anything) and the second being the index of that item (here called i). The preceding example ignores the index and simply has the function return the value d of the data. The *vertical* location of each bar, though, is not dependent on the value of the data. You want the bars to stack one on top of the next, so you need to keep the same x coordinate, but increment the *y* value by the bar height for each new data point. That means you need not the data, d, but the index i:

```
.attr("x", 100)
.attr("y", function(d, i){ return (50 + i*30) })
```

The complete code is shown in Listing 25.1

LISTING 25.1   The Bar Chart Using Bound Data

```
<!DOCTYPE html>
<html>
<head>
    <title>A D3 Bar Chart</title>
    <script src="https://d3js.org/d3.v4.min.js"></script>
</head>
<body>
    <div id="out"></div>
    <script>

    var myData = [];
    for(let i=0; i<10; i++){
        myData[i] = Math.round(Math.random()*100);
    }

    var mySVG = d3.select("#out")
        .append("svg")
        .attr("width", 600)
        .attr("height", 600);

    mySVG.selectAll("rect")
        .data(myData)
        .enter()
        .append("rect")
        .style("stroke", "black")
        .style("fill", "#88cc88")
        .attr("x", 100)
        .attr("y", function(d, i){ return (50 + i*30) })
        .attr("height", 30)
        .attr("width", function(d, i){ return d });

    </script>
</body>
</html>
```

If you save this code to an .html file and open it in your browser, you should see that it displays a bar chart that's identical to the one made earlier and shown in Figure 25.4

This is still pretty basic, so what can you do to improve it? First, it would be handy if you could easily alter the *scale* of the data and maybe add some *text labels*.

Using Scales

You can define a linear scale in D3 by using the keyword `scale`, like this:

```
var x_scale = d3.scale.linear()
    .domain([0, 100]) // the min and max of your data values
    .range([0, 300]); // will map to this range of pixel values
```

The variable `x_scale` in this snippet now contains a function that will scale the data, in this case stretching the values by a factor of three. You can apply the scale simply by passing this function as a callback:

```
.attr("x", x_scale)
```

Of course, you could build this scaling into your custom callback function, but abstracting the scaling logic into a separate scale statement can clean up your code and let you deal with scaling all in one place.

Adding Text

You can add text elements to your D3 visualizations using the SVG `text` element.

Now that you have your head around other SVG elements like `rect`, adding text items is pretty straightforward. You can specify the text style using CSS-like style attributes and the text location (the coordinates of the first character) in just the same way:

```
mySVG.append("text")
        .attr("text-anchor", "middle")
        .attr("style", "font: 10px arial, sans-serif;")
        .text("Hello world!");
```

TIP

Transformations

See the D3 documentation for the many ways you can transform text with translation and rotation using commands like

```
.attr("transform", "translate(100,150) rotate("-60")")
```

There are far too many options here to go into details in this lesson!

Loading Data

So far you've generated some basic displays based on random numbers. But how do you apply these techniques to real-world data?

In a real application you might have your data in a file (say, a .csv file), or it might arrive packaged as XML or JSON data.

D3 can load data from various file formats including .csv, .xml, and .json.

CAUTION

Beware of Security Gotchas

Like the module examples in Lesson 21, to import data in external files, you need to use a web server rather than use local files.

In the following Try It Yourself project, you see how to deal with remote data when you collect some real-world data with the help of jQuery.

▼ TRY IT YOURSELF

Near Earth Objects

Let's bring together what you've learned so far to make a real application.

NASA publishes a JSON data feed about Near-Earth Objects—asteroids and comets that pass near (in astronomical terms!) to Earth. Here, you create a D3 web app that

▶ Grabs that JSON data and builds a dataset to display

▶ Builds a horizontal bar chart showing the magnitude of these objects as seen from Earth

▶ Makes the chart display further information via a pop-up when the mouse pointer enters each chart entry

First, you need to grab the data. If you point your browser at https://data.nasa.gov/resource/2vr3-k9wn.json, you'll see the JSON data feed. Here's a sample entry, giving details of the object's designation, discovery date, and various pieces of data about its orbit:

```
{"designation":"386847 (2010 LR33)","discovery_date":"2010-06-
06T00:00:00.000","h_mag":"18","i_deg":"5.84","moid_au":"0.029",
"orbit_class":"Apollo","period_yr":"2.2","pha":"Y","q_au_1":"0.91","q_au_2":"2.48"}
```

There are a number of ways you could capture this data in JavaScript, but this example uses jQuery, since it has a handy .getJSON() method that takes a URL as a parameter:

```
$.getJSON('https://data.nasa.gov/resource/2vr3-k9wn.json',
    function(data) {
        //data is the JSON string
        for(let i=0; i<data.length; i++) {
            var dt = data;
            if(dt[i].orbit_class == "Aten") {
                myData.push({ "Designation":dt[i].designation,
                            "Magnitude":dt[i].h_mag,
                            "Period":dt[i].period_yr,
                            "Discovery_date":dt[i].discovery_date,
                            "moid_au":dt[i].moid_au,
                            "q_au_1":dt[i].q_au_1,
                            "q_au_2":dt[i].q_au_2
                });
            }
        }
    }
```

TIP
_____

All About Orbits

To have a manageable dataset, this example selects only those items with an orbit class of "Aten". If you want to know about the various orbit classes—and lots of other cool stuff—visit https://cneos.jpl.nasa.gov/about/basics.html and read all about it!
_____

You also use an extra `div` element as the information pop-up. It will be styled with CSS and made visible on `mouseover` by altering its `opacity` value.

The code is shown in Listing 25.2.

This example may look a little daunting at first, but on closer inspection, you'll see that (apart from a little CSS styling) it simply combines the preceding jQuery data capture routine, the bar chart techniques from Listing 25.1, and the techniques discussed earlier for adding and positioning text.

LISTING 25.2   Displaying NASA's Feed of Near Earth Objects

```
<!DOCTYPE html>
<html>
<head>
    <title>Near Earth Objects</title>
    <style>
        body {background-image: url("starfield.jpg");}
        h1 {
            font: 28px arial, sans-serif;
            color: white;
        }
        #out1 {
            position: absolute;
            border: 0px;
        }
        div.popup {
            position: absolute;
            text-align: left;
            width: 300px;
            height: 100px;
            padding: 20px;
            font: 12px arial, sans-serif;
            background: #bb88bb;
            border: 2px solid black;
            border-radius: 20px;
            pointer-events: none;
        }
    </style>
    <script src="http://code.jquery.com/jquery-latest.min.js"></script>
    <script src="https://d3js.org/d3.v4.min.js"></script>;
    <script>
        var myData = [];

        $(document).ready(function() {
            // jQuery is used to process the JSON feed
            $.getJSON('https://data.nasa.gov/resource/2vr3-k9wn.json', function(data) {
                //data is the JSON string
```

```
for(let i=0; i<data.length; i++) {
    var dt = data;
    if(dt[i].orbit_class == "Aten") {
        myData.push({ "Designation":dt[i].designation,
                      "Magnitude":dt[i].h_mag,
                      "Period":dt[i].period_yr,
                      "Discovery_date":dt[i].discovery_date,
                      "moid_au":dt[i].moid_au,
                      "q_au_1":dt[i].q_au_1,
                      "q_au_2":dt[i].q_au_2
        });
    }
}

// Create and attach the canvas
var mySVG = d3.select("#out1")
    .append("svg")
    .attr("width", 500)
    .attr("height", 500);

// Bar height for the chart
var barHeight = 30;

// Define the div for the popup box
var popup = d3.select("body").append("div")
                    .attr("class", "popup")
                    .style("opacity", 0);

// Build the data-bound bar chart
// using mouseover and mouseout to
// toggle the opacity of the popup
mySVG.selectAll("rect")
    .data(myData)
    .enter().append("rect")
    .style("stroke", "black")
    .style("fill", "#8888aa")
    .attr("width", function(d) { return parseInt(200 * (d.Period)); })
    .attr("height", barHeight)
    .attr("y", function(d, i){ return (50 + i*barHeight)})
    .attr("x", function(d){ return 200 })
    .on("mouseover", function(d) {
        d3.select(this).style("fill", "#000088");
        popup.style("opacity", .8);
        popup.html("Designation: " + d.Designation +
            "<br/>Magnitude: " + d.Magnitude +
            "<br/>Period (years): " + d.Period +
            "<br/>Discovered: " + d.Discovery_date +
            "<br/>Min distance from Earth (au): " + d.moid_au +
```

```
                    "<br/>Perigee (au): " + d.q_au_1 +
                    "<br/>Apogee (au): " + d.q_au_2)
                .style("left", (d3.event.pageX) + "px")
                .style("top", (d3.event.pageY - 28) + "px");
            })
            .on("mouseout", function(d) {
                d3.select(this).style("fill", "#8888aa");
                popup.style("opacity", 0);
            });

            //Column Headers
            mySVG.append("text")
                .attr("style", "font: 16px bold arial, sans-serif")
                .attr("style", "fill: white")
                .attr("x", 50)
                .attr("y", 30)
                .text("Designation");
            mySVG.append("text")
                .attr("style", "font: 16px bold arial, sans-serif")
                .attr("style", "fill: white")
                .attr("x", 250)
                .attr("y", 30)
                .text("Magnitude");

            // Left hand column shows object Designation
            mySVG.selectAll("text.desig")
                .data(myData)
                .enter()
                .append("text")
                .attr("class", "desig")
                .attr("x", 50 )
                .attr("y", function(d, i){ return 50 + i * barHeight })
                .attr("dy", 5 + barHeight/2)
                .attr("text-anchor", "left")
                .attr("style", "font: 14px arial, sans-serif;")
                .attr("style", "fill: white")
                .text(function(d) { return d.Designation; });
            });
        });
    </script>
</head>
<body>
    <h1>NEAR EARTH OBJECTS</h1>
    <div id="out1"></div>
</body>
</html>
```

▼ Save the code from Listing 25.2 in an HTML file and open it in your browser. You should see something like the contents of Figure 25.5, but since this data is from a live, updating feed, your content might be different from mine.

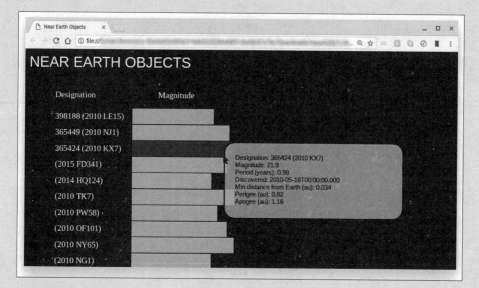

FIGURE 25.5
The completed data visualization

If you want to further examine the elements that D3 has generated, simply pop open your browser's developer tools, as done in Figure 25.6. This is a useful technique when you're building and debugging your data visualizations.

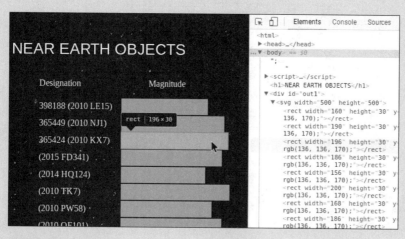

FIGURE 25.6
Using the browser's developer tools

Summary

This lesson introduced the D3 library for building data visualizations and data-driven documents.

You learned the basics of how the library can be used to create SVG graphics and attach them to a `canvas` element on your web page. You also learned how such graphics can have their attributes bound to data to form interactive presentations, and built a working example using a live data feed from NASA.

D3 is a complex and immensely capable library, and this lesson has barely scratched the surface of what it can do, but I hope it will form a basis for you to experiment further and devise your own interactive web pages and data visualizations.

Q&A

Q. Can D3 be used for applications other than web pages?

A. Although it's a little beyond the scope of this lesson, it's possible to export SVG graphics in other formats such as PNG or PDF. This makes graphics generated by D3 suitable for use in other media such as print.

Q. What are the licensing terms for D3?

A. D3 is distributed under a BSD license, allowing it to be used free of charge for both private and commercial projects provided that some simple licensing conditions are met (such as the inclusion of the D3 copyright notice in any applications distributed). You can read the licensing information at https://github.com/d3/d3/blob/master/LICENSE.

Workshop

Quiz questions and exercises to test your understanding and to stretch your skills.

Quiz

1. SVG files contain data in which of the following formats?

   a. Binary

   b. XML

   c. JSON

2. What would you use to select a page element having `id = "myDiv"`?

   a. `myDiv.select()`

   b. `d3.select("myDiv")`

   c. `select("d3.myDiv")`

3. What would you use to attach a canvas element to a selected element?

   a. `.append("svg")`

   b. `.attach("svg")`

   c. `.add("svg")`

4. Which of the following has the correct syntax to define a linear scale?

   a. `d3.linear.scale`

   b. `d3.scale(linear)`

   c. `d3.scale.linear()`

5. Which file formats can D3 read natively?

   a. CSV

   b. JSON

   c. XML

   d. All of the above

TIP
_____

Register Your Book

Just a reminder for those of you reading these words in the print or e-book edition of this book: If you go to www.informit.com/register and register this book (using ISBN 978-0-672-33809-0), you can receive free access to an online Web Edition that not only contains the complete text of this book but also features an interactive version of this quiz.
_____

Answers

   1. b. XML

   2. b. `d3.select("myDiv")`

   3. a. `.append("svg")`

   4. c. `d3.scale.linear()`

   5. d. All of the above

Exercises

A Near-Earth Object above a given size and with an orbit that could let it make exceptionally close approaches to Earth is termed a Potentially Hazardous Object (PHO). These objects are defined as having a `moid` value of less than 0.05 AU and an absolute magnitude of 22 or greater.

Can you modify the code in Listing 25.2 to make any such objects display differently to the others? You might, for instance, make the magnitude bar of these objects turn red, instead of blue, on `mouseover`.

Game Programming Using EaselJS

What You'll Learn in This Lesson:

▶ How to include the EaselJS library in your pages

▶ How to use EaselJS to employ the `<canvas>` element more easily

▶ How to build an animated game

EaselJS is a library to help you code high-performance interactive 2D content such as games, artwork, advertisements, data visualizations, and more in HTML5. It does this by offering an easy-to-use interface layer for the `<canvas>` element, which you read about in Lesson 15, "Programming HTML with JavaScript."

EaselJS forms one part of the CreateJS suite of libraries, which you can find at www.createjs.com/.

In this lesson you explore the features of EaselJS while creating a fully playable animated shooting game.

NOTE

Get EaselJS for Free

EaselJS is released for free under the MIT license, which means you can use it for almost any purpose, including your commercial projects.

Introducing EaselJS

As you found out in earlier lessons, one of the coolest new features of HTML5 is the `<canvas>` element. This element offers a blank canvas on which you can render graphics such as shapes, lines, and bitmap images.

Working directly with the `<canvas>` element can be challenging, however. Out of the box, `<canvas>` doesn't understand ideas such as a display list of items to render (as does, for instance, the Flash Player). It just gives you a single area on which you can draw. What needs to be drawn, when, and in what order are up to you.

EaselJS tries to provide a Flash-like Display List API. Don't worry if you're not yet sure what that means; in the course of this lesson, you use EaselJS to develop a fully playable game that you can later go on to expand further if you wish.

Downloading EaselJS

You can download the latest version of EaselJS for free from www.createjs.com/.

Download the .zip package and extract it to a convenient place on your computer. The .zip archive contains lots of information, including examples, tools, comprehensive documentation, and more. The important bit that you'll need to re-create the code in this lesson, though, is the EaselJS JavaScript file.

In the package I downloaded, this file is called easeljs-1.0.0.min.js and is in a folder called lib.

Including EaselJS in Your Pages

There are two easy ways to include the library in your page. If you downloaded the library as described in the preceding section, simply use this line:

```
<script src="lib/easeljs-1.0.0.min.js"></script>
```

Alternatively, you can include the library via a Content Delivery Network (CDN) like this:

```
<script src="https://code.createjs.com/1.0.0/easeljs.min.js"></script>
```

TIP

Get the Latest Version

Check the websites at www.createjs.com and http://code.createjs.com/ for the latest available versions of the downloadable and CDN libraries, respectively.

Using the Stage

All the action in an EaselJS application takes place on a stage. The Stage object is a container to hold all the other objects that EaselJS will render, animate, show, hide, or otherwise manipulate.

Setting the Stage

The foundation on which to build the stage is an HTML5 <canvas> element, which has the ID attribute canvas1. You can then create the stage like this:

```
var stage = new createjs.Stage('canvas1');
```

With that done, it's time to create some objects to display on the stage.

Using `Text` Objects

A `Text` object holds, as you might expect, a string of text. The parameters accepted are the text string, font, and color. The font and color parameters are described as they would be in CSS. Here's an example:

```
var txt = new createjs.Text("My text string", "24px arial", "#333");
```

With our Text object created, we can position it on the stage:

```
txt.x = 200;
txt.y = 100;
stage.addChild(txt);
```

WARNING

Your Text Is Converted to an Image

Text entered this way is not accessible. It becomes pixel data; that is, it is converted to an image when rendered on the screen.

Adding Images

Of course, EaselJS can handle images as well as text. It does so by means of the `Bitmap` object:

```
var img = new Image();
img.src = "path/to/imagefile.png";
var bmap = new createjs.Bitmap(img);
```

Then, as before with the `Text` object, you can position the `Bitmap` object and add it to the stage:

```
bmap.x = 250;
bmap.y = 120;
stage.addChild(bmap);
```

Updating the Stage

Unfortunately, none of what you've done so far can yet be seen on the screen. That won't happen until you update the stage:

```
stage.update();
```

This way, you can make all the edits you want to the various elements that make up the scene and display the whole new stage in one fell swoop.

Rendering a Canvas

Let's put that all together into an example. Here you build a simple composition using a `Text` object and a `Bitmap` object, add them to the stage, and display it in the browser.

▼ TRY IT YOURSELF

Displaying a Stage

Here's the basic HTML code. Apart from including the EaselJS library file, all you have is a `<canvas>` element, which is placed in the `<body>` of the page and given an ID of `"canvas1"`:

```html
<!DOCTYPE html>
<html>
<head>
    <title>First Steps with EaselJS</title>
    <script src="https://code.createjs.com/1.0.0/easeljs.min.js"></script>
</head>
<body>
    <canvas id="canvas1" width="800" height="600"></canvas>
</body>
</html>
```

Now let's build the scene. First, you create the stage. Then you need to preload the resources the page needs. That's done inside a function called `init()`, which is called when the page body has finished loading.

The final resource to load is the image file blimp.png. You'll see from the line

```
img.onload = doImg;
```

that, once this file has loaded, a further function named `doImg()` is called. Inside that function you create the `Bitmap` object and then add it and the previously made `Text` object to the stage:

```html
<!DOCTYPE html>
<html>
<head>
    <title>First Steps with EaselJS</title>
    <script src="https://code.createjs.com/1.0.0/easeljs.min.js"></script>
    <script>

        var stage;
        var txt;
        var img;
        var bmap;
        var canvas;

    function init() {

        canvas = document.getElementById('canvas1');
        stage = new createjs.Stage(canvas);

        txt = new createjs.Text("My text string", "24px arial", "#333");
        txt.x = 200;
        txt.y = 100;
```

```
        img = new Image();
        img.src = "blimp.png";
        img.onload = doImg;
    }


function doImg(event) {
        bmap = new createjs.Bitmap(img);
        stage.addChild(bmap);
        stage.addChild(txt);
        stage.update();
    }


    </script>
</head>
<body onLoad = "init();">
    <canvas id="canvas1" width="800" height="600"></canvas>
</body>
</html>
```

Finally, you update the stage to display the scene. Enter the preceding code into an .html file. You can replace blimp.png with any small image file you have at hand and simply edit the code to use the file's name.

When you load the file into your browser, you should see something similar to my result, shown in Figure 26.1.

FIGURE 26.1
The rendered canvas

Animating an Image

Building a stage to display is all very well, but to make a playable game, you need to move things around.

EaselJS lets you animate your display in the same way that animation has been carried out for decades: by displaying each object, moving it a little, then displaying it again. Rinse and repeat.

But to help orchestrate all that activity, you need a conductor. That's where the `Ticker` object comes in.

Using the `Ticker` Object

The `Ticker` object provides a background "heartbeat" repeating at a set interval. Listeners can be attached to objects in the browser, subscribing them to the tick event so they can be notified when a set interval has elapsed.

The `Ticker` class doesn't need to be instantiated; you can use it directly in your code. Here's how to set the animation's frame rate to 30 frames per second and add an event listener to the ticker:

```
createjs.Ticker.setFPS(30);
createjs.Ticker.addEventListener("tick", handler);
```

At each tick event, the `handler()` event handler will be executed. Then you need to create a function called `tick()` to be the event handler, so the code becomes

```
createjs.Ticker.addEventListener("tick", tick);
```

Creating the `tick()` Function

To control the animation, you need to tell EaselJS what changes to make between ticks of the ticker. You do that with the `tick()` event handler:

```
function tick() {
    // move the image
    bmap.x -= 3;

    // redraw the canvas element
    stage.update();
}
```

Note that, if you were not using EaselJS, you'd have to erase all the elements on the canvas and redraw them at each update. But EaselJS takes care of all of that, leaving you free just to concentrate on the animation process.

Although you can't see the animation in the static screenshot of Figure 26.2, the blimp is now traversing the screen right to left, moving three pixels at each tick, as defined in the `tick()` function. The `Text` object `txt` has also been edited to form a placeholder for the scoreboard for the game.

The canvas also has a background image set via CSS (I could have used another `Bitmap` element to achieve the same effect, but since the background will be static, the CSS approach is a little easier).

FIGURE 26.2
The blimp is now animated

Now let's add an anti-aircraft gun at the lower edge of the canvas. In the `init()` function, you can preload the required image like this:

```
gun = new Image();
gun.src = "cannon.png";
gun.onload = drawCannon;
```

NOTE

Preloading Images

When your game has lots of assets to preload, such as images, sound files, and so on, you may be better off using the PreloadJS library, which is part of the CreateJS suite. Check out the documentation at www.createjs.com/.

After the image has loaded, you can call a `drawCannon()` function to position it on the screen:

```
function drawCannon(event) {
    cannon = new createjs.Bitmap(gun);
    cannon.x = 200;
    cannon.y = 530;
    stage.addChild(cannon);
    stage.update();
}
```

The basic game field is now set up, as shown in Figure 26.3. I bet you can already see where this game is going....

FIGURE 26.3
The cannon in place

Handling Keyboard Input

The game will be controlled from the keyboard. The player should be able to move the gun right and left using the arrow keys. To do that, you can use the `onkeydown` method of the `document` object:

```
document.onkeydown = handleKeyDown;
```

The `handleKeyDown()` function will look for the keycodes corresponding to the left- and right-arrow keys being pressed. For the moment, all other key presses will be ignored. When a left- or right-arrow key is detected, the x position of the gun will be changed accordingly:

```
function handleKeyDown(e) {
    var key = e.keyCode;
    if(key == 37) {
        //left arrow; move gun left
        if(cannon.x > 3) cannon.x -= 3;
    }
    if(key == 39) {
        //right arrow; move gun right
        if(cannon.x < 400) cannon.x += 3;
    }
}
```

The `if()` statement is used here to limit the gun's movement range.

Adding a Projectile

A gun's not much use if it can't fire anything! You could use another image to provide the projectile, but instead use the EaselJS shape-drawing methods:

```
function drawBullet(event) {
    bullet = new createjs.Shape();
    bullet.graphics.beginFill("black").drawCircle(0, 0, 5);
    bullet.x = 100;
    bullet.y = 100;
    stage.addChild(bullet);
}
```

Skip back to Lesson 15 and see how simple this is, with EaselJS doing the heavy lifting, compared to the native routines for the <canvas> element described there.

In the handleKeyDown() function, you can now add code to catch the pressing of the spacebar, which will be used to fire the projectile:

```
if(key == 32) {
    //space bar; fire bullet
    drawBullet();
}
```

Of course, you don't want the bullet object to be static; you want it to appear at the gun barrel and shoot off, as depicted in Figure 26.4.

FIGURE 26.4
Shooting a projectile

In the following section, we develop the `drawBullet()` function to do just that.

Employing Some Game Logic

It's time to start gluing together the various parts of the game.

First, you need to create a new global variable, `shooting`, which has a value of Boolean `true` while a bullet is flying across the screen, and `false` otherwise:

```
var shooting = false;
```

When a bullet is flying, you can animate it by changing its location using code in the `tick()` function. You also need to detect when the bullet has left the screen, or when it collides with a target, and return it to its offscreen (and therefore invisible) position:

```
// move bullet if one exists
if(shooting) {
    bullet.x += 6;
    bullet.y -= 8;
    if((bullet.x > 800)||(bullet.y < 0)||(blimpHit())) {
        shooting = false;
        bullet.x = -20;
        bullet.y = -20;
    }
}
```

The function `blimpHit()` does nothing for now, but later it will detect when the bullet hits a target and deal with that situation. For now, it's just an empty "stub" function:

```
function blimpHit() {
    return false;
}
```

Ending the Game

When five ships have successfully crossed the screen and disappeared at the left side without being hit, you can declare that the game has finished. Let's count them in another global variable, `ships_crossed`. Here's some more code to add to `tick()`, in this case to detect when a ship has safely crossed, increment the counter, and invisibly move the ship back to the right side of the screen:

```
// if ship now off-screen, wrap the image to RHS
if (bmap.x < -200) {
    bmap.x = 800;
    ships_crossed++;
    if(ships_crossed > 5) endGame();
}
```

The function `endGame()` is also a stub for now, but we get to it shortly:

```
function endGame() {
    return false;
}
```

Scoring a Hit

Now it's time to deal with the situation where the player successfully hits a ship. To do that, you need to create one more new global variable:

```
var exploding = 0;
```

There's a reason this variable has an initial value of zero, rather than Boolean `false`. When a ship is hit, an explosion should stay visible onscreen for a few ticks. When an explosion begins, this variable will be set to a positive number and then counted down inside the `tick()` function. When its value reaches zero, the image of the explosion will be moved offscreen on the next tick of the `Ticker`:

```
// show explosion if one is happening
if(exploding > 0) {
    // count down
    exploding--;
} else {
    // reset explosion image
    bang.x = -100; // off-screen
    bang.y = -100;
}
```

The final step in gluing together the basic game logic is to detect when a target is hit. This game uses simple box geometry to test when the bullet and a ship occupy the same region of the screen. When that happens, you need to set the value of the exploding variable to something positive (I've chosen 5, so the explosion will stay visible for five ticks), increment the player's score, show the explosion, hide the bullet, and hide the ship. That sounds like a lot, but it's pretty simple:

```
function blimpHit() {
    if((bullet.x - bmap.x < 100 )&&(bullet.x - bmap.x > 0)&&(bullet.y - bmap.y < 75)
    ➡&&(bullet.y - bmap.y > 0)) {
        // we have a hit
        exploding = 5;

        // add score
        score++;
        txt.text = "Score " + score;

        // show explosion
        bang.x = bullet.x - 50;
        bang.y = bullet.y - 40;
```

```
            // take bullet back off screen
            bullet.x = -20;
            bullet.y = -20;

            // reset ship position
            bmap.x = 800;

        }
    }
```

The game is now quite playable, if rather rudimentary. You can see it in action in Figure 26.5, where a ship has just been destroyed.

FIGURE 26.5
A direct hit!

Now to add a few extra features to make the game more playable.

Tidying Up the Game Logic

To add an extra challenge, you can add a random element to the height and speed of each blimp that crosses the screen. To make things tidier, move the code that moves each ship to the right side of the screen into its own function that you can call from anywhere in the game:

```
function restartShip() {
    bmap.x = 800;
    bmap.y = Math.floor(0.6 * canvas.height * Math.random());
    bmap.speed = (Math.random()*4)+3;
}
```

This code adds both a static and a random element to both altitude and speed for each new craft that appears onscreen.

Finally, you need to deal with the end of the game. To do that, simply set the ship speed to zero (so no new ships will appear) and move the Text object `txt`, which has been displaying the score, into the center of the screen, where it will display a closing message, as shown in Figure 26.6:

```
function endGame() {
    bmap.speed = 0;
    txt.x = 300;
    txt.y = 200;
    txt.text = "GAME OVER!\n\nYou scored " + score + " hits!\n\nRefresh to play again ...";
    stage.update();
};
```

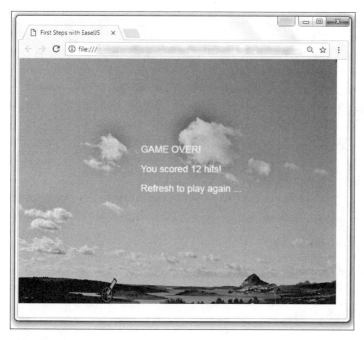

FIGURE 26.6
The closing message

Examining the Final Game Code

The completed code for the game is shown in Listing 26.1.

LISTING 26.1   The Completed Game Code

```html
<!DOCTYPE html>
<html>
<head>
    <title>First Steps with EaselJS</title>
    <style>
        body {
            background:url(bg.jpg);
            background-repeat:no-repeat;
        }
    </style>
    <script src="https://code.createjs.com/1.0.0/easeljs.min.js"></script>
    <script>

        var stage;
        var txt;
        var img;
        var bg;
        var gun;
        var bmap;
        var cannon;
        var canvas;
        var bullet;
        var shooting = false;
        var exploding = 0;
        var ships_crossed = 0;
        var score = 0;
        document.onkeydown = handleKeyDown;

    function init() {

        canvas = document.getElementById('canvas1');
        stage = new createjs.Stage(canvas);

        txt = new createjs.Text("Score " + score, "24px arial", "#fff");
        txt.x = 700;
        txt.y = 0;

        gun = new Image();
        gun.src = "cannon.png";
        gun.onload = drawCannon;

        boom = new Image();
        boom.src = "boom.png";
        boom.onload = drawExplosion;
```

```
    blimp = new Image();
    blimp.src = "blimp.png";
    blimp.onload = drawBlimp;

    drawBullet();

    createjs.Ticker.setFPS(30);
    createjs.Ticker.addEventListener("tick", tick);
}

function drawBlimp(event) {
    bmap = new createjs.Bitmap(blimp);
    bmap.x = 800;
    bmap.y = 300;
    bmap.speed = 3;
    stage.addChild(bmap);
    stage.addChild(txt);
    stage.update();
}

function drawCannon(event){
    cannon = new createjs.Bitmap(gun);
    cannon.x = 200;
    cannon.y = 530;
    stage.addChild(cannon);
    stage.update();
}

function drawBullet() {
    bullet = new createjs.Shape();
    bullet.graphics.beginFill("black").drawCircle(0, 0, 5);
    bullet.x = -20; // initially off-screen
    bullet.y = -20;
    stage.addChild(bullet);
    stage.update();
}

function drawExplosion() {
    bang = new createjs.Bitmap(boom);
    bang.x = 100;
    bang.y = 100;
    stage.addChild(bang);
    stage.update();
}

function tick() {
  // move the image
  bmap.x -= bmap.speed;
```

```
    // if ship off-screen, wrap the image to RHS
    if (bmap.x < -200) {
        restartShip();
        ships_crossed++;
        if(ships_crossed > 5) endGame();
    }

    // move bullet if one exists
    if(shooting) {
        bullet.x += 6;
        bullet.y -= 8;
        if((bullet.x > 800)||(bullet.y < 0)||(blimpHit())) {
            shooting = false;
            bullet.x = -20;
            bullet.y = -20;
        }
    }

    // show explosion if one is happening
    if(exploding > 0) {
        exploding--;
    } else {
        // reset explosion image
        bang.x = -100; // off-screen
        bang.y = -100;
    }

    // redraw the canvas element
    stage.update();
}

function blimpHit() {
    if((bullet.x - bmap.x < 100 )&&(bullet.x - bmap.x > 0)&&(bullet.y - bmap.y < 75)
    ➥&&(bullet.y - bmap.y > 0)) {
        // we have a hit
        exploding = 5;

        // add score
        score++;
        txt.text = "Score " + score;

        // show explosion
        bang.x = bullet.x - 50;
        bang.y = bullet.y - 40;

        bullet.x = -20;
        bullet.y = -20;

        // reset ship position
        restartShip();
```

```
        }
    }

    function endGame() {
        bmap.speed = 0;
        txt.x = 300;
        txt.y = 200;
        txt.text = "GAME OVER!\n\nYou scored " + score + " hits!\n\nRefresh to play again ...";
        stage.update();
    };

    function handleKeyDown(e) {
        // execute things on KeyDown
        var key = e.keyCode;
        if(key == 37) {
            //left arrow; move gun left
            if(cannon.x > 3) cannon.x -= 3;
        }
        if(key == 39) {
            //right arrow; move gun right
            if(cannon.x < 400) cannon.x += 3;
        }
        if(key == 32) {
            //space bar; fire bullet
            if(!shooting) {
                bullet.x = cannon.x + 40;
                bullet.y = cannon.y + 5;
                shooting = true;
            }
        }
    }

    function restartShip() {
        bmap.x = 800;
        bmap.y = Math.floor(0.6 * canvas.height * Math.random());
        bmap.speed = (Math.random()*4)+3;
    }

    </script>
</head>
<body onLoad = "init();">
    <canvas id="canvas1" width="800" height="600"></canvas>
</body>
</html>
```

This is a basic but playable game that you can adapt further to suit your needs or use as a basis for your own animation experiments.

Improving Your Game Further

There's plenty of scope to make the game better, both in coding style and playability.

First, too many variable values are hard-coded. For example, if you want to change the static or random parts of the ship speed, you currently need to edit the `restartShip()` function. These items would be better extracted as constants defined at the start of the script and included in `restartShip()` using the constants' names. The same is true for other quantities that remain unchanged in the game such as canvas dimensions, bullet speed, length of the explosions, and so on. It would then be a very quick job to tweak the playability of the game to suit your tastes simply by editing the values of these constants.

You might also display more information, such as a counter showing how many "lives" the player has lost (that is, how many ships have successfully crossed the screen).

It would be better to remove the `init()` function from the inline `onload` handler of the `<body>` tag, and handle it instead using a more unobtrusive method, as described elsewhere in these lessons.

I've suggested another possibility in the "Exercises" section at the end of this lesson. Hopefully, you'll expand on this prototype game and make something much more advanced.

Summary

In this lesson you learned about the EaselJS JavaScript library and used it to create an animated 2D game. EaselJS is part of a suite of related libraries collectively known as ScriptJS. Together these libraries help you get the best out of the many interactive features available in HTML5.

Along the way you saw how to render shapes, images, and text; how to animate them; and how to bind the whole thing together with some simple game logic.

I hope you found it a useful starting point for creating your own games or other interactive applications.

Q&A

Q. What are the other libraries that form CreateJS?

A. In addition to EaselJS, the CreateJS suite includes TweenJS (a tweening and animation library), SoundJS (for handling audio), PreloadJS (for controlling the preloading of assets into your scripts), and Zoë (for converting SWF animations).

Q. I'm stuck! Where can I get more help with EaselJS?

A. There's an active online community at www.reddit.com/r/createjs/ where you can post your questions or help others to answer theirs.

Workshop

Quiz questions and exercises to test your understanding and to stretch your skills.

Quiz

1. What is the correct syntax to create a `Shape` object in a variable named `x`?

    a. `new createjs.Shape(x);`

    b. `var x = new createjs.Shape();`

    c. `new Shape(createjs);`

2. Which of these statements redraws the stage?

    a. `redraw.stage();`

    b. `stage.update();`

    c. `update.stage();`

3. What does the `Ticker` class do?

    a. Creates an audible tick

    b. Creates the image of a clock face

    c. Helps control timing for objects and animations

4. The CreateJS library is released

    a. In the public domain

    b. Free of charge under an MIT license

    c. At cost under a proprietary closed-source license

5. EaselJS draws its graphics using

    a. An HTML5 `<canvas>` element

    b. Flash animation

    c. Animated GIFs

TIP

Register Your Book

Just a reminder for those of you reading these words in the print or e-book edition of this book: If you go to www.informit.com/register and register this book (using ISBN 978-0-672-33809-0), you can receive free access to an online Web Edition that not only contains the complete text of this book but also features an interactive version of this quiz.

Answers

1. b. `var x = new createjs.Shape();`

2. b. `stage.update();`

3. c. Helps control timing for objects and animations

4. b. Free of charge under an MIT license

5. a. An HTML5 `<canvas>` element

Exercise

How could you animate the explosion in Listing 26.1? (Hint: Use a different explosion image for each value of the variable exploding as it counts down from 5 to 1. You can change the image associated with a bitmap by setting its image property.)

Tools for JavaScript Development

JavaScript development doesn't require any special tools or software other than a text editor and a browser.

Most operating systems come bundled with at least one of each, and in many cases, these tools will be more than sufficient for you to write your code.

However, many alternative and additional tools are available, some of which are described here.

TIP

Be sure to check the license terms on the individual websites or included in the download package.

Editors

The choice of an editor program is a personal thing, and most programmers have their favorite. Listed in the following sections are some popular, free editors that you can try.

Notepad++

If you develop on the Windows platform, you're probably already aware of the Notepad editor usually bundled with Windows. Notepad++ (http://notepad-plus-plus.org/) is a free application that aims to be a more powerful replacement, while still being light and fast.

Notepad++ offers line numbering, syntax and brace highlighting, macros, search and replace, and a whole lot more.

jEdit

jEdit is a free editor written in Java. It can therefore be installed on any platform having a Java virtual machine available, such as Windows, Mac OS X, OS/2, Linux, and so on.

A fully featured editor in its own right, jEdit can also be extended via 200+ available plug-ins to become, for example, a complete development environment or an advanced XML/HTML editor.

Download jEdit from www.jedit.org.

SciTE

Initially developed as a demonstrator for the Scintilla editing component, SciTE has developed into a complete and useful editor in its own right.

A free version of SciTE is available for Windows and Linux users via download from www.scintilla.org/SciTE.html, while a commercial version is available via the Mac App Store for Mac OS X users.

Geany

Geany (www.geany.org/) is a capable editor that can also be used as a basic Integrated Development Environment (IDE). It was developed to provide a small and fast IDE, and can be installed on pretty much any platform supported by the GTK toolkit, including Windows, Linux, Mac OS X, and FreeBSD.

Geany is free to download and use under the terms of the GNU General Public License.

Validators

To make sure your pages work as intended regardless of the user's browser and operating system, it's always advisable to check your HTML code for correctness and conformance to standards.

A number of online tools and facilities are available to help you, as discussed next.

The W3C Validation Services

The W3C offers an online validator at http://validator.w3.org/ that will check the markup validity of web documents in HTML, XHTML, SMIL, MathML, and other markup languages. You can enter the URL of the page to be checked, or cut and paste your code directly into the validator.

CSS can be validated in a similar way at http://jigsaw.w3.org/css-validator/validator.html.en.

Web Design Group

Web Design Group (or WDG) also offers an online validation service at www.htmlhelp.com/tools/validator/.

It is similar to the W3C validator, but in some circumstances, it gives slightly more helpful information. For example, it warns about valid but dangerous code, or highlights undefined references instead of simply listing them as errors.

CodeBeautify JavaScript Validator

The CodeBeautify JavaScript Validator (https://codebeautify.org/jsvalidate) is an easy-to-use online JavaScript validation tool. Simply copy and paste your JavaScript code into the interface.

Verifying and Testing Tools

Verifying tools help you write tidy, concise, readable, and problem-free code.

JSLint

JSLint (www.jslint.com/), written by Douglas Crockford, analyzes your JavaScript source code and reports potential problems, including both style conventions and coding errors.

JSONLint

JSONLint (https://jsonlint.com/) is an online validator for JSON-encoded data.

Online Regex Tester

The online Regular Expression Tester at www.regextester.com/ allows you to enter and test your regular expressions before applying them in your applications. It has specific support for JavaScript regexes.

Index

Q-R

S

Accessing the Free Web Edition

Your purchase of this book in any format, print or electronic, includes access to the corresponding Web Edition, which provides several special features to help you learn

- ▶ The complete text of the book online

- ▶ Interactive quizzes and exercises to test your understanding of the material

- ▶ Updates and corrections as they become available

The Web Edition can be viewed on all types of computers and mobile devices with any modern web browser that supports HTML5.

To get access to the Web Edition of *Sams Teach Yourself JavaScript in 24 Hours*, Seventh Edition, all you need to do is register this book:

1. Go to www.informit.com/register.

2. Sign in or create a new account.

3. Enter the ISBN: **9780672338090**.

4. Answer the questions as proof of purchase.

The Web Edition will appear under the Digital Purchases tab on your Account page.

Click the Launch link to access the product.